KU-601-977

# CHAMBERS
# CHILDREN'S
# POCKET
# THESAURUS

# CHAMBERS
# CHILDREN'S
# POCKET
# THESAURUS

GEORGE MARSHALL

CHAMBERS

CHAMBERS

An imprint of Larousse plc
Elsley House, 24-30 Great Titchfield Street,
London W1P 7AD

This edition published by
Chambers 1996

2 4 6 8 10 9 7 5 3 1

Copyright © Larousse plc 1994, 1996

A CIP catalogue record for this book is
available from the British Library.

ISBN 0550 10672 3

The material in this revised and reillustrated
pocket edition was previously published in the
*Chambers Children's Illustrated Thesaurus* (1994)

All rights reserved. No part of this publication
may be reproduced, stored in a retrieval system
or transmitted by any means electronic, mechanical,
photocopying or otherwise, without the prior
permission of the publisher.

**Editor:** John Grisewood

**Illustrations:** David Ashby (Garden Studio)
Julian Baker  Julie Banyard  Ian Howatson  Mark Iley
Josephine Martin (Garden Studio)
John Marshall  Clive Spong (Linden Artists)

**DTP operators:** Tracey McNerney, Primrose Burton

Printed in Hong Kong

# Introduction

This book is called a thesaurus, which is a Latin word of Greek origin, meaning 'a treasury or storehouse of information', particularly when it deals with words and collections of words. If you examine what this book contains, you will see that is exactly what it is: a collection of words. It is a kind of dictionary, with a list of words in alphabetical order.

Instead of simply giving the *meaning* of a word, it tells you of other words that have a *similar* meaning. Suppose you began a letter to a friend with the sentence *I hope you have a nice time on your holiday*. The word *nice* sounds dull in this case. If you look up the word *nice* in this thesaurus, you will find that it gives you a short list of words that you could use instead: *pleasant, agreeable, amiable, charming, delightful*. Such words are known as **synonyms**. The word *nice* also has another meaning, which is quite different: *precise, accurate, fine, subtle*.

To go back to our letter, you could now write *I hope you have a **pleasant** time on your holiday*. Your friend could write back to you and tell you that *I am having a **delightful** time on my holiday!* As you can see, the thesaurus helps you to write in a better style, and to use words other than the very ordinary, perhaps even boring ones.

In addition to giving these alternative words, this thesaurus also shows you *opposite* words. In the case of *nice*, you will find the opposite word *nasty*. These opposite words are called **antonyms**. In many cases, there are cross-references to other words of similar meaning which are to be found elsewhere in the book. Below is a key to show you how to find the various words and their meaning.

**Parts of speech:** *adj.* = adjective; *adv.* = adverb; *conj.* = conjunction; *n.* = noun; *prep.* = preposition; *v.* = verb

**Opposite words:** These are shown with a star (★) and in ★**bold type.**

**Cross-reference to other meanings:** If a word is shown with an arrow ▷ and in *italics*, it means that you can look up that word to find further, similar meanings. For example, if you look up the word *ruffian*, you find, at the end of the list, the word ▷ *rascal*. So, if you look under *rascal* you will find other, similar words.

A **homonym** is a word that sounds the same as another, but means something quite different.Such words are shown in small capitals, like this: HERE.

If a word has a number of different meanings, each different meaning is shown by a figure in a circle: ①, ②, ③.

George Marshall

# A a

**abandon** v. forsake, give up, leave in the lurch, surrender, sacrifice ▷ *leave, quit*

**abate** v. lessen, slacken, dwindle, fade

**abbey** n. monastery, priory, cloister, church

**abbreviate** v. shorten, cut, contract, reduce ▷ *abridge* ★**expand**

**abdicate** v. resign, retire, renounce ▷ *quit*

**ability** n. aptitude, knack, flair, talent, gift, skill ★**inability**

**able** adj. skilful, competent, talented, strong ▷ clever ★**incapable**

**abnormal** adj. unusual, exceptional, erratic ★**normal**

**abode** n. home, residence, haunt, dwelling, lodging

**abolish** v. destroy, cancel, do away with, exterminate ★**restore**

**abominable** adj. detestable, foul, hateful, horrible, loathsome, atrocious, ▷ *awful* ★**desirable**

**about** prep. & adv. near, nearly, touching, concerning, around

**above** prep. & adv. over, beyond, exceeding, on high, aloft ★**below**

**abridge** v. condense, compact ▷ *abbreviate*

**abroad** adv. overseas, far, away, apart, adrift ★**home**

**abrupt** adj. ① sudden, curt, blunt, brusque ② steep, hilly ★**smooth**

**absent** adj. not present, away, elsewhere, missing ★**present**

**absent-minded** adj. distracted, heedless, forgetful ★**attentive**

**absolute** adj. perfect, complete, certain, positive ▷ *utter* ★**imperfect**

**absorb** v. take in, soak up, assimilate, devour, pull in, swallow, consume ★**emit**

**absorbed** adj. intent, rapt, engrossed, preoccupied

**abstain** adj. refuse, refrain, give up, keep from, avoid, forbear ★**indulge**

**abstract** ① adj. theoretical, intangible ② v. withdraw, steal, remove, take away

**absurd** adj. preposterous, nonsensical, foolish ▷ *silly* ★**sensible**

**abundant** adj. ample, profuse, rich, plentiful, overflowing ★**scarce**

**abuse** ① v. damage, injure, spoil, maltreat, hurt, misuse ★**protect** ② n. maltreatment, attack, exploitation

**accelerate** v. speed up, hasten, quicken, urge ▷ *hurry* ★**delay**

**accent** n. ① stress, beat, rhythm, emphasis ② brogue *Eileen speaks with an Irish brogue,* drawl, pronunciation, twang

**accept** v. receive, take, admit, adopt, take on ★**refuse**

**accident** n. chance, casualty, disaster, calamity, mishap ★**purpose**

**acclaim** v. applaud, praise, approve ★**denounce**

**accommodate** v. oblige, lodge, receive, admit, adapt ★**deprive**

**accompany** v. be with, go with, escort, attend, convoy ★**abandon**

**accomplice** n. ally, confederate, helper, partner, conspirator, henchman

**accomplish** v. perform, fulfil, finish, complete ▷ *achieve* ★**fail**

**accord** ① v. agree, consent, harmonize, allow ★**differ** ② n. agreement, harmony

**account** n. ① bill, invoice, record, score ② tale, story *Mary told us the story of her trip to Australia,* narrative, history

**accumulate** v. collect, grow, gather, hoard, increase, amass ★**scatter**

**accurate** adj. careful, exact, faithful, precise ▷ *correct* ★**defective**

**accuse** v. charge, incriminate, taunt, denounce ★**defend**

**accustom** v. acclimatize, get used to, familiarize ★**estrange**

**ache** ① n. pain, twinge ② v. hurt, pain, sting, smart

**achieve** v. fulfil, accomplish, reach ▷ *attain* ★**fail**

**achievement** n. accomplishment, attainment, exploit, deed, completion ▷ *feat*

**acid** adj. sharp, vinegarish, acrid, sour, tart ★**sweet, mellow**

**acknowledge** *v.* admit, avow, recognize, own, accept, yield ★**disclaim**

**acquaint** *v.* inform, tell, teach, notify, advise ★**deceive**

**acquaintance** *n.* ① friend, pal, associate ② knowledge *You will need some knowledge of Spanish if you visit Mexico*, familiarity, experience

**acquainted** *adj.* aware, familiar, informed

**acquire** *v.* gain, earn, obtain, get, capture ★**forfeit, lose**

**acquit** *v.* discharge, release, exonerate, dismiss, liberate ★**accuse**

**acrid** *adj.* bitter, harsh, sour ▷ *acid* ★**mellow**

**across** *adj. & prep.* crosswise, athwart, slantingly, over against ★**along**

**act** ① *n.* deed, performance, action, step, presentation ② *v.* operate, work, function, perform *Our class will perform a play by Ibsen*

**action** *n.* operation, movement, feat, deed, exercise ★**rest**

**actual** *adj.* correct, true, positive, certain ★**possible**

**acute** *adj.* sharp, pointed, keen, penetrating, severe, distressing ★**blunt**

**adapt** *v.* fit, adjust, accommodate, suit, conform

**adaptable** *adj.* flexible, usable, adjustable

**add** *v.* ① total, combine, tot up ★**subtract** ② affix, annex, connect ★**detach**

**address** ① *n.* residence, place, home, domicile ② *v.* talk to, speak to, accost, call

**adept** *adj.* expert, adroit, handy, skilful ▷ *clever* ★**clumsy**

**adequate** *adj.* ① sufficient, ample *The boat was small, but there was ample room for two*, plenty ② equal, able, qualified

**adjacent** *adj.* near, neighbouring, next, bordering, touching ★**separate**

**adjoin** *v.* border, touch, verge, annex

**adjust** *v.* ① regulate, rectify, correct, amend, revise ② get used to *Our puppy quickly got used to her new home*

**administer** *v.* ① execute, perform, carry out, conduct, direct, manage ② give, dole out *The nurse doled out the pills each morning*

**admirable** *adj.* praiseworthy, commendable, excellent ★**despicable**

**admiration** *n.* adoration, affection, approval, delight, respect ★**contempt**

**admire** *v.* approve, esteem, appreciate ▷ *respect* ★**despise**

**admit** *v.* ① pass, permit, grant, concede, allow, let in, acknowledge ② confess, own up ★**deny**

**ado** *n.* hubbub, commotion, fuss *Let's start the meeting without any more fuss*, excitement

**adopt** *v.* assume, select, choose, employ, apply, take over

**adore** *v.* worship, idolize, admire, revere, venerate ★**despise**

**adorn** *v.* beautify, decorate, embellish, deck, garnish ★**deface**

**adrift** *adv.* loose, afloat, floating, distracted

**adroit** *adj.* handy, skilful, dexterous, expert ▷ *adept* ★**awkward**

**adult** *adj.* grown-up, mature, full-grown ★**immature**

**advance** *v.* ① progress, increase, further, go,

**Adequate**

*The boat was small, but there was ample room for two.*

go on, proceed ★**retreat** ② lend *Helen said she will lend me the money,* loan

**advanced** *adj.* beforehand, ahead, modern

**advantage** *n.* benefit, upper hand, opportunity, assistance, boon ★**hindrance**

**adventure** *n.* experience, escapade, venture, undertaking

**adversary** *n.* foe, opponent, antagonist, rival ▷*enemy* ★**ally**

**adverse** *adj.* unfavourable, hard, hostile, unfortunate ▷*unlucky* ★**fortunate**

**advice** *n.* counsel, suggestion, guidance

**advise** *v.* counsel, urge, suggest, prompt, inform, persuade ★**deter**

**afar** *adv.* far, far off, away, abroad ★**near**

**affable** *adj.* courteous, gracious, easy, frank, open ★**haughty**

**affair** *n.* ① matter, business, concern ② romance, liaison, love affair

**affect** *v.* ① assume, adopt, feign, sham, put on airs ② influence, change, sway *Your argument did not sway my opinion*

**affection** *n.* desire, fondness, feeling, kindness, liking ▷*love* ★**indifference**

**affectionate** *adj.* warmhearted, fond, loving ▷*tender* ★**indifferent**

**affirm** *v.* assert, state, declare, endorse, maintain ★**deny**

**affix** *v.* attach, fasten, unite, append ★**detach**

**afflict** *v.* trouble, ail, distress, upset

**afford** *v.* ① be wealthy, be rich ② produce, provide *The stream provided good, clean water,* yield, bear ★**deny**

**afraid** *adj.* timid, cautious, frightened, alarmed ▷*fearful* ★**fearless**

**after** *prep.* behind, later, following, succeeding ★**before**

**again** *adv.* ① frequently, repeatedly, anew, afresh ② furthermore, moreover

**against** *prep.* opposite, over, opposing, resisting ★**for**

**age** ① *n.* period, date, time ② *n.* old age, senility ★**youth** ③ *v.* grow old, mature

**aged** *adj.* ancient, antiquated ▷*old* ★**youthful**

**agent** *n.* doer, actor, performer, operator,

**Aircraft**

Hot air balloon

Microlight

Seaplane

worker, representative, go-between

**aggravate** *v.* ① increase, make worse, worsen ★**mitigate** ② irritate, annoy

**aggressive** *adj.* offensive, warlike, military, pushy ★**peaceful**

**aghast** *adj.* astonished, dumbfounded, bewildered ★**calm**

**agile** *adj.* nimble, active, fleet, brisk, alert ▷*lithe* ★**clumsy**

**agitate** *v.* disturb, trouble, excite, stir, fluster ★**smooth**

**ago** *adv.* past, gone, since ★**hence**

**agony** *n.* torture, torment, distress, pangs,

Airship

VTOL (Vertical Take Off and Landing)

Airliner

Glider

Biplane

Helicopter

anguish, woe ▷*pain* ★**comfort**
**agree** *v.* accord, fit, harmonize, combine, tally, suit ★**differ**
**agreeable** *adj.* obliging, welcome, acceptable, grateful ▷*pleasant* ★**disagreeable**
**agreement** *n.* understanding, harmony, concord ★**dispute**
**ahead** *adv.* ① forward, onwards ② before, in advance ★**behind**
**aid** *v.* assist, support, encourage, serve ▷*help* ★**hinder**
**aim** *n.* object, goal, purpose, end, intention

**aisle** *n.* path, corridor, passage, way ISLE
**akin** *adj.* related, similar, allied, like ★**dissimilar**
**alarm** *v.* frighten, terrify, startle ▷*scare* ★**comfort**
**alert** *adj.* active, ready, wakeful, watchful ▷*agile* ★**drowsy**
**alien** ① *adj.* foreign, strange, remote ★**akin** ② *n.* foreigner, stranger
**alike** *adj.* similar, resembling, allied, like ★**unlike**
**alive** *adj.* living, breathing, warm, alert, brisk ★**dead**

9

**all** *adj.* whole, entire, complete, total ★**none**

**allot** *v.* apportion, give, allocate, dispense, grant ★**retain**

**allow** *v.* grant, permit, concede, owe, tolerate, entitle ★**forbid**

**ally** *n.* friend, companion, supporter, accomplice, colleague ★**foe**

**almost** *adj.* nearly, about, approximately, well-nigh

**alone** *adj.* lone, lonely, lonesome, forlorn ★**together**

**aloud** *adv.* loudly, noisily, clamorously, audibly ★**silently** ALLOWED

**already** *adv.* at this time, now, just now, previously

**alter** *v.* modify, vary, convert, transform ▷*change* ★**retain** ALTAR

**altogether** *adv.* completely, wholly, outright, totally ★**partially**

**always** *adv.* ever, forever, eternally ★**never**

**amass** *v.* collect, accumulate, heap, pile ★**scatter**

**amaze** *v.* astound, surprise, stun, dumbfound ▷*astonish*

**ambition** *n.* aspiration, desire, longing, zeal, aim ▷*goal*

**amend** *v.* revise, mend, correct, repair, improve, put right, remedy ▷*alter*

**amiable** *adj.* affable, kindly, pleasant, amicable ▷*agreeable* ★**unfriendly**

**amount** *n.* figure, volume, sum, number, total

**ample** *adj.* bountiful, liberal, sufficient, plentiful ▷*abundant* ★**insufficient**

**amplify** *v.* increase, raise, enlarge, elaborate *Our teacher explained the problem and went on to elaborate the details,* make louder ★**abbreviate**

**amuse** *v.* entertain, charm, beguile, please ★**bore**

**ancestor** *n.* forebear, parent, forefather, antecedent, predecessor ★**descendant**

**ancient** *adj.* aged, antique, primeval, time-honoured ▷*old* ★**modern**

**anger** *n.* wrath, ire, resentment, indignation, fury ▷*rage*

**angry** *adj.* wrathful, irate, resentful, furious, infuriated, indignant ★**good-tempered**

**angle** *n.* ① corner, bend, fork, branch ② aspect, phase, point of view *We quarrelled at first, but then I saw Tom's point of view*

**anguish** *n.* torment, torture, pain ▷*agony* ★**ease**

**announce** *v.* broadcast, declare, propound,

## Alphabets

Arabic

Cyrillic (Russian)

Egyptian hieroglyphs

Sanskrit

Greek

Hebrew

Thai

Latin

Japanese

Runes

reveal, herald ▷*proclaim* ★**conceal**

**annoy** *v.* tease, vex, irritate, disturb, harass ▷*upset* ★**soothe**

**answer** *n.* reply, response, solution *It was a difficult puzzle, but Emma came up with the solution* ★**question**

**anticipate** *v.* expect, prepare, hope for, foresee, predict

**anxious** *adj.* fearful, afraid, apprehensive, worried ★**carefree**

**apart** *adv.* away, separately, asunder, loosely ★**together**

**aperture** *n.* slit, hole, orifice, opening, cleft

**apologize** *v.* express regret, excuse, explain, plead, atone ★**insult**

**apparel** *n.* clothes, robes, vestments, raiment, trappings, attire

**apparent** *adj.* plain, conspicuous, unmistakable, clear ▷*obvious* ★**obscure**

**appeal** *v.* address, request, urge, entreat, invite, ask ▷*atttract*

**appear** *v.* emerge, become visible, seem, look, come into view ★**disappear**

**appearance** *n.* aspect, look, shape, form, impression, likeness

**appease** *v.* pacify, moderate, satisfy, stay, soften ★**provoke**

**appetite** *n.* hunger, palate, relish, liking

**applaud** *v.* clap, cheer, praise, approve, encourage ★**denounce**

**apply** *v.* ① use, utilize, employ ② devote, direct, dedicate *Sue was dedicated to her job and worked very hard*

**appoint** *v.* name, assign, nominate, engage

**appreciate** *v.* esteem, recognize, respect, value, enjoy

**appropriate** ① *v.* use, employ, adopt ② *adj.* fitting, proper *To do a job well, you should use the proper tools,* timely

**approve** *v.* acclaim, admire, appreciate, favour, agree ★**disapprove**

**approximate** *adj.* near, close, rough

**apt** *adj.* ① fit, apposite, appropriate, timely ★**unfitted** ② liable, prone, inclined *Jack and Meg are both inclined to be late.* ③ clever, intelligent, expert

**ardent** *adj.* passionate, warm, eager, fervent,

**Apes**

Gibbon
Gorilla
Orangutan
Chimpanzee

intense, keen, dedicated ★**indifferent**

**arduous** *adj.* hard, laborious, tough, strenuous ▷*difficult* ★**easy**

**area** *n.* district, region, place, expanse, tract

**argue** *v.* ① discuss, debate, talk over ② quibble, quarrel, disagree

**arid** *adj.* parched, sterile ▷*dry* ★**moist**

**arise** *v.* ① awaken, get up ② begin, come into existence, originate, crop up, take place

**army** *n.* troops, legion, force, soldiery

**around** *adv.* about, encircling, on every side ★**within**

**arouse** *v.* awaken, excite, disturb, alarm ★**pacify**

**arrange** *v.* sort, order, dispose, deal, classify ★**confuse**

**arrest** *v.* seize, take prisoner, hold, detain, stop ★**release**

**arrive** *v.* reach, attain, land, get to, appear ★**depart**

**arrogant** *adj.* supercilious, proud, haughty, disdainful, conceited ★**modest**

**art** *n.* skill, artistry, cleverness, talent

**artful** *adj.* cunning, knowing, crafty, wily, sly ★**innocent**

**article** *n.* ① thing, object, substance ② essay, treatise, typescript

**artificial** *adj.* invented, fictitious, fabricated, man-made, synthetic ★**real**

**ascend** *v.* climb, rise, go up, get up, move up, scale, mount ★**descend**

**ashamed** *adj.* shamefaced, abashed, confused ★**proud**

**ask** *v.* demand, query, inquire, appeal ▷*request* ★**answer**

**aspect** *n.* front, face, side, appearance, presentation, look, expression

**aspire** *v.* wish, long, desire, aim, hope, crave

**ass** *n.* ① donkey, mule ② fool, dunce, idiot, dolt, wally, clot

**assault** *v.* attack, assail, set upon, charge, invade ★**defend**

**assemble** *v.* meet, gather, convene, come together, muster, collect ★**disperse**

**assent** *v.* agree, comply, accept, consent ★**dissent**

**assert** *v.* pronounce, maintain, state, aver ▷*declare* ★**deny**

**assess** *v.* estimate, evaluate, appraise

**assign** *v.* appoint, name, apportion, entrust

**assist** *v.* aid, support, protect, maintain, sustain ▷*help* ★**obstruct**

**association** *n.* union, connection, companionship, society, company, club

**assortment** *n.* variety, kind, sort, batch, parcel, collection

**assume** *v.* ① believe, accept, suppose, admit ② confiscate, take, possess oneself of

**assure** *v.* promise, guarantee, warrant, encourage ★**deter**

**astonish** *v.* startle, surprise, confound, alarm, scare ▷*amaze*

**astound** *v.* stagger, stupefy ▷*astonish*

**astray** *adj.* lost, gone, vanished, missing, loose ★**safe**

**astute** *adj.* shrewd, brainy, knowing, sharp, acute, crafty ★**simple**

**atrocious** *adj.* monstrous, enormous, shameful, cruel, abominable, vile

**attach** *v.* fasten, append, unite, tie ▷*connect* ★**unfasten**

**attack** *v.* assault, invade, set upon, pounce, descend upon ★**defend**

**attain** *v.* extend, master, obtain, acquire, grasp ▷*reach* ★**fail**

**attempt** *v.* endeavour, strive, seek, tackle ▷*try* ★**abandon**

**attend** *v.* ① listen, heed, notice, observe, follow ★**disregard** ② be present

**attentive** *adj.* mindful, particular, heedful, observant ★**careless**

**attire** *n.* costume, robes, clothes, garments ▷*apparel*

**attitude** *n.* disposition, bearing, outlook, posture, position, aspect

**attract** *v.* ① draw, influence, tempt, prompt, pull, drag ② fascinate, enchant, captivate ★**repel**

**attractive** *adj.* agreeable, beautiful, handsome, pretty, tempting ★**repellent**

**avail** *n.* benefit, advantage, use, help, profit

**available** *adj.* convenient, handy, ready, attainable, accessible, within reach

**avenge** *v.* retaliate, revenge, pay back, take vengeance for ★**pardon**

**average** *adj.* usual, ordinary, mediocre, so-so, normal, standard ★**extreme**

**avid** *adj.* eager, greedy, grasping

**avoid** *v.* shun, elude, quit, keep clear of, evade ▷*dodge* ★**seek**

**awake** *v.* wake, rouse, arouse, awaken, stir

**award** *v.* reward, give, bestow, grant, donate ★**withdraw**

**aware** *adj.* conscious, sensible, informed, assured ★**unaware oblivious**

**away** *adv.* absent, not present, afar, elsewhere ★**near**

**awe** *n.* fear, dread, shock, consternation, wonder

**awful** *adj.* fearful, terrible, alarming, dreadful ★**commonplace**

**awkward** *adj.* ungainly, unwieldy, uncouth, clownish, gawky ▷*clumsy* ★**dexterous**

**awry** *adj.* crooked, askew, amiss, twisted, wrong ★**straight**

# B b

**babble** *v.* prattle, blab, cackle, chatter, gossip

**baby** *n.* babe, infant, child, toddler, tot

**back** ① *adj.* after, rear, hind, posterior ★**front** ② *v.* uphold, support *The party will support Tina Johnson at the next election,* endorse, be loyal to

**backer** *n.* supporter, ally, champion, sponsor

**backward** *adj.* slow, shy, reluctant, unwilling, retarded ▷ *dull* ★**forward**

**bad** *adj.* ① imperfect, dreadful, unsound, awful, atrocious ② naughty, wrong, wicked, ill-behaved ③ rotten *This barrel is full of rotten apples,* spoiled ★**good**

**badge** *n.* emblem, hallmark, symbol, crest

**badger** *v.* bother, annoy, nag ▷ *pester*

**bad-mannered** *adj.* impolite, boorish, uncivil ▷ *rude* ★**polite**

**baffle** *v.* puzzle, perplex, frustrate, bewilder, mystify ▷ *puzzle*

**bag** *n.* net, sack, pouch, purse, knapsack

**bail** *v.* scoop, ladle, dip

**bait** ① *v.* tease, bother, goad, rib, needle ▷ *pester* ② *n.* decoy, lure, snare BATE

**bake** *v.* cook, roast, harden, fire

**balance** *v.* weigh, adjust, equalize, compare

**bald** *adj.* hairless, severe, stark, bare, unadorned

**balk** *v.* hinder, baffle, thwart, obstruct, foil ★**aid**

**ball** *n.* ① dance, masquerade ② globe, orb, sphere

**ballad** *n.* song, serenade, ditty

**ballot** *n.* vote, election, franchise, poll

**ban** *v.* prohibit, forbid, deny, stop

**band** *n.* ① stripe, strip, zone, belt ② orchestra, ensemble, group BANNED

**bandit** *n.* outlaw, robber, highwayman, thief, crook

**bang** *v.* crash, slam, smash, collide

**banish** *v.* expel, eject, exclude, exile, deport, cast out ▷ *dismiss* ★**welcome**

**bank** *n.* ① shore, terrace, coast, embankment ② safe, vault, treasury

**banner** *n.* ensign, standard, streamer ▷ *flag*

**banquet** *n.* meal, feast, repast

**banter** *v.* chaff, tease, ridicule, joke

**bar** *v.* ① obstruct, block, blockade, forbid, shut out ② fasten, bolt, lock, latch

**bare** *adj.* ① barren, empty, void ② naked, unclothed, severe, blunt *We expected a polite reply, but got a blunt refusal,* bald BEAR

**barely** *adv.* hardly, scarcely *The well had run dry, and there was scarcely enough water for all of us,* just, simply

**bargain** ① *n.* pact, deal ② *adj.* low-priced, cheap

**bark** *n.* ① rind, husk, peel ② yelp, growl, cry

**barrel** *n.* cask, keg, drum, tub, cylinder

**barren** *adj.* bare, unfertile, empty ▷ *arid* ★**fertile** BARON

**barrier** *n.* obstruction, obstacle, block, fence

**barter** *v.* swap, exchange, trade

**base** ① *adj.* low, sordid, cheap, corrupt ② *adj.* dishonourable, vile ③ *adj.* humble, menial ④ *n.* bottom, foundation ⑤ *v.* found *The book* Robinson Crusoe *was founded on a true story* BASS

**Band**

**Banned**

**bashful** *adj.* shy, timid, modest, coy ★**bold**

**basin** *n.* bowl, pot, sink, tub, depression

**batch** *n.* lot, amount, assortment, collection

**batter** *v.* beat, strike, shatter, break, smash

**battle** *v.* clash, combat, fight, struggle, wrestle

**bawl** *v.* shout, yell, roar, bellow ★**whisper**

**bay** ① *n.* inlet, gulf, basin, bight ② *v.* bark, yelp BEY

**be** *v.* exist, live, breathe

**beach** *n.* shore, sands, seaside, strand BEECH

**beacon** *n.* signal, lamp, light, guide

**beak** *n.* snout, bill, nose

**beam** *n.* ① ray, light, streak ② plank, joist, girder

**bear** *v.* ① tolerate, put up with, endure, suffer ★**protest** ② bring, fetch, carry BARE

**bearing** *n.* manner, behaviour, appearance, attitude, posture *He was a tall man with a military bearing* BARING

**bearings** *n.* direction, whereabouts, location *In the storm we totally lost our bearings*

**beat** *v.* ① strike, pound, thrash ▷*batter* ② throb, flutter, thump *My heart thumped when I heard the sound of shouting in the street* BEET

**beautiful** *adj.* handsome, lovely, graceful, delicate, gorgeous ▷*pretty* ★**ugly**

**beauty** *n.* elegance, charm, loveliness, grace ★**ugliness**

**because** ① *conj.* for, owing to, by reason of, since *Since Tom and Jane are here, I will stay too,* as ② *adv.* consequently

**beckon** *v.* signal, call, nod, summon

**becoming** *adj.* graceful, suitable, comely, fitting, attractive

**before** ① *prep.* ahead, in front of, forward, preceding ② *adv.* earlier *Here is a pie that I baked earlier,* previously ★**after**

**beg** *v.* ask, request, entreat, beseech, plead, pray

**begin** *v.* commence, initiate, found, launch ▷*start* ★**end**

**beginner** *n.* novice, recruit, learner, pupil

**beginning** *n.* start, opening, origin, outset, foundation ★**end**

**behaviour** *n.* conduct, demeanour, manners

**Bell**

Handbell

Belfry
Bell tower
Bicycle bell
Church bell
Doorbell
Gong

▷*bearing* ★**misbehaviour**

**behind** ① *prep.* after, following *Bill arrived to meet us, with his dog following* ② *adv.* in the rear of, later, afterwards ★**before**

**being** *n.* creature, animal

**belief** *n.* faith, confidence, opinion, trust ★**disbelief**

**believe** *v.* trust, assent, have faith in, think, suspect ★**disbelieve**

**bellow** *v.* roar, shout, cry ▷*bawl*

**belong** *v.* relate to, pertain, be owned by

**below** *adv.* under, beneath, underneath ★**above**

**belt** *n.* strap, sash, girdle, strip

**bend** *v.* curve, incline, turn, yield, relax ★**straighten**

**benefit** *n.* advantage, profit, good, favour, aid, blessing ★**disadvantage**

**beside** *adv.* alongside, side by side, next to, abreast, together ★**apart**

**besides** *adv.* in addition, furthermore, also, moreover

**best** *adj.* choice, prime, unequalled, finest ★**worst**

**bestow** *v.* award, donate, confer, present ★**deprive**

**betray** *v.* deceive, dupe, expose, unmask, inform on, reveal ★**protect**

**better** *adj.* superior, finer, preferable *I think it would be preferable to visit the museum this afternoon instead of this morning* ★**worse**

**between** *prep.* amid, among, betwixt

**beware** *v.* be careful, refrain from, heed,

avoid, mind, watch out, guard against

**bewilder** *v.* confound, dazzle, mystify, confuse ▷*astonish* ★**enlighten**

**beyond** *adv.* over, farther, past, more, after ★**near**

**bicker** *v.* quarrel, dispute, wrangle, argue ★**converse**

**bid** *v.* proffer, present, tender, request, propose

**big** *adj.* ① large, great, wide, huge, bulky, fat, ② important ★**small**

**bill** *n.* ① statement *This is a statement of your investments with us,* account, invoice, score, chit, reckoning ② beak, mouth ③ poster, advertisement, notice

**bin** *n.* box, can, case, chest, crate, tub

**bind** *v.* tie, fasten, secure, lace, swathe ★**untie**

**birth** *n.* origin, beginning, source, creation ★**death** BERTH

**bit** *n.* morsel, piece, fragment, part, crumb ★**whole**

**bite** *v.* gnaw, chew, rend, chomp BIGHT

**bitter** *adj.* ① harsh, sour, tart ▷*acid* ② severe, stern ▷*sarcastic* ★**mellow**

**blame** *v.* chide, rebuke, reproach, criticize, accuse, condemn ★**praise**

**bland** *adj.* soft, mild, gentle, soothing, tasteless

**blank** *adj.* empty, bare, void, bleak ★**full**

**blare** *v.* blast, boom, clang, roar, sound

**blast** *v.* explode, split, discharge, burst

**blaze** *v.* burn, flare, glare, flicker

**bleak** *adj.* bare, open, exposed, dismal, stormy, chilly, raw, desolate *The farm was a cold and desolate place in winter* ★**sheltered**

**blemish** *n.* spot, stain, mark, speck, flaw, blotch, defect

**blend** *v.* mix, unite, harmonize, merge, fuse, combine ★**separate**

**bless** *v.* hallow, praise, exalt, endow, enrich, consecrate ★**curse**

**blessing** *n.* advantage, boon, approval, godsend ★**curse**

**blight** *n.* pest, plague, disease

**blind** *adj.* ① eyeless, sightless *These salamanders live in underground caves and are sightless,* unsighted, unseeing ② ignorant, uninformed

**blink** *v.* wink, twinkle, glitter, gleam

**bliss** *n.* joy, ecstasy, rapture, blessedness, happiness ★**misery**

**block** ① *n.* lump, mass, chunk ② *v.* obstruct, bar, arrest BLOC

**bloom** ① *n.* flower, blossom, bud ② *v.* blossom, flourish, flower, thrive ★**decay**

**blot** *n.* stain, blotch ▷*blemish*

**blow** ① *v.* puff, gust, blast ② *n.* shock, stroke, impact, bang

**blue** *adj.* azure, turquoise, indigo, navy, ultramarine, cobalt BLEW

**bluff** ① *adj.* frank, brusque, abrupt, outspoken *Freda Jones will never be elected mayor; she's too outspoken* ② *v.* deceive, pretend *The lion closed its eyes, pretending it had not seen the antelope,* conceal

**blunder** ① *n.* mistake, error, slip, fault *It was my fault that the plates were broken,* oversight ② *v.* slip, err, bungle ★**correct**

**blunt** *adj.* ① plain, abrupt, curt ▷*bluff* ② dull, not sharp

**blush** *v.* redden, colour, crimson, flush

### The Body

Head
Hair
Ears
Eyes
Back
Arm
Elbow
Nails
Leg
Knee
Ankle
Foot

**board** ① *n.* plank, table ② *n.* committee, council ③ *v.* live *The new teacher is going to live at our house,* lodge, accommodate BORED

**boast** *v.* swagger, swell, bluster ▷*brag*

**boat** *n.* ship, vessel, craft, bark, barge

**body** *n.* ① corpse, trunk, carcase ② corporation, company, society

**bog** *n.* swamp, morass, marsh, quagmire

**bogus** *adj.* fake, false, spurious, sham, counterfeit ★**genuine**

**boil** *v.* cook, steam, poach, seethe, foam

**boisterous** *adj.* tempestuous, stormy, uncontrolled, loud, noisy ★**serene**

**bold** *adj.* fearless, courageous, adventurous, valiant, daring ▷*brave* ★**fearful** BOWLED

**bolt** ① *v.* run away, take flight, flee *After the revolution, the queen had to flee the country* ② *v.* devour, gorge, eat ▷*gulp* ③ *n.* lock, latch, fastening

**bond** *n.* tie, link, joint, band, fastening

**bonny** *adj.* fair, handsome, healthy, shapely, buxom ▷*pretty* ★**plain**

**bonus** *n.* premium, benefit, award, prize

**booby** *n.* blockhead, noodle, oaf, chump, nincompoop, dunce, noodle, numbskull, blast ★**oracle**

**boom** *n.* ① thunder, roar, rumble ② prosperity *After the recession came years of prosperity*

**boon** *n.* blessing, windfall, advantage ▷*benefit* ★**drawback**

**boorish** *adj.* unrefined, loutish, bad-mannered, rude, clumsy ★**refined**

**boost** *v.* strengthen, raise up, heighten

**border** *n.* fringe, edge, margin, frontier

**bore** *v.* ① tire, weary, fatigue *We were fatigued by the long bus ride home* ② drill, punch, perforate BOAR

**bored** *adj.* uninterested, tired, jaded, fed-up BOARD

**borrow** *v.* take, imitate, adopt, assume, raise money ★**lend**

**boss** *n.* ① stud, knob ② chief, manager *Helen is manager of the new beauty salon,* employer

**bossy** *adj.* domineering, tyrannical, despotic, overbearing ▷*arrogant* ★**modest**

**bother** *v.* alarm, annoy, concern, distress ▷*disturb*

**bottom** *n.* underside, deepest part, floor ▷*base* ★**top**

**bough** *n.* branch, limb, shoot BOW

**boulder** *n.* rock, slab, stone

**bounce** *v.* leap, spring, bound, bump, jump

**bound** *v.* rebound, prance ▷*bounce*

**boundary** *n.* bounds, limits, border, frontier, verge, perimeter ▷*barrier*

**bounty** *n.* donation, gift, grant ▷*bonus*

**bow** *v.* bend, nod, stoop, kneel, incline, kowtow, yield, submit BOUGH

**bowl** *n.* plate, basin, dish, vessel, casserole BOLL

**box** ① *n.* carton, case, chest, coffer *The town's coffers were empty, so they had to raise taxes,* pack ② *v.* fight, spar, punch

**boy** *n.* lad, youth, child, youngster BUOY

**brag** *v.* crow, swagger, gloat ▷*boast*

**braid** *v.* entwine, weave, plait BRAYED

**branch** *n.* ① shoot, limb, twig ▷*bough* ② department, office, division

**brand** *n.* ① trade-mark, emblem, label ② blot, stigma, stain

**brandish** *v.* flourish, parade, shake, swing, wave, wield, flaunt

**brash** *adj.* brazen, foolhardy, hasty, impetuous, impudent ▷*rash*

**brave** ① *adj.* audacious, fearless, daring, dauntless, gallant, heroic, courageous ▷*bold* ★**cowardly** ② *v.* dare, defy, endure

**break** *v.* batter, burst, crack, snap, fracture, shatter BRAKE

**breathe** *v.* draw in, gasp, inhale, sniff, gulp, wheeze, emit

**breed** *v.* reproduce, produce, cause, bear, rear, bring forth, multiply, propagate

**bribe** *v.* corrupt, buy, grease the palm, fix

**brief** *adj.* short, little, concise, terse, crisp, curt ★**lengthy**

**bright** *adj.* ① clear, cloudless, fair, airy ② cheerful, genial *We were pleased to find so many genial members in the club* ③ clever, ingenious, acute ★**dull**

**Bridges**

Cantilever

Suspension

Beam

Arch

Bascule bridge
Drawbridge
Footbridge

Rope bridge
Swing span bridge
Viaduct

**brilliant** *adj.* ① lustrous, shining, radiant, dazzling, luminous ② clever, intelligent ★**dull**

**brim** *n.* edge, brink, rim, fringe

**bring** *v.* bear, fetch, deliver, carry, convey

**bring about** *v.* bring off, accomplish, achieve, cause, make happen

**bring up** *v.* breed, develop, raise, educate, foster

**brink** *n.* margin, border, boundary, limit

**brisk** *adj.* agile, alert, busy, energetic, active, nimble, invigorating ★**sluggish**

**brittle** *adj.* breakable, fragile, delicate ▷*frail*

**broad** *adj.* wide, expansive, roomy, open, vast, large ★**narrow**

**brood** *v.* sigh, agonize, dwell upon *You must try to forget your disappointment and not dwell upon it,* languish BREWED

**brook** *n.* stream, rivulet, watercourse, burn

**brow** *n.* forehead, face, front, brink, edge, summit

**bruise** *v.* damage, discolour, blemish, injure, wound BREWS

**brusque** *adj.* abrupt, discourteous, gruff ▷*blunt* ★**polite**

**brutal** *adj.* cruel, inhumane, savage, barbarous, bloodthirsty ★**humane**

**bubble** *n.* drop, droplet, blob, bead

**buckle** *n.* catch, clasp, clip, fastening

**bud** *n.* sprout, germ, shoot

**budge** *v.* move, propel, push, shift, slide

**build** *v.* make, form, assemble, construct, erect, put up ★**demolish** BILLED

**bulge** *n.* bump, swelling, lump, billow

**bulky** *adj.* big, huge, unwieldy, massive, cumbersome *I never liked that chair; it's too big and cumbersome to move*

**bully** ① *n.* ruffian, tormentor, bruiser, tyrant, tough ② *v.* cow, harass, oppress, terrorize

**bump** *v.* collide, hit, knock, strike, jab, jolt

**bunch** *n.* batch, bundle, cluster, collection, lot, clump, stack

**bundle** *n.* group, mass, heap, pack, parcel

**bungle** *v.* botch, blunder, mess up, ruin, fumble ★**succeed**

**burden** *n.* ① load, weight ② strain, hardship *We suffered great hardship during the war*

**burly** *adj.* beefy, big, hefty, brawny, husky, muscular ★**frail**

**burn** *v.* blaze, flare, glow, singe, scorch, char, incinerate, smoulder

**burst** *v.* break open, crack, explode, shatter, erupt

**bury** *v.* inter, conceal, cover up, hide, entomb, lay to rest BERRY

**business** *n.* ① occupation, career, profession, ② company, enterprise, firm ③ problem, duty, affair

**busy** *adj.* active, brisk, industrious, lively, bustling ★**lazy**

**buy** *v.* acquire, get, purchase, procure *If I can procure a computer, I'll do the job for you* ★**sell** BY, BYE

# Cc

**cab** *n.* taxi, taxicab, hackney carriage

**cabin** *n.* ① hut, chalet, cottage, shack ② berth, compartment

**cabinet** *n.* ① cupboard, dresser, closet ② council, committee

**cackle** *v.* chuckle, giggle, snigger

**café** *n.* restaurant, coffee bar, snack bar

**cage** *v.* shut up, confine, imprison ★**free**

**calamity** *n.* catastrophe, disaster, misadventure ▷*mishap* ★**blessing**

**calculate** *v.* reckon, figure, estimate ▷*count*

**call** *v.* ① cry out, shout, hail ② name, designate ③ summon, telephone ④ visit *We will visit you next week,* drop in

**calling** *n.* occupation, job, profession

**callous** *adj.* unfeeling, harsh, hard-bitten ★**sensitive**

**calm** ① *v.* soothe, ease, pacify, comfort ② *adj.* easy, composed, mild ▷*peaceful* ★**excited**

**can** *n.* tin, jar, container, canister

**cancel** *v.* abolish, erase, put off, obliterate ★**confirm**

**candid** *adj.* fair, honest, open, sincere, truthful, blunt ▷*frank* ★**devious**

**capable** *adj.* talented, able, competent, ▷*clever* ★**incompetent**

**capacity** *n.* ① space, volume, extent ② ability, aptitude *Jenny has an aptitude for learning languages,* intelligence

**caper** ① *v.* dance, gambol, frolic ② *n.* (*old*) prank, joke, jest, lark

**capital** ① *n.* cash, assets, funds, finance ② *adj.* chief, excellent, important

**captain** *n.* chief, head, commander, master, skipper

**capture** *v.* seize, arrest, trap ▷*catch* ★**release**

**car** *n.* automobile, motor-car, vehicle, conveyance, carriage, coach

**carcase** *n.* body, corpse, skeleton

**care** ① *v.* take care, beware, heed, mind ② *n.* attention, protection ★**carelessness**

**careful** *adj.* heedful, prudent, watchful ▷*cautious* ★**careless**

**careless** *adj.* neglectful, slack, casual, thoughtless ★**careful**

**carelessness** *n.* inaccuracy, negligence, slackness ★**care**

**caress** *v.* hug, stroke, cuddle, embrace, pet, pat, fondle

**carriage** *n.* car, coach, cab, chariot

**carry** *v.* bring, convey, lift, support ▷*bear*

**carry on** *v.* continue, maintain, persist

**carry out** *v.* perform, achieve, fulfill, do

**cart** *n.* wagon, pushcart, handcart, wheelbarrow

**carton** *n.* bin, case, package, crate ▷*box*

**carve** *v.* sculpt, cut, chisel, fashion, whittle ▷*shape*

**case** *n.* chest, bin, suitcase, trunk ▷*box*

**cash** *n.* money, coins, funds, coinage CACHE

**cask** *n.* barrel, keg, drum

**cast** *v.* ① mould, form, shape ② fling, heave, sprinkle ▷*throw* CASTE

**casual** *adj.* accidental, chance, random ▷*occasional* ★**regular**

**catch** *v.* grasp, seize, arrest ▷*capture* ★**miss**

**catching** *adj.* infectious, contagious

**cause** ① *v.* bring about, create, provoke ② *n.* reason, source, origin CAWS

**caution** *n.* watchfulness, heed, vigilance, prudence ▷*care* ★**recklessness**

**cautious** *adj.* careful, discreet, prudent ▷*watchful* ★**heedless**

**cavity** *n.* dent, hole, gap, hollow

**cease** *v.* stop, conclude, end, refrain, terminate ★**begin**

**celebrate** *v.* commemorate, observe, honour, glorify, rejoice, praise

**cell** *n.* chamber, cavity, cubicle, compartment SELL

**cellar** *n.* basement, vault, crypt, cave SELLER

**cement** ① *v.* glue, stick, bind, gum, unite ② *n.* plaster, mortar, adhesive

**censor** *v.* cut, examine, take out CENSER

**censure** *v.* blame, rebuke, reprimand, chide ▷*scold* ★**praise**

**centre** *n.* middle, core, heart, nucleus

**ceremony** *n.* ritual, custom, performance

**certain** *adj.* ① decided, definite, undoubted ▷*sure* ★**dubious** ② particular *I had a particular reason for inviting you,* special

**certainty** *n.* confidence, assurance, trust, sureness ★**doubt**

**certificate** *n.* document, permit, deed, diploma, testimonial

**chafe** *v.* rub, rasp, grate, irritate

**chain** *v.* bind, fetter, shackle, tether, bond

**challenge** *v.* dare, demand, dispute, defy, object to

**chamber** *n.* room, apartment, bedroom, compartment, hollow

**champion** *n.* defender, victor, master, winner ★**loser**

**chance** *n.* ① fortune, hazard, luck, gamble, lottery, wager ② opportunity, occasion, risk ★**certainty**

**change** *v.* alter, vary, turn, shift, reform, transform ★**preserve**

**chant** *v.* intone, drone, croon, recite ▷*sing*

**chaos** *n.* turmoil, confusion, disorder, pandemonium ★**order**

**chapter** *n.* clause, division, part, period *It was a period in my life that I will never forget,* phase

**character** *n.* ① letter, mark, emblem, device ② reputation *She had the reputation of being very generous,* temperament, qualities

**charge** *n.* ① attack, stampede, advance ② cost, amount, price ③ accusation, blame *The men were all guilty, but it was Harry Smith who took the blame,* indictment

**charm** *v.* please, delight, enchant, bewitch, fascinate ▷*attract* ★**irritate**

**charming** *adj.* delightful, appealing, lovely, pleasant ▷*attractive* ★**disgusting**

**chart** *n.* map, sketch, diagram, plan

**chase** *v.* hunt, pursue, follow, run after, hurry, track

**chaste** *adj.* virgin, pure, virtuous, innocent ★**immodest** CHASED

**chastise** *v.* punish, whip, flog, beat, scold, tell off, reprove, berate

**chat** *v.* converse, gossip ▷*talk*

**chatter** *v.* babble, gossip ▷*talk*

Chest

Chest

**cheap** *adj.* inexpensive, low-priced, bargain, reasonable, inferior, ★**expensive**

**cheat** *v.* swindle, bilk, defraud, fleece, diddle, rip off ▷*trick*

**check** ① *v.* inspect, compare, examine *The customs officer examined our luggage,* make sure ② *n.* curb, setback, reverse

**cheek** *n.* audacity, boldness, impertinence, insolence

**cheer** *v.* ① comfort, console, elate, buck up ② applaud *The audience applauded the leading soprano,* clap, hail

**cheerful** *adj.* lively, bright, happy, merry, joyful ▷*happy* ★**sad**

**cheery** *adj.* blithe, breezy, bright, merry ★**downcast**

**cherish** *v.* caress, hold close, care for, shelter, treasure

**chest** *n.* ① case, coffer ▷*box* ② bosom, torso

**chew** *v.* bite, gnaw, grind, munch ▷*eat*

**chide** *v.* scold, criticize, blame, tell off

**chief** *adj.* main, principal, leading, foremost ★**minor**

**child** *n.* baby, infant, youth, juvenile, bairn

**chilly** *adj.* cool, crisp, brisk, cold, unfriendly ★**warm**

**chip** *v. & n.* crack, splinter, dent, flake

**chirp** *v. & n.* warble, trill, cheep, twitter

**choice** ① *n.* option *I had no option but to take the job,* preference, alternative ② *adj.* select, dainty, precious, cherished, special

**choke** *v.* throttle, suffocate, gag, strangle, smother ▷*stifle*

**Churches and Places of Worship**

Cathedral
Chapel
Church
Mosque
Oratory
Pantheon
Synagogue
Temple

**choose** *v.* pick, elect, decide, prefer ▷ *select* CHEWS

**chop** *v.* cut, hack, clip, cleave, sever, lop

**chubby** *adj.* plump, buxom, portly, round, stout ★**slim**

**chum** *n.* comrade, pal, friend, mate, companion, crony

**chuck** *v.* throw, toss, fling, heave, sling

**chuckle** *v.* cackle, chortle, snigger, giggle ★**laugh**

**chunk** *n.* piece, lump, mass, portion, slab

**churlish** *adj.* brusque, harsh, impolite, morose *Dad had a headache and was in a morose mood* ▷ *surly* ★**polite**

**circle** *n.* ① ring, band, hoop ② company, group, class, clique

**circular** ① *adj.* round, disc-like ② *n.* handbill, notice, poster

**circulate** *v.* broadcast, distribute, publicize

**cistern** *n.* tank, sink, basin, reservoir

**cite** *v.* mention, specify, name, quote SIGHT, SITE

**civil** *adj.* polite, courteous, polished ▷ *affable* ★**churlish**

**claim** *v.* demand, ask, require, insist, call for

**clamour** *n.* babel, blare, din, row, hubbub, racket ▷ *noise* ★**silence**

**clamp** *v.* fasten, fix, hold, grasp

**clap** *v.* applaud, acclaim, cheer

**clarify** *v.* ① make clear, explain, simplify ② cleanse, purify

**clash** *v.* ① battle, conflict, quarrel ② bang, crash, clang, clatter

**clasp** ① *v.* grasp, grip, seize, hold, fasten ② *n.* buckle, catch, pin

**class** *n.* category, type, sort, grade, group, species

**classical** *adj.* pure, refined, scholarly, elegant, polished, well-proportioned

**classify** *v.* grade, sort, arrange, catalogue

**clean** ① *adj.* pure, fresh, spotless, unsoiled ② *v.* cleanse, scrub ▷ *wash* ★**dirty**

**cleanse** *v.* purify, scour ▷ *clean* ★**defile**

**clear** *adj.* ① bright, fair, fine, light ★**dim** ② distinct, audible, lucid ★**vague** ③ free, open, empty

**cleft** *n.* crack, cranny, slit, split, aperture

**clever** *adj.* able, astute, apt, brainy, skilful, talented ▷ *expert* ★**foolish**

**cliff** *n.* precipice, height, bluff, crag, overhang

**climax** *n.* crisis, head, summit, turning point

**climb** *v.* mount, scale, ascend, soar, go up

**cling** *v.* adhere, attach, embrace, grasp, hold

**clip** ① *n.* fastener, clasp ② *v.* trim, prune, snip, cut

**clog** *v.* block, dam up, hinder, jam, impede

**close** ① *v.* (kloz) shut, bolt, bar, obstruct *The curtains were thick and obstructed a lot of light,* end ② *adj.* (klos) near, neighbouring, adjacent ★**far** ③ *adj.* heavy, stuffy, uncomfortable

**closet** *n.* wardrobe, cabinet

**clothing** *n.* garments, dress, attire, raiment

**cloud** *n.* vapour, fog, billow, haze

**clown** *n.* buffoon, comedian, jester, joker

**club** *n.* ① cudgel, stick, truncheon ② company, group, society

**clue** *n.* evidence, inkling, lead, sign CLEW

**clump** *n.* cluster, group, bunch

**clumsy** *adj.* awkward, gawky, ungainly, blundering ★**graceful**

**clutch** *v.* snatch, clasp, grasp, seize, grip

**clutter** *n.* litter, muddle, mess

**coach** *n.* ① bus, car, carriage, vehicle ② trainer, tutor, instructor

## Clothing

**Dresses and trousers**
Bermuda shorts
cocktail dress
dress
evening gown
jeans
jodhpurs
kilt
miniskirt
petticoat
sari
sarong
skirt

**Coats and jackets**
anorak
blazer
cloak
poncho
raincoat
suit
tuxedo

**Tops**
blouse
cardigan
pullover
sweater
sweatshirt
T-shirt

**Headwear** see page 56

**Foot and legwear**
boots
galoshes
moccasins
shoes
socks
stockings
tights
trainers

**coarse** *adj.* ① rough, unrefined, unpolished ② brutish, rude, uncivil ★**refined** COURSE

**coat** *n.* ① jacket, blazer, windcheater ② fleece, fur, skin, hide

**coax** *v.* cajole, wheedle, urge, persuade, beguile *We sat for hours as Aunt Anna beguiled us with stories* ★**dissuade** COKES

**coddle** *v.* pamper, spoil, indulge, baby, mollycoddle

**coffer** *n.* casket, case, chest, treasury

**cog** *n.* tooth, prong

**coil** *v.* twist, wind, loop, curl

**coincide** *v.* match, agree, accord, synchronize, tally

**cold** *adj.* cool, chilly, frigid, freezing, frosty, frozen ★**hot**

**collapse** *v.* founder, topple, break down, crumple, fall down

**collect** *v.* accumulate, amass, assemble, save ▷*gather* ★**scatter**

**collide** *v.* crash, smash, hit, strike, meet

**colossal** *adj.* enormous, gigantic, immense, massive ▷*huge* ★**tiny**

**column** *n.* ① pillar, post, shaft, support, upright ② file *The file of soldiers marched on parade,* line, procession, queue, rank

**combat** *v.* battle, contend, contest, oppose, defy ★**submit**

**combine** *v.* unite, join, link, fuse, merge, mix, bond, blend ★**separate**

**come** *v.* arrive, appear, enter, reach, advance ★**go**

**come by** *v.* get, procure, acquire *I acquired a new television set in the sale*

**comfort** *v.* cheer, hearten, calm, soothe, console ★**torment**

**comfortable** *adj.* restful, convenient, cosy, agreeable ★**uncomfortable**

**comforting** *adj.* cheering, encouraging, consoling

**command** *v.* ① order, dictate, direct, demand, require ② rule, dominate

**commence** *v.* start, begin, initiate, originate, embark on ★**finish**

**comment** *v.* mention, remark, observe, point out, note

**commiserate** *v.* sympathize, show pity, be sorry for

**commit** *v.* carry out, do, enact, perform, promise, entrust

**common** *adj.* ① ordinary, vulgar, habitual, customary ② public, social, communal

**commonplace** *adj.* everyday, humdrum, ordinary, obvious ★**rare**

**commotion** *n.* excitement, flurry, stir, uproar ▷*fuss*

**communicate** *v.* tell, disclose, impart, reveal

**community** *n.* society, partnership, association ▷*group*

**compact** *adj.* dense, close, tight, firm, condensed, concise

**companion** *n.* comrade, friend, chum, mate, colleague, comrade, escort ★**rival**

**company** *n.* association, league, alliance, business, firm

**compare** *v.* match, liken, equal, parallel

**compartment** *n.* cubicle, alcove, bay, cell, carriage

**compassion** *n.* kindness, mercy, sympathy, charity, understanding ▷*pity* ★**indifference**

**compel** *v.* make, coerce, drive, force *We could not understand the signs so we were forced to guess where to check in*, urge ★**coax**

**compensate** *v.* make good, refund, reimburse, repay, reward ★**injure**

**compete** *v.* contest, contend, rival, strive, oppose, challenge, emulate

**Compel**

**competent** *adj.* able, adapted, capable ▷*clever* ★**incompetent**

**competition** *n.* game, match, contest, rivalry, race, tournament

**compile** *v.* amass, put together, unite ▷*collect*

**complacent** *adj.* self-satisfied, contented ▷*smug* ★**diffident**

**complain** *v.* protest, gripe, grumble, grouse ▷*nag* ★**rejoice**

**complement** *v.* complete, round off, add to, supplement, match COMPLIMENT

**complete** ① *v.* finish, accomplish, achieve ② *adj.* finished, full, entire

**complex** *adj.* complicated, intricate, mixed, tangled ★**simple**

**complicated** *adj.* entangled, involved ▷*complex*

**compliment** *v.* flatter, admire, congratulate ▷*praise* ★**insult** COMPLEMENT

**comply** *v.* agree to, assent to, abide by, perform, yield ★**refuse**

**compose** ① *v.* make up, put together, form, construct, write ② calm, quell

**composure** *n.* assurance, calm, confidence ★**exuberance**

**compound** *n.* mixture, alloy, blend, combination

**comprehend** *v.* grasp, discern, take in ▷*understand* ★**misunderstand**

**compress** *v.* condense, contract, abbreviate ▷*squeeze* ★**expand**

**comprise** *v.* contain, consist of, include, embody, encompass

**compromise** *v.* ① meet halfway, strike a balance, adjust, agree ② imperil, weaken, jeopardize

**compulsory** *adj.* forced, necessary, obligatory *Everyone in the school has to go*

*We could not understand the signs so we were forced to guess where to check in.*

to the meeting; it's obligatory, required
★**voluntary**

**compute** v. calculate, figure, reckon, estimate

**computer** n. calculator, word processor

**comrade** n. companion, pal, chum, mate ▷*friend* ★**enemy**

**conceal** v. bury, camouflage, cover ▷*hide* ★**reveal**

**concede** v. allow, admit, yield, acknowledge, surrender ★**dispute**

**conceit** n. vanity, self-importance, arrogance ▷*pride* ★**modesty**

**conceited** adj. proud, vain, arrogant ★**modest**

**conceive** v. create, design, devise *We devised a way to sharpen the scissors,* form, think up, develop

**concentrate** v. focus on, centralize, heed, pay attention

**concept** n. idea, thought, theory, view

**concern** ① v. affect, touch ② n. affair, matter, interest, business

**concerning** prep. as regards, respecting, about, with reference to

**concise** adj. brief, condensed, short ▷*compact* ★**expansive**

**conclude** v. ① finish, terminate ▷*end* ② deduce, judge, reckon, presume

**conclusion** n. result, termination, end

**concoct** v. contrive, hatch, plan, devise, invent

**concord** n. agreement, understanding, good-will, harmony ★**discord**

**concrete** ① adj. actual, definite, real ② n. cement, mortar

**concur** v. approve, agree, coincide, consent ★**disagree**

**condemn** v. blame, denounce, reprove, sentence, disapprove ★**approve**

**condense** v. compress, concentrate, abridge, thicken ★**expand**

**condition** n. shape, way, state, position, plight, situation ▷*predicament*

**condone** v. overlook, disregard, forgive, excuse ★**censure**

**conduct** ① n. attitude, bearing, behaviour

② v. guide, direct, lead, pilot, steer, usher

**confederate** n. accomplice, ally, associate, partner

**confer** v. bestow, grant, award, give, present

**conference** n. discussion, meeting, forum

**confess** v. admit, acknowledge, own up, divulge ★**deny**

**confide** v. tell, divulge, reveal, whisper, entrust, unburden

**confidence** n. assurance, belief, boldness, firmness ★**doubt**

**confident** adj. certain, assured, poised, fearless ★**diffident**

**confine** v. restrict, limit, detain, imprison, constrain, intern ★**free**

**confirm** v. verify, assure, approve, endorse, attest ★**deny**

**confiscate** v. seize, impound, commandeer *The house was commandeered by the army*

**conform** v. agree with, comply with, yield, adjust

**confound** v. perplex, mystify, puzzle, baffle, fluster ▷*bewilder* ★**enlighten**

**confront** v. challenge, defy, face, oppose, menace

**confuse** v. baffle, bemuse, mystify ▷*bewilder* ★**clarify**

**congenial** adj. companionable, natural, sympathetic, agreeable ▷*friendly* ★**disagreeable**

**congested** adj. jammed, crowded, clogged, packed, teeming ★**clear**

**congratulate** v. rejoice, compliment, praise, wish well ★**commiserate**

**congregate** v. assemble, meet, come together, converge ★**disperse**

**congress** n. meeting, assembly, council, convention

**conjecture** v. guess, surmise, suspect, imagine, assume

**connect** v. unite, join, combine, fasten, link ★**disconnect**

**conquer** v. beat, crush, overcome, overpower, triumph ▷*defeat* ★**surrender**

**conscientious** adj. moral, scrupulous, careful, diligent ▷*honest* ★**careless**

**conscious** adj. alert, alive, aware, sensible,

mindful, responsible ★**unconscious**

**consecutive** *adj.* chronological, in sequence, successive, continuous

**consent** *v.* assent, permit, concur, approve, comply ▷*agree* ★**oppose**

**conserve** *v.* keep, preserve, protect, save, store up, safeguard ★**waste**

**consider** *v.* discuss, examine, ponder, reflect *Alone on the island, I reflected on all that had happened,* take account of ★**ignore**

**considerable** *adj.* abundant, ample, great, large, noteworthy, important ★**insignificant**

**consist of** *v.* comprise, be composed of, contain, include

**consistent** *adj.* uniform, constant, regular, steady ★**inconsistent**

**console** *v.* comfort, cheer, sympathize, soothe, solace ★**upset**

**conspicuous** *adj.* noticeable, marked, apparent, obvious, prominent ★**inconspicuous**

**conspire** *v.* intrigue, scheme, plot *He was gaoled for plotting against the government*

**constant** *adj.* ① regular, stable, uniform ▷*consistent* ② loyal, faithful, staunch, true ★**fickle**

**consternation** *n.* dismay, horror, fear, awe, stupefaction ▷*alarm* ★**composure**

**constitute** *v.* compose, comprise, set up, fix, form, establish ★**destroy**

**constrict** *v.* tighten, strain, tauten, draw together, choke, pinch ★**expand**

**construct** *v.* erect, compose, compound, assemble ▷*build* ★**demolish**

**consult** *v.* ask, seek advice, discuss, confer, debate, refer to

**consume** *v.* use up, absorb, eat up, devour

**contact** *n.* touch, connection, meeting, communication, association

**contagious** *adj.* catching, infectious

**contain** *v.* comprise, consist of, hold, accommodate, enclose

**contaminate** *v.* pollute, soil, stain, sully, taint, infect

**contemplate** *v.* think, reflect, deliberate, consider, ponder

**contempt** *v.* disdain, scorn, disregard, derision ★**admiration**

**contend** *v.* compete, contest, conflict, strive, struggle ★**concede**

**content** ① *adj.* (con-*tent*) satisfied, smug ② *v.* satisfy, delight, gratify ③ *n.* (*con*-tent) matter, text, subject

**contest** ① *n.* (*con*-test) competition, match, tournament ② *v.* (con-*test*) dispute, argue

**continue** *v.* go on, keep up, endure, last, persist ★**stop**

**contract** ① *v.* (con-*tract*) condense, lessen, shrink ② *n.* (*con*-tract) agreement, pact, understanding

**contradict** *v.* deny, dispute, challenge, oppose, gainsay

**contrary** *adj.* opposed, adverse, counter, opposite ★**agreeable**

**contrast** ① *n.* (*con*-trast) difference, disparity, comparison ② *v.* (con-*trast*) compare, differ, oppose, distinguish

**contribute** *v.* donate, present, bestow, provide, assist, help ★**withhold**

**contrive** *v.* form, fashion, construct, create, design, invent

**control** *v.* command, direct, dominate, lead, supervise, oversee, superintend

**convene** *v.* call together, rally, meet, muster *We mustered on the dock before boarding the ship,* assemble ★**dismiss**

**convenient** *adj.* handy, fit, helpful, suitable, accessible ★**awkward**

**conversation** *n.* talk, chat, communication, discussion, discourse, exchange

**convert** *v.* alter, change, transform, adapt

**convey** *v.* carry, transport, conduct, bear, transmit

**convict** ① *n.* (*con*-vict) prisoner, captive, criminal ② *v.* (con-*vict*) find guilty, condemn, sentence

**convince** *v.* assure, persuade, prove to, win over, sway, bring round

**cook** *v.* boil, broil, heat, warm, steam, fry, stew, bake, grill, roast

**cool** *adj.* ① chilly, frigid ▷*cold* ② self-composed, calm, relaxed

**cooperate** *v.* collaborate, combine, aid,

assist, join forces, unite, conspire
**cope (with)** v. deal, handle, struggle, grapple, manage
**copy** v. duplicate, reproduce, imitate, mimic, simulate, crib, plagiarize
**cord** n. string, rope, twine, line CHORD
**cordial** adj. hearty, sincere, congenial, jovial, affable ★**hostile**
**core** n. heart, kernel, pith, crux *Now we're getting to the crux of the problem,* centre CORPS
**corner** n. angle, bend, crook, cavity, cranny, niche, compartment
**corpse** n. body, carcase, remains
**correct** adj. true, actual, accurate, exact, precise ★**wrong**
**correspond** v. ① fit, harmonize, agree, coincide ② write letters
**corridor** n. hallway, passage, aisle
**corroborate** v. confirm, certify, endorse, establish ★**contradict**
**corrode** v. erode, waste, eat away, rust
**corrupt** ① adj. dishonest, fraudulent, rotten

② v. bribe, deprave, entice, lead astray
**cost** n. ① charge, amount, price, outlay
② penalty, forfeit, sacrifice
**costly** adj. expensive, valuable, precious
**costume** n. suit, outfit, ensemble, attire, dress, uniform, get-up
**cot** n. bed, bunk, berth
**cottage** n. bungalow, cabin, chalet, shack, lodge
**couch** n. sofa, settee, chaise-longue
**council** n. assembly, committee, congress, convention COUNSEL
**counsel** ① n. lawyer, attorney, advocate
② v. advise, instruct, recommend COUNCIL
**count** v. add up, calculate, check, compute, reckon, tally
**counter** ① n. token, coin, disc ② n. bar, bench ③ adj. against, opposed
**counterfeit** adj. forged, fraudulent, fake, bogus *She entered the country on a bogus passport,* false
**country** ① n. nation, people, realm, state
② adj. rural, farmland, sticks

**Cooking utensils**

| | | |
|---|---|---|
| Blender | Grill | Rolling pin |
| Bottle | Jar | Saucepan |
| Bowl | Kettle | Sieve |
| Casserole | Ladle | Skillet |
| Colander | Lemon | Spatula |
| Cup | squeezer | Spoon |
| Cutting | Masher | Tureen |
| board | Measuring | Urn |
| Dish | jug | Whisk |
| Frying pan | Pan | Wok |
| Funnel | Peeler | |
| Grater | Plate | |
| Griddle | Pot | |
| | Ramekin | |

**couple** ① *n.* pair, brace, two ② *v.* link, yoke, unite, join, connect

**courage** *n.* bravery, valour, boldness, gallantry, daring, pluck ★**cowardice**

**courageous** *adj.* brave, bold, fearless, valiant ▷*plucky* ★**cowardly**

**course** *n.* ① route, channel, path, road, track, trail ② policy, plan, manner COARSE

**court** ① *n.* alley, courtyard, atrium, quad ② *n.* bar, bench, tribunal ③ *n.* palace, retinue ④ *v.* make love, woo, flatter

**courteous** *adj.* considerate, polite, refined, elegant ★**discourteous**

**courtesy** *n.* politeness, civility, manners, gentility, gallantry, respect

**cove** *n.* inlet, bay, creek, firth

**cover** ① *v.* conceal, hide, secrete ② *v.* include, embody, incorporate ③ *n.* cap, case, lid, canopy

**covet** *v.* want, envy, fancy, hanker after, long for, crave

**cow** *v.* frighten, bully, terrorize, scare, subdue

**coward** *n.* weakling, craven, funk, sneak ★**hero** COWERED

**cowardice** *n.* fear, funk, faint-heartedness ★**courage**

**cowardly** *adj.* fearful, weak, scared,

**Creature**

*It was a huge brute – the biggest crocodile I'd ever seen.*

spineless, timorous ★**courageous**

**cower** *v.* cringe, grovel, flinch, crouch

**coy** *adj.* demure, skittish, blushing, bashful, shy ★**forward**

**crack** ① *n.* slit, split, cleft, cranny, crevice, breach ② *v.* snap, split, splinter

**craft** *n.* ① cunning, deceit ② ability, cleverness, expertise ③ occupation, business ④ boat, ship, plane

**crafty** *adj.* cunning, artful, wily, shrewd

**cram** *v.* ram, stuff, squeeze, press

**cramp** *v.* restrict, obstruct, hinder, confine

**crash** *v.* bang, clash, clatter, break, fall, topple, plunge, collapse

**crass** *adj.* stupid, oafish, boorish, obtuse, slow-witted ★**sensitive**

**crave** *v.* long for, hanker after, need, yearn for, beg, plead

**crawl** *v.* creep, drag, slither, grovel

**crazy** *adj.* insane, mad, beserk, deranged, idiotic ★**sane**

**creak** *v.* grate, grind, rasp, groan CREEK

**crease** *n.* fold, pucker, ridge, pleat, tuck

**create** *v.* bring into being, compose, concoct, make, invent, coin, devise

**creation** invention, handiwork, foundation, production ★**destruction**

**creature** *n.* animal, beast, being, brute *It was a huge brute – the biggest crocodile I'd ever seen,* person

**credible** *adj.* believable, likely, plausible ★**incredible**

**credit** *n.* ① acclaim, kudos, merit ② belief, faith, confidence

**creek** *n.* bay, cove, bight, stream, CREAK

**creep** *v.* crawl, slither, squirm, wriggle

**crest** *n.* top, crown, pinnacle

**crestfallen** *adj.* downcast, dejected, discouraged ★**elated**

**crevice** *n.* cleft, chink, crack, cranny, gap

**crew** *n.* team, company, party, gang

**crime** *n.* misdeed, offence, fault, felony

**criminal** ① *n.* culprit, convict, felon, crook ② *adj.* unlawful, wicked

**cringe** *v.* cower, flinch, duck, shrink, grovel

**cripple** *v.* disable, mutilate, paralyse, weaken, damage

**Creek**

**Creak**

**crisis** *n.* climax, turning point, catastrophe, disaster, crunch

**crisp** *adj.* brittle, crumbly, crunchy, firm, crusty ★**soggy**

**critical** *adj.* crucial, all-important, acute, grave, pressing, decisive

**criticize** *v.* find fault with, disapprove of, condemn ★**praise**

**crony** *n.* accomplice, ally, confederate, comrade, chum ▷*friend*

**crooked** *adj.* ① bent, bowed, distorted, twisted ② dishonest, criminal

**crop** ① *n.* harvest, gathering, yield ② *v.* graze, shorten, browse

**cross** ① *adj.* angry, annoyed, crusty ② *v.* bridge, pass over ③ *n.* crucifix

**crouch** *v.* stoop, squat, bow, cringe

**crow** ① *v.* gloat, shout, brag, bluster ② *n.* blackbird, raven

**crowd** *n.* mob, multitude, flock, assembly, swarm, throng

**crowded** *adj.* jammed, packed, congested, cramped

**crucial** *adj.* decisive, critical, acute

**crude** *adj.* raw, unrefined, rustic, unpolished ▷*coarse* ★**refined**

**cruel** *adj.* unkind, brutal, inhuman, ruthless ▷*savage* ★**kind**

**cruise** *n.* voyage, trip, sail, crossing CREWS

**crumb** *n.* bit, morsel, seed, grain, scrap, shred

**crumble** *v.* decay, grind, powder, crunch

**crumple** *v.* crinkle, crush, wrinkle, pucker

**crunch** *v.* chew, grind, masticate, munch ▷*crush*

**crush** *v.* squash, mash, pound, compress

**cry** *v.* ① exclaim, call, shout, shriek ② weep, bawl, blubber, sob

**cuddle** *v.* hug, embrace, fondle, cosset, pet, snuggle, fondle

**cue** *n.* hint, key, nod, sign, signal QUEUE

**cull** *v.* choose, pick, thin out, amass, collect

**culprit** *n.* criminal, convict, felon, offender, malefactor

**cultivated** *adj.* refined, civilized, cultured, educated, trained ★**neglected**

**cumbersome** *adj.* bulky, awkward, clumsy, hefty ★**convenient**

**cunning** *adj.* artful, astute, crafty

**curb** *v.* check, tame, restrain

**cure** ① *n.* remedy, medicine, drug ② *v.* heal, remedy, treat, attend

**curious** *adj.* ① odd, peculiar, singular ② inquisitive, prying, nosy

**curl** *v.* coil, twist, curve, crimp

**current** ① *adj.* present, contemporary, topical, fashionable ② *n.* stream, course, flow, electrical flow CURRANT

**curse** ① *v.* swear, condemn, damn ② *n.* oath, denunciation

**curt** *adj.* brusque, blunt, churlish, crusty, gruff ▷*terse* ★**polite**

**curtail** *v.* trim, shorten, clip, truncate ▷*abbreviate* ★**lengthen**

**curve** *n.* loop, hook, curl, twist, wind, coil ▷*bend*

**cushion** *n.* pillow, bolster, pad, support

**custom** *n.* habit, usage, convention, rite ▷*fashion*

**customer** *n.* purchaser, buyer, client, patron

**cut** *v.* carve, whittle, chisel, cleave, sever, gash, slice, shear, shave

**cut off** *v.* disconnect, interrupt, stop

**cute** *adj.* charming, attractive, pretty, dainty

**cutting** *adj.* sharp, biting, bitter, sarcastic

# D d

**dab** *v.* blot, swab, touch, pat

**dabble** *v.* toy, meddle, tinker, trifle, potter

**daft** *adj.* crazy, silly, innocent, idiotic, cracked, dopey ★**bright**

**dagger** *n.* knife, dirk, bayonet, stiletto

**daily** ① *adj.* everyday, normal, common *It is quite common to see squirrels in the woods* ② *n.* newspaper

**dainty** *adj.* delicate, charming, exquisite, choice, tasty

**dally** *v.* play, trifle, dawdle, linger, loiter

**damage** *n.* harm, sabotage, vandalism, injury, hurt

**damn** *v.* curse, swear, condemn, criticize ★**bless**

**damp** *adj.* humid, clammy, dank ▷*moist* ★**dry**

**damsel** *n.* girl, maiden, lady, woman

**dance** *v.* hop, skip, jump, prance, frolic, gambol

**danger** *n.* peril, hazard, risk, jeopardy, menace ★**safety**

**dangerous** *adj.* perilous, precarious, unsafe, risky, hazardous, reckless, hairy ★**safe**

**dangle** *v.* hang, swing, sway

**dank** *adj.* sticky, muggy, moist, soggy ▷*damp*

**dapper** *adj.* spruce, natty, neat, stylish, trim ▷*smart* ★**scruffy**

**dare** *v.* brave, face, risk, defy, challenge, venture

**daring** *adj.* adventurous, dashing, bold, fearless ▷*brave* ★**timid**

**dark** *adj.* dusky, swarthy, shady, dim, dingy, shadowy ★**light**

**darling** *n.* pet, love, dear, favourite, beloved, precious

**darn** *v.* mend, sew, patch, repair

**dart** ① *n.* arrow, missile ② *v.* dash, hurtle *The express train hurtled through the tunnel,* charge, gallop

**dash** *v.* rush, gallop, run, career, fly, hasten

**date** ① *n.* time, point ② *n.* appointment *I have an appointment to see the doctor,* engagement ③ *v.* become old, become dated

**daub** *v.* plaster, spread, smear, coat, paint

**daunt** *v.* intimidate, terrify, scare, confront

**dauntless** *adj.* fearless, gallant, courageous ▷*brave* ★**discouraged**

**dawdle** *v.* linger, loiter, lag, waste time,

## Dances

| | |
|---|---|
| Ballet | Polonaise |
| Bolero | Quadrille |
| Bop | Quickstep |
| Cha-cha | Rumba |
| Charleston | Samba |
| Conga | Square dance |
| Country dance | Tango |
| Disco | Tarantella |
| Fandango | Two-step |
| Flamenco | Twist |
| Fox-trot | Waltz |
| Gavotte | |
| Highland fling | |
| Jitterbug | |
| Jive | |
| Mazurka | |
| Minuet | |
| Morris dance | |
| Polka | |

hang about, dilly-dally ▷*dally* ★**hurry**

**dawn** *n.* beginning, daybreak, daylight, morning, sunrise ★**dusk**

**daze** *v.* deaden, muddle, blind, dazzle ▷*bewilder* DAYS

**dazzle** *v.* blind, glare, confuse ▷*daze*

**dead** *adj.* deceased, departed, gone, lifeless, dull ★**alive**

**deaden** *v.* paralyse, blunt, muffle, drown

**deadly** *adj.* fatal, lethal, mortal, baleful, venomous

**deaf** *adj.* hard of hearing, unhearing, heedless

**deal** *v.* bargain, trade, market, communicate, traffic, give out

**dealer** *n.* merchant, trader, tradesman

**dear** ① *adj.* darling, beloved, loved, cherished *These old records are some of my cherished possessions* ② expensive, high-priced, costly DEER ★**cheap**

**death** *n.* decease, end of life, mortality ★**life**

**debate** *v.* argue, discuss, dispute, question, contend

**debris** *n.* trash, junk ▷*rubbish*

**debt** *n.* obligation, debit, dues, liability ★**credit**

**decay** *v.* ① decompose, rot *The potatoes had been left too long and had rotted,* spoil ② decline, sink, dwindle, waste

**deceive** *v.* dupe, hoax, trick, cheat, mislead ▷*betray* ★**enlighten**

**decent** *adj.* respectable, chaste, proper, fair, modest ★**indecent**

**decide** *v.* determine, rule, judge, resolve

**declare** *v.* avow, state, profess, proclaim, announce

**decline** ① *v.* descend, dwindle *The profits of the business had dwindled,* drop, fall ② *v.* refuse, say no ★**assent** ③ *n.* descent, slope, slant, dip, pitch

**decorate** *v.* embellish, adorn, ornament

**decoy** ① *v.* entice *We were enticed into the café by the smell of roasting coffee,* ensnare, mislead, tempt ② *n.* lure, bait

**decrease** *v.* diminish, lessen, wane, decline, reduce ★**increase**

**decree** *n.* law, edict, manifesto, rule, decision, order, statute, proclamation

**decrepit** *adj.* senile, infirm, crippled, feeble, frail ★**robust**

**dedicate** *v.* devote, apportion, assign, surrender, pledge

**deduce** *v.* draw, infer, conclude, glean, surmise, reason

**deduct** *v.* subtract, take from, remove, withdraw ★**add**

**deed** *n.* ① act, feat, stunt ② document, paper, contract *Michael was under contract to play rugby for the team for three years*

**deep** *adj.* ① profound *The accident taught us a profound lesson about friendship,* bottomless, low ② learned, wise, sagacious

**deface** *v.* disfigure, deform, injure, mar, blemish ★**adorn**

**defeat** *v.* beat, conquer, overcome, vanquish, overthrow, overwhelm ★**triumph**

**defect** *n.* flaw, fault, weak point, blemish, error, imperfection

**defective** *adj.* imperfect, faulty, deficient, insufficient ★**perfect**

**defend** *v.* protect, guard, fortify, support, sustain, uphold ★**attack**

**defer** *v.* postpone, put off, adjourn, waive, yield ★**hasten**

**defiant** *adj.* mutinous, rebellious, resistant, aggressive ★**submissive**

**deficient** *adj.* wanting, imperfect, defective, faulty ★**superfluous**

**defile** *v.* taint, infect, pollute, sully, disgrace ★**cleanse**

**define** *v.* explain, interpret, designate, mark out, specify ★**obscure**

**definite** *adj.* clear, certain, clear-cut, distinct ▷*sure* ★**vague**

**deform** *adj.* misshape, distort, contort, twist, warp

**defraud** *v.* fleece, swindle, embezzle, diddle ▷*cheat*

**defy** *v.* resist, withstand, disregard, challenge, disobey ★**obey**

**degrade** *v.* humble, debase, corrupt, downgrade, cheapen ★**improve**

**degree** *n.* grade, step, measure, rate, scale *Our answers were scored on a scale from* *one to ten,* class, step, level, standard

**dejected** *adj.* depressed, downcast, crestfallen, disheartened, disconsolate ▷*gloomy* ★**elated**

**delay** *v.* postpone, put off, detain, halt, hinder, impede ★**hurry**

**deliberate** ① *adj.* wilful, calculated, intentional, planned ★**unintentional** ② *v.* reflect, contemplate, discuss

**delicate** *adj.* dainty, refined, soft, luxurious, modest, fragile, tender ★**harsh**

**delicious** *adj.* palatable, luscious, mellow, savoury, choice, mouth-watering ▷*scrumptious* ★**unpleasant**

**delight** *n.* enjoyment, pleasure, rapture, bliss ▷*happiness* ★**displease**

**delightful** *adj.* enjoyable, cheery, enchanting, lovely ▷*agreeable* ★**horrible**

**deliver** ① *v.* transfer, hand over, bear *She came bearing gifts for the whole family,* carry, convey ② free, liberate, release

**delude** *v.* cheat, hoax, hoodwink, mislead ▷*deceive* ★**guide**

**deluge** *n.* inundation, swamp, spate ▷*flood*

**demand** *v.* ① request, ask, appeal, entreat ② badger, pester, nag *My sister has been nagging me to take her to the park*

**demeanour** *n.* bearing, manner, conduct, air

**demented** *adj.* distracted, foolish, insane ▷*mad* ★**sane**

**demolish** *v.* destroy, wreck, ruin, smash, overthrow, knock down ★**build**

**demon** *n.* fiend, imp, devil, evil spirit

**demonstrate** *v.* prove, exhibit, illustrate ▷*show*

**demote** *v.* degrade, downgrade, relegate ★**promote**

**demur** *v.* hesitate, object, protest, doubt, waver ★**consent**

**demure** *adj.* coy, sedate, staid, sober, prudish, discreet ★**indiscreet**

**den** *n.* ① nest, cave, haunt, lair ② hideaway, retreat *This little room is my retreat, where I can sit and think,* study

**denote** *v.* designate, indicate, mean, show, point out

**denounce** *v.* decry, defame, attack, brand, condemn, vilify ▷*accuse* ★**praise**

**dense** *adj.* ① thick, solid, stout, compact ★**sparse** ② stupid, thick, stolid, obtuse ★**clever** DENTS

**dent** *n.* notch, cavity, chip, dimple, hollow

**deny** *v.* ① refuse, reject, repudiate ② disagree with *I am afraid that I disagree with what you say,* oppose, contradict ★**admit**

**depart** *v.* quit, go, retire, withdraw, vanish ▷*leave* ★**arrive**

**department** *n.* section, division, office, branch, province

**depend on** *v.* lean on, rely upon, trust in

**depict** *v.* describe, sketch, portray, outline, draw

**deplorable** *adj.* distressing, disastrous, shameful, scandalous ★**excellent**

**deplore** *v.* regret, lament, mourn ★**celebrate**

**deport** *v.* banish, exile, expel, oust

**deposit** *v.* drop, lay, place, put, bank, entrust, save ★**withdraw**

**depot** *n.* ① warehouse, storehouse ② terminus, station

**depraved** *adj.* corrupted, immoral, evil, sinful, vile *After calling me vile names, he left* ★**upright**

**depreciate** *v.* ① devalue, lessen, lose value *From the moment it was bought the car began losing value,* reduce ② belittle, disparage, deride ★**appreciate**

**depress** ① *v.* dishearten, dispirit, cast down ★**cheer** ② flatten, push down

**depressed** *adj.* dispirited, disheartened, despondent, fed up

**deprive** *v.* take away, rob, starve, divest *The traitor had been divested of all her honours* ★**bestow**

**depth** *n.* pit, shaft, well, chasm, gulf, abyss

**deputy** *n.* agent, delegate, lieutenant, assistant, councillor

**derelict** *adj.* abandoned, deserted *The* Mary Celeste *sailing ship was found deserted in the Atlantic,* forlorn

**deride** *v.* laugh at, jeer at, ridicule ▷*mock* ★**praise**

**derive** *v.* develop *Many English words developed from Norman-French,* obtain, arise from, originate

**descend** *v.* fall, drop, lower, decline, collapse ▷ *sink* ★**ascend**

**describe** *v.* depict, portray, detail, define, tell

**desert** ① *n.* (*dez*-ert) wasteland, wilderness ② *adj.* desolate, arid, barren ③ *v.* (dez-*ert*) forsake, leave ▷ *abandon* DESSERT

**deserve** *v.* be worthy of, merit, warrant, be entitled to ★**forfeit**

**design** *n.* drawing, painting, plan, pattern, scheme

**desirable** *adj.* ① agreeable, pleasing, good ② attractive, alluring, adorable

**desire** *v.* ① wish, require, need, crave ② long for, yearn after, pine for *My sister lived abroad, but always pined for home* ★**detest**

**desist** *v.* abstain, avoid, break off, cease, end

**desolate** *adj.* lonely, forlorn, miserable, wretched, alone ★**cheerful**

**despair** *n.* depression, misery, hopelessness, sorrow ▷ *gloom* ★**hope**

**desperate** *adj.* drastic, reckless, frantic, rash, wild ★**hopeful**

**despicable** *adj.* contemptible, low, detestable, degrading ★**noble**

**despise** *v.* abhor, detest, loathe, look down upon ▷ *hate* ★**prize**

**despite** *prep.* in spite of, notwithstanding

**despondent** *adj.* depressed, dispirited, broken-hearted ▷ *miserable* ★**cheerful**

**destination** *n.* goal, terminus, end, objective, journey's end

**destiny** *n.* fate, lot, fortune, future, prospect, doom

**destitute** *adj.* poor, needy, bankrupt, penniless, poverty-stricken ★**wealthy**

**destroy** *v.* ruin, demolish, spoil, smash, exterminate ▷ *wreck* ★**create**

**destruction** *n.* desolation, downfall, ruin, defeat, havoc ★**creation**

**detach** *v.* separate, part, divide, loosen, undo ★**attach**

**detail** *n.* item, fact, circumstance, point

**detain** *v.* delay, retard, restrain, arrest, hold

**Dessert**

**Desert**

up, hinder, impede, stop ★**release**

**detect** *v.* notice, discover, observe, scent, track down ★**miss**

**deter** *v.* prevent, hold back, check, stop ▷ *detain* ★**encourage**

**deteriorate** *v.* become worse, worsen, corrode, decline, decompose ★**improve**

**determine** *v.* find out, decide, identify, choose, regulate

**detest** *v.* abhor *Lucy was a peaceful person and abhorred violence,* loathe, despise ▷ *hate* ★**adore**

**devastate** *v.* lay waste, ravage, overwhelm ▷ *destroy*

**develop** *v.* mature, ripen, grow up, evolve, extend ★**restrict**

**deviate** *v.* diverge, differ, vary, contrast, wander ★**conform**

**device** *n.* apparatus, contrivance, instrument, appliance

**devil** *n.* imp, evil spirit, demon, fiend, Satan

**devious** *adj.* tricky, sly, subtle, cunning, roundabout ▲**forthright**

**devise** *v.* contrive, fashion, form, plan, conceive

**devoid** *adj.* barren, empty, free, without, lacking ★**endowed**

**devote** *v.* allocate, allot, give, assign, dedicate

**devoted** *adj.* dedicated, devout, loyal, caring, ardent ★**indifferent**

**devour** *v.* swallow, gulp, gorge, consume ▷*eat*

**devout** *adj.* pious, devoted, religious, faithful, passionate ★**insincere**

**dexterous** *adj.* able, active, deft, nimble ▷*skilful* ★**clumsy**

**diagram** *n.* outline, plan, sketch, draft, chart, drawing

**dictate** *v.* speak, utter, say, instruct, ordain, command

**die** *v.* expire, finish, end, pass away, perish, cease ★**live** DYE

**differ** *v.* ① vary, contrast, diverge *In this case, my views diverge strongly from yours* ② argue, conflict, clash

**difference** *n.* variance, distinctness, divergence, subtlety ★**agreement**

**different** *adj.* contrary, variant, distinct, original, unusual ★**same**

**difficult** *adj.* hard, puzzling, baffling, complex, laborious ★**easy**

**difficulty** *n.* trouble, bother, predicament ★**plight**

**diffident** *adj.* bashful, reserved, retiring, timid, unsure ▷*shy* ★**confident**

**dig** *v.* burrow, excavate, grub, delve, scoop

**digest** ① *v.* (di-*gest*) absorb, assimilate, dissolve ② *n.* (*di*-gest) abridgment, condensation, précis

**digit** *n.* ① number, figure, cipher ② finger, toe, thumb

**dignified** *adj.* grave, majestic, noble, lofty, grand ★**undignified**

**dignity** *n.* grandeur, merit, fame, gravity, nobility

**dilapidated** *adj.* neglected, unkempt, crumbling, decayed

**dilemma** *n.* quandary, plight, difficulty, predicament

**dilute** *v.* water down, weaken, reduce, thin

**dim** *adj.* dark, faint, pale, gloomy ▷*obscure* ★**bright**

**diminish** *v.* reduce, lessen, decrease, become smaller ★**enhance**

**din** *n.* uproar, racket, babble, pandemonium, commotion, hubbub ▷*noise* ★**quiet**

**dingy** *adj.* murky, dark, dreary, sombre, gloomy ▷*dismal* ★**bright**

**dip** *v.* sink, subside, immerse, plunge

**dire** *adj.* alarming, appalling, awful, horrible ▷*terrible* DYER

**direct** ① *adj.* straight, even, blunt, candid ② *v.* aim, level, train, point

**direction** *n.* course, trend, way, track, route

**dirt** *n.* impurity, filth, grime, muck, soil

**dirty** *adj.* unclean, impure, filthy, sordid, squalid, nasty ★**clean**

**disable** *v.* cripple, lame, maim, disarm

**disadvantage** *n.* inconvenience, burden, damage, loss, obstacle ★**advantage**

**disagree** *v.* differ, revolt, decline, refuse, dissent, argue ★**agree**

**disagreeable** *adj.* unpleasant, obnoxious,

**Dogs**

Afghan hound
Airedale
Bassett hound
Beagle
Bloodhound
Borzoi
Boxer
Bulldog
Chihuahua

unwelcome, offensive ★**agreeable**

**disappear** *v.* vanish, dissolve, fade, melt, depart, expire ★**appear**

**disappoint** *v.* frustrate, disillusion, let down, dismay, dissatisfy ★**please**

**disapprove** *v.* condemn, denounce, criticize, reproach ★**approve**

**disaster** *n.* calamity, catastrophe, accident, misfortune ★**triumph**

**disbelief** *n.* incredulity, distrust, doubt, suspicion ★**belief**

**discard** *v.* eliminate, get rid of, reject, scrap *Once we got a new car, I scrapped the old one,* throw away ★**adopt**

**discern** *v.* note, discover, distinguish

**discharge** *v.* ① dismiss, give notice to, expel ② detonate, emit, fire

**disciple** *n.* follower, learner, pupil, attendant

**discipline** *n.* correction, training, self-control, obedience

**disclaim** *v.* repudiate, disown, renounce, deny, reject ★**acknowledge**

**disclose** *v.* discover, show, reveal, expose, betray ▷*divulge* ★**conceal**

**disconcert** *v.* abash, confuse, confound, upset, baffle ★**encourage**

**disconnect** *v.* separate, detach, cut off, sever, uncouple ★**connect**

**disconsolate** *adj.* distressed, sad, forlorn, melancholy, desolate ▷*unhappy* ★**cheerful**

**discontented** *adj.* displeased, disgruntled, unsatisfied, reluctant ★**content**

**discord** *n.* disagreement, strife ★**concord**

**discourage** *v.* depress, dismay, dispirit, dishearten *I don't want to dishearten you, but our holiday is cancelled,* put off ★**encourage**

**discouraged** *adj.* crestfallen, daunted, depressed, downcast ★**encouraged**

**discourteous** *adj.* blunt, crude, churlish,

Chow chow
Collie
Dachshund
Dalmatian
Doberman
 pinscher
Foxhound

German shepherd
Golden retriever
Great Dane
Greyhound
Irish setter
Labrador
Old English
 sheepdog
Pekinese
Pointer

Poodle
Pug
St. Bernard
Saluki
Spaniel
Terrier

outspoken, abrupt ★**courteous**

**discover** v. locate, surprise, unearth, uncover ▷*find* ★**conceal**

**discreet** adj. prudent, cautious, careful, tactful, sensible ★**indiscreet** DISCRETE

**discriminate** v. distinguish, penetrate, favour, judge, assess ★**confound**

**discuss** v. confer, consider, talk over, debate, argue

**disdain** n. ridicule, scorn, contempt, derision ★**admiration**

**disease** n. infection, contagion, illness, plague, ailment, sickness

**disfigure** v. blemish, deface, deform, mar, scar, spoil ★**adorn**

**disgrace** n. scandal, dishonour, shame, infamy, stigma ★**honour**

**disguise** v. conceal, mask, falsify, cloak, deceive, fake

**disgust** ① n. revulsion, loathing, distaste *The room was messy, and I entered it with distaste* ② v. repel, revolt, nauseate ★**admire**

**dish** n. plate, platter, bowl

**dishearten** v. depress, cast down, deter, deject ▷*discourage* ★**encourage**

**dishonest** adj. deceitful, unscrupulous, shady, crooked ★**honest**

**disintegrate** v. crumble, moulder, decompose, rot, fall apart ★**unite**

**dislike** v. hate, loathe, detest, abhor, abominate ▷*despise* ★**like**

**dismal** adj. dreary, ominous, cheerless, depressing ▷*hopeless* ★**cheerful**

**dismiss** v. banish, discard, abandon, dispel, repudiate, release ★**appoint**

**disobey** v. rebel, transgress, resist, defy, ignore ★**obey**

**disorder** n. confusion, disarray, commotion, chaos ★**order**

**dispel** v. disperse, drive away, dismiss, allay, scatter ★**collect**

**dispense** v. distribute, arrange, allocate, supply, measure out ★**accept**

**disperse** v. scatter, separate, break up, spread abroad, distribute ★**gather**

**display** v. show, exhibit, unfold, expose,

flaunt *He flaunts his expensive clothes to his friends,* flourish ▷*reveal* ★**hide**

**displease** v. annoy, anger, irritate, upset, vex, offend, infuriate, incense ★**please**

**dispose** v. arrange, place, position, regulate, order

**dispose of** v. discard, dump, destroy, eliminate, throw away ★**keep**

**dispute** ① n. conflict, quarrel, argument ② v. argue, refute, contend

**disregard** v. overlook, misjudge, despise, ignore, snub ★**heed**

**disreputable** adj. discreditable, dishonourable, disgraceful ▷*shameful* ★**honourable**

**dissect** v. examine, scrutinize, analyse, dismember

**dissent** n. disagreement, difference, repudiation, opposition ★**assent**

**dissimilar** adj. different, diverse, unlike, various ★**similar**

**dissolve** v. melt, thaw, break up, fade

**dissuade** v. deter, discourage, warn, put off ★**persuade**

**distance** n. extent, remoteness, range, reach, span, stretch

**distinct** adj. ① separate, independent, detached ② clear, conspicuous, lucid ★**hazy**

**distinguish** v. discern, discover, differentiate

**distinguished** adj. important, notable, great, famed, celebrated ★**ordinary**

**distort** v. deform, misshape, twist, bend, buckle

**distract** v. ① beguile, bewilder, disturb, confuse ② entertain

**distress** v. harass, embarrass, trouble, grieve ▷*worry* ★**soothe**

**distribute** v. give out, deliver, disperse, circulate ▷*dispense* ★**collect**

**district** n. area, community, locality *Pat and Mike have moved to a new locality,* neighbourhood, region

**distrust** v. suspect, discredit, doubt, disbelieve ★**trust**

**disturb** v. annoy, bother, disquiet, unsettle, upset, confuse ★**calm**

## Domesticated Animals

| | |
|---|---|
| Camel | Goat |
| Canary | Goose |
| Cat | Horse |
| Cattle | Parakeet |
| Chicken | Parrot |
| Dog | Pig |
| Donkey | Pigeon |
| Duck | Sheep |
| Elephant | |

**dither** *v.* waver, hesitate, falter, oscillate

**dive** *v.* plunge, pitch, swoop, descend, drop

**diverse** *adj.* different, various, dissimilar, numerous, separate ★**identical**

**divert** *v.* ① alter, change, deflect ② entertain, gratify

**divest** *v.* disrobe, undress, strip

**divide** *v.* separate, dissect, part, divorce, distribute, apportion, split ★**join**

**division** *n.* portion, fragment, section, compartment, department

**divorce** *v.* annul, cancel, separate, divide, part, split up

**divulge** *v.* betray, disclose, tell, announce, broadcast, uncover

**dizzy** *adj.* giddy, confused, shaky, wobbling, muddled, staggering

**do** *v.* ① carry out, perform, act ② be adequate, suffice

**do away with** *v.* destroy, abolish, eliminate, kill

**do up,** *v.* fasten, tie, fix

**docile** *adj.* amenable, tame, meek, orderly, manageable ★**unco-operative**

**doctrine** *n.* article, belief, creed, dogma, teaching

**document** *n.* paper, deed, certificate, form

**dodge** *v.* avoid, parry, duck, elude, fend off

**dogged** *adj.* obstinate, morose, sullen, persistent, steadfast ★**docile**

**doleful** *adj.* dismal, woebegone, depressing, rueful, sad ▷*gloomy* ★**merry**

**domestic** ① *adj.* homely, household *The children always help with the household chores,* family, internal ② domesticated, tame

**dominant** *adj.* masterful, superior, supreme, prevalent ★**subordinate**

**dominate** *v.* rule, control, direct, tyrannize, overbear ★**yield**

**donation** *n.* gift, present, contribution

**doom** *n.* judgement, fate, verdict, destiny, destruction

**door** *n.* entrance, doorway, gate, gateway, portal

**dose** *n.* draught, potion, quantity, amount

**doubt** *v.* hesitate, waver, demur, suspect, mistrust, be dubious ★**trust**

**doubtful** *adj.* suspicious, dubious, indefinite, uncertain, unclear ★**certain**

**dour** *adj.* austere, dreary, grim, hard, severe ★**cheery**

**dowdy** *adj.* dull, plain, dingy, frumpish ▷*shabby* ★**elegant**

**downcast** *adj.* crestfallen, downhearted, dejected ▷*miserable* ★**happy**

**downfall** *n.* ruin, overthrow, misfortune, disgrace, failure

**downright** *adj.* blunt, candid, absolute, forthright, straightforward

**doze** *v.* snooze, slumber, sleep, nod off, drowse DOES

**drab** *adj.* colourless, cheerless, dull, gloomy, grey ▷*dreary* ★**bright**

**draft** *v.* sketch, outline, draw, design, plan

**drag** *v.* draw, pull, haul, tug, tow, lug

**drain** ① *v.* draw, strain, drip, percolate, empty, dry, drink up ② *n.* conduit, sewer, pipe

**dramatic** *adj.* theatrical, exciting, surprising, sensational ★**ordinary**

**drape** *v.* hang, suspend, droop, cover

**drastic** *adj.* extreme, dire, desperate, harsh, radical ★**mild**

**draw** *v.* ① pull, tug, drag, haul ② sketch, design, depict, portray

**drawback** *n.* weakness, shortcoming, failing, defect, handicap ★**advantage**

**dread** *n.* fear, terror, horror, alarm, awe, dismay ▷*fright* ★**confidence**

**dreadful** *adj.* fearful, terrible, horrible, alarming ▷*awful* ★**comforting**

**dream** *n.* trance, vision, fancy, reverie, fantasy, illusion

**dreary** *adj.* dingy, gloomy, sombre, cheerless ▷*dismal* ★**bright**

**drench** *v.* saturate, soak, steep, flood

**dress** ① *n.* clothing, vestments, costume, garb, apparel, attire ② *v.* wear, put on, don

**dress up** *v.* play-act, don, fancy-dress

**drift** *v.* float, flow, wander, stray, meander
*The little stream meandered through lush countryside*

**drill** ① *v.* teach, exercise, train, discipline ② bore, penetrate, pierce

**drink** *v.* imbibe, swallow, absorb, quaff, sip

**drip** *v.* drop, ooze, percolate, drizzle, trickle

**drive** *v.* ① make, compel, force, oblige, prod, goad ② propel, direct, operate, actuate

**drivel** *n.* nonsense, babble, twaddle, bunkum, gibberish

**drizzle** *v.* dribble, mizzle, shower, spit, spray ▷*rain*

**droll** *adj.* whimsical, comical, comic ▷*funny*

**droop** *v.* flag, sink, decline, languish, drop, bend, wilt

**drop** ① *v.* fall, sink, dip, plunge, plummet ② *n.* droplet, globule, drip

**drown** *v.* sink, immerse, swamp, submerge, extinguish

**drowsy** *adj.* sleepy, somnolent, dazed, tired

**drudge** *v.* toil, labour, struggle, plod, slave

**drug** *v.* dope, deaden, sedate, stupefy, poison

**dry** *adj.* ① arid, parched, moistureless, dried up ★**wet** ② uninteresting, boring, tedious, prosaic, dull

**dubious** *adj.* suspicious, fishy, suspect, untrustworthy ▷*doubtful* ★**trustworthy**

**duck** ① *n.* water fowl ② *v.* plunge, submerge, dip, dodge, lurch

**due** *adj.* ① owing, unpaid, payable ② just, fair, proper ③ scheduled, expected DEW

**duel** *n.* combat, contest, battle, swordplay

**duffer** *n.* blunderer, bungler, booby, dolt

**dull** *adj.* ① stupid, stolid, obtuse, dim-witted ② blunt, not sharp ③ boring, uninteresting, tedious, monotonous, lifeless

**dumb** ① *adj.* silent, speechless, mute ② foolish, stupid ▷*dull* ★**intelligent**

**dummy** ① *n.* mannequin, puppet, doll ② *n.* blockhead, dimwit ③ *adj.* artificial, fake, false

**dump** *v.* deposit, ditch, empty, throw away

**dunce** *n.* dimwit, dolt, blockhead, duffer, ignoramus ★**genius**

**dungeon** *n.* cell, prison, jail, vault, gaol

**dupe** *v.* cheat, defraud, deceive, outwit

**duplicate** *n.* copy, facsimile, replica, reproduction

**durable** *adj.* lasting, enduring, permanent, stable, reliable ★**fragile**

**dusk** *n.* twilight, nightfall, evening, gloaming ★**dawn**

**dusty** *adj.* grimy, dirty, filthy, grubby ★**polished**

**duty** *n.* ① obligation, responsibility, allegiance, trust, task ② impost, tax, excise

**dwell** *v.* stop, stay, rest, linger, tarry, live, reside

**dwell on** *v.* emphasize, linger over, harp on

**dwindle** *v.* diminish, decrease, decline, waste, shrink, become smaller ★**increase**

**dye** *n.* pigment, colouring matter, colour, stain, tint DIE

# E e

**eager** *adj.* avid, enthusiastic, ambitious, ardent, zealous ▷*keen* ★**indifferent**

**early** *adj.* advanced, forward, soon ★**late**

**earn** *v.* make money, deserve, merit, rate, win, acquire ★**spend** URN

**earnest** *adj.* serious, sincere, determined, eager, zealous ★**flippant**

**earth** *n.* ① soil, dust, dry land world, globe, sphere

**ease** *n.* ① calm, repose, rest, quiet, peace ② dexterity, deftness ★**difficulty**

**easy** *adj.* effortless, smooth, simple, practicable ★**difficult**

**eat** *v.* consume, dine, chew, swallow, gorge

**ebb** *v.* flow back, fall back, recede, decline, wane ★**flow**

**eccentric** *adj.* queer, strange, odd, erratic, whimsical ▷*peculiar* ★**normal**

**echo** *v.* vibrate, reverberate, imitate

**economical** *adj.* moderate, reasonable, frugal ▷*thrifty* ★**expensive**

**ecstasy** *n.* joy, happiness, delight, elation ▷*bliss* ★**torment**

**edge** *n.* border, rim, brink, fringe, margin, tip ▷*end*

**edible** *adj.* eatable, comestible, safe, wholesome ★**inedible**

**edit** *v.* revise, correct, adapt, censor, publish

**educate** *v.* instruct, teach, tutor, coach, train

**educated** *adj.* learned, cultured, erudite, literate, well-bred ★**ignosant**

**eerie** *adj.* weird, unearthly, uncanny, awesome

**effect** ① *n.* outcome *What was the outcome of your interview?,* end, result ② *v.* cause, make, bring about, accomplish

**effective** *adj.* operative, serviceable, competent ★**useless**

**efficient** *adj.* competent, proficient, able ▷*effective* ★**inefficient**

**effort** *n.* exertion, toil, labour, accomplishment ▷*feat*

**eject** *v.* drive out, force out, expel, evict, oust, discharge

**elaborate** *adj.* complex, elegant, ornate, intricate ★**simple**

**elated** *adj.* excited, gleeful, joyous, overjoyed ▷*pleased* ★**downcast**

**elderly** *adj.* old, aged, ancient ★**youthful**

**elect** *v.* choose, determine, vote, select, pick

**elegant** *adj.* refined, luxurious, polished, classical ▷*graceful* ★**inelegant**

**elementary** *adj.* easy, effortless, basic, clear ▷*simple* ★**complex**

## Eating verbs

bolt  breakfast
chew  chomp  consume
devour  dig in  dine  drink
eat  eat up
feast  feed  finish off
gobble  gorge  gulp  guzzle
imbibe
lap up  lunch
masticate  munch
nibble  nosh
partake  peck at  pick at
quaff
relish
sample  savour  set to  sip  slurp
snack  swallow  sup  swig  swill
taste  tuck in
wash down  wine and dine
wolf down

**elevate** *v.* raise, erect, hoist, upraise ▷ *lift* ★**lower**

**eligible** *adj.* qualified, suitable, acceptable, proper ▷ *fit* ★**unfit**

**eliminate** *v.* do away with, abolish *The government has abolished many old laws,* exterminate, erase, delete ★**keep**

**elude** *v.* evade, avoid, depart, dodge, escape

**embarrass** *v.* abash, confuse, disconcert, fluster, shame

**emblem** *n.* badge, mark, brand, sign, crest, device

**embrace** *v.* ① hug, squeeze, cuddle, caress, hold ② include *The census figures include new arrivals this year,* encompass, enclose

**emerge** *v.* come out, exit, appear, arise, turn up ★**disappear**

**emergency** *n.* crisis, danger, extremity, predicament ▷ *plight*

**eminent** *adj.* famous, noted, renowned, well-known, esteemed ▷ *important* ★**unknown**

**emit** *v.* give off, belch, radiate, discharge, eject, vent ★**absorb**

**emotion** *n.* sentiment, feeling, fervour, passion

**emotional** *adj.* affected, sensitive, responsive, temperamental ★**cold**

**emphasize** *v.* accentuate, accent, intensify ▷ *stress* ★**understate**

**employ** *v.* engage, hire, retain, apply, adopt ▷ *use*

**employee** *n.* worker, workman, staff member, job-holder, hand

**empty** ① *adj.* bare, barren, vacant *That house has been vacant for months,* hollow, unoccupied ★**full** ② *v.* discharge, drain, unload, pour out ★**fill**

**enchant** *v.* enthral, bewitch, delight, gratify ▷ *charm* ★**bore**

**enclose** *v.* surround, encircle, encompass, contain, include ★**open**

**encounter** *v.* come upon, meet, experience, face

**encourage** *v.* cheer, hearten, console, comfort, support ▷ *urge* ★**dissuade**

**encroach** *v.* intrude, transgress, overstep, trespass, infringe, make inroads, invade

**end** ① *n.* conclusion, finish, limit, boundary *This river marks the boundary of the county* ② *v.* complete, close, terminate ▷ *finish* ★**start**

**endanger** *v.* hazard, imperil, jeopardize ▷ *risk* ★**protect**

**endeavour** *v.* aspire, aim, strive, struggle, try ▷ *aim*

**endless** *adj.* ceaseless, continuous, everlasting, limitless

**endorse** *v.* undersign, uphold, support, guarantee, vouch for ★**disapprove**

**endow** *v.* settle upon, invest, award, bequeath, provide ▷ *bestow* ★**divest**

**endowed** *adj.* talented, gifted, enhanced

**endure** *v.* bear, tolerate, suffer, go through, experience, cope with

**enemy** *n.* foe, adversary, rival, antagonist, opponent ★**friend**

**energetic** *adj.* dynamic, lively, vigorous, brisk ▷ *active* ★**sluggish**

**energy** *n.* vigour, endurance, stamina, vitality, force, power

**enforce** *v.* apply, administer, carry out

**engage** *v.* ① employ, hire, charter, rent ② occupy *That new book has occupied my mind for weeks,* oblige, operate ③ pledge, betroth

**engine** *n.* machine, device, motor, turbine, appliance

**engrave** *v.* etch, stipple, incise, sculpture, carve, chisel

**engrossed** *adj.* absorbed, fascinated, enthralled ★**bored**

**enhance** *v.* intensify, strengthen, amplify, improve ★**decrease**

**enigma** *n.* riddle, puzzle, cryptogram, mystery, problem

**enjoy** *v.* like, be fond of, delight in, appreciate, savour ▷ *relish* ★**detest**

**enjoyable** *adj.* likeable, amusing, delicious ▷ *agreeable* ★**disagreeable**

**enlarge** *v.* amplify, make bigger, expand, extend, magnify, increase, broaden ▷ *swell* ★**shrink**

**enlighten** *v.* inform, teach, explain to,

## Engines

Diesel engine
Internal combustion engine
Jet engine
Piston engine
Steam engine
Turbojet engine
Turboprop engine
Wankel engine

educate, instruct ★**confuse**

**enlist** *v.* conscript, employ, engage, muster, sign up, volunteer

**enmity** *n.* animosity, acrimony, bitterness, hostility, antagonism, antipathy ▷*hatred* ★**friendship**

**enormous** *adj.* immense, vast, tremendous, massive ▷*huge* ★**tiny**

**enough** *adj.* sufficient, adequate, ample, plenty ★**insufficient**

**enrage** *v.* aggravate, incite, incense, infuriate ▷*anger* ★**soothe**

**enrich** *v.* decorate, embellish, adorn, improve ★**impoverish**

**enrol** *v.* sign up, enlist, register, accept, admit ★**reject**

**enslave** *v.* bind, conquer, dominate, overpower, yoke ★**free**

**ensue** *v.* develop, follow, result, arise ▷*happen* ★**precede**

**ensure** *v.* confirm, guarantee, insure, protect, secure

**entangle** *v.* tangle, snarl, ensnare, complicate ▷*bewilder* ★**extricate**

**enter** *v.* go in, arrive, enrol, invade, commence, penetrate ★**leave**

**enterprise** *n.* endeavour, adventure, undertaking, concern, establishment

**entertain** *v.* amuse, charm, cheer, please, divert, beguile ★**bore**

**enthral** *v.* captivate, charm, entrance, fascinate ★**bore**

**enthusiasm** *n.* fervour, ardour, interest, hobby, passion, eagerness

**entice** *v.* attract, beguile, coax, lead on, wheedle

**entire** *adj.* complete, intact, total, whole, full ★**partial**

**entirely** *adj.* absolutely, wholly, utterly *Our old dog came home, utterly tired and exhausted,* altogether ★**partially**

**entitle** *v.* ① allow, authorize, empower *As president, I am empowered to sign this document,* enable ② call, christen, term, name

**entrance** ① *n.* (*en*-tranee) way in, access *There is an access to the garden on the far side,* doorway, gate, opening ② *v.* (en-*trance*) bewitch, captivate, charm ★**repel**

**entreat** *v.* beg, beseech, implore, ask

**entry** *n.* access, admission, admittance ▷*entrance* ★**exit**

**envelop** *v.* wrap, wind, roll, cloak, conceal, enfold

**envious** *adj.* jealous, grudging, covetous *Arlene cast a covetous eye at my new jacket,* resentful ★**content**

**environment** *n.* surroundings, neighbourhood, vicinity, background

**envy** *v.* covet, grudge, desire, crave, resent

**episode** *n.* occasion, affair, circumstance, happening, instalment

**equal** *adj.* ① matching, like, alike, same ★**different** ② fit *I'm not sure if Joe is really fit for this job*

**equip** *v.* furnish, provide, supply, fit out, rig

**equipment** *n.* stores, supplies, outfit, tackle *When we arrived at the lake, Sam found he'd left his fishing tackle behind,* gear

**equivalent** *adj.* equal, comparable, alike, similar, interchangeable ★**unlike**

**era** *n.* epoch, age, generation, period, time

**eradicate** *v.* uproot, weed out, remove, stamp out ▷*abolish*

**erase** *v.* cancel, rub out, obliterate, eliminate ▷*delete* ★**mark**

**erect** ① *adj.* upright, upstanding, rigid *The tent had a rigid metal frame* ★**relaxed** ② *v.* build, construct, put up ★**demolish**

**err** *v.* be mistaken, blunder, go astray,

mistake, misjudge, sin, slip up

**errand** *n.* mission, assignment, duty, job ▷*task*

**erratic** *adj.* eccentric, irregular, unstable, unreliable ★**stable**

**erroneous** *adj.* untrue, false, faulty, inaccurate ▷*wrong* ★**correct**

**error** *n.* mistake, fault, flaw, fallacy, untruth ▷*blunder* ★**truth**

**erupt** *v.* blow up, explode, burst, vent ▷*discharge*

**escape** *v.* break free, get away, dodge, elude, evade ▷*flee* ★**capture**

**escort** ① *n.* (*es*-cort) guard, conductor, aide, attendant, procession ② *v.* (es-*cort*) accompany, conduct

**especially** *adv.* chiefly, principally, notably

**essay** *n.* ① effort, trial ② theme, manuscript, composition *Whoever writes the best composition gets a prize*

**essence** *n.* ① extract, juice, perfume ② substance *He spoke well, but there was no substance to his speech,* core, pith, character

**essential** *adj.* necessary, needed, vital, requisite ★**superfluous**

**establish** *v.* situate, place, station, found, organize, set up ★**upset**

**estate** *n.* property, land, fortune, inheritance

**esteem** *v.* honour, respect, admire ▷*like* ★**dislike**

**estimate** *v.* consider, calculate, figure, assess, reckon

**estrange** *v.* alienate, antagonize, separate ★**unite**

**eternal** *adj.* endless, ceaseless, forever, immortal, undying ★**temporary**

**evacuate** *v.* leave, desert, quit ▷*abandon* ★**occupy**

**evade** *v.* elude, avoid, get away from, escape from ★**face**

**evaporate** *v.* vanish, dissolve, disappear, condense, dry up

**even** *adj.* ① smooth, plane, flat, flush ② balanced, equal ★**uneven** ③ yet, still

**evening** *n.* eve, eventide, sunset ▷*dusk* ★**morning**

**event** *n.* occurrence, incident, happening

**ever** *adv.* always, evermore, perpetually, forever ★**never**

**everlasting** *adj.* continual, endless, permanent, lasting ★**temporary**

**everyday** *adj.* common, frequent, daily, familiar ★**occasional**

**everything** *n.* all, the whole, the lot

**evict** *v.* expel, eject, cast out, remove, kick out

**evidence** *n.* appearance, proof, sign, token, testimony

**evident** *adj.* obvious, apparent, plain, visible, conspicuous ★**obscure**

**evil** *v.* wicked, sinister, wrong, bad, hurtful, sinful ★**good**

**exact** *adj.* accurate, precise, definite, correct ▷*right* ★**inexact**

**exaggerate** *v.* magnify, overstate, overestimate, amplify ★**minimize**

**examine** *v.* check, inspect, scrutinize, test, quiz, question

**example** *n.* case, sample, specimen, pattern, model, illustration

**exasperate** *v.* provoke, anger, annoy, aggravate ★**soothe**

**excavate** *v.* mine, quarry, shovel, dig up, discover, unearth ★**bury**

**exceed** *v.* excel, surpass, better, beat, outstrip

**excel** *v.* outdo ▷*exceed*

**excellent** *adj.* admirable, good, superb, exquisite ▷*splendid* ★**inferior**

**except** *prep.* with the exception of, barring, save, saving, omitting

**exceptional** *adj.* unique, unusual, rare *Margaret has a rare gift for the piano,* uncommon ★**common**

**excess** *n.* too much, extreme, glut, extravagance, extreme ▷*surplus* ★**scarcity**

**exchange** *v.* trade, barter, swap, convert, change

**excite** *v.* inflame, inspire, provoke, rouse, thrill ★**quell**

**excited** *adj.* ablaze, wild, ecstatic, frantic, thrilled ★**bored**

**exclaim** v. state, say, utter, ejaculate, declare, cry out

**exclude** v. bar, shut out, prevent, boycott, forbid, leave out ★**include**

**exclusive** adj. only, personal, choice, particular, special ★**inclusive**

**excuse** v. forgive, pardon, absolve, exempt, release ★**accuse**

**execute** v. ① accomplish, do, carry out *The work was carried out just as I had expected,* achieve ② put to death, hang

**exempt** v. excuse, release, discharge, relieve, exonerate

**exercise** ① n. performance, lesson, lecture, training ② v. apply, train, practise *We have been practising our tennis for months*

**exert** v. apply, exercise, strain, struggle, toil

**exhale** v. breathe out, expel, expire ★**inhale**

**exhaust** ① v. use up *We have used up all our butter,* consume, deplete, empty ② overtire, fatigue, weaken

**exhibition** n. spectacle, show, fair, pageant, display

**exhilarate** v. invigorate, animate, stimulate, thrill ★**discourage**

**exile** v. deport, banish, relegate, transport, dismiss

**exist** v. be, live, breathe, subsist, stand

**exit** n. way out, outlet, egress, door

**expand** v. inflate, spread, dilate, extend, amplify ▷*swell* ★**contract**

**expansive** adj. affable, genial, friendly, open, comprehensive

**expect** v. look out for, anticipate, assume, foresee, contemplate

**expedition** n. ① outing, excursion, exploration, quest *As a child I spent long hours in the library in the quest for knowledge* ② speed, dispatch, alacrity

**expel** v. evict, eject, discharge, throw out ★**admit**

**expend** v. spend, lay out, waste, consume, use up ▷*exhaust* ★**save**

**expensive** adj. costly, high-priced, valuable, rich ★**cheap**

**experience** ① n. training, practice, wisdom, knowledge ② v. encounter, try, undergo,

endure, meet, know, live through

**experiment** n. trial, test, check, venture

**expert** n. specialist, master, authority, professional ★**novice**

**expire** v. ① breathe out, exhale ② die, lapse *The lease on this house will lapse at the end of the year,* run out ★**begin**

**explain** v. elucidate, spell out, define, expound, teach ★**mystify**

**explanation** n. definition, outline, answer, meaning

**explode** v. detonate, blow up, go off, burst, discharge

**exploit** ① n. deed, feat, act, stunt ② v. take advantage of, profit by

**export** v. ship, send out, send abroad

**expose** v. show, reveal, exhibit, present, lay bare, betray ★**cover**

**express** ① v. phrase, voice, put into words, utter ② v. squeeze out ③ adj. speedy, fast

**expression** n. ① phrase, idiom, sentence, statement ② look, countenance, appearance

**exquisite** adj. dainty, subtle, fine, refined ▷*beautiful* ★**coarse**

**extend** v. stretch, reach, lengthen ▷*expand* ★**shorten**

**extent** n. breadth, expanse, width, bulk, mass, reach, duration

**exterior** ① n. outside, surface ② adj. external, outer, outdoor ★**interior**

**extinct** adj. defunct, dead, exterminated ★**living**

**extinguish** v. put out, blow out, abolish, destroy, quench ★**establish**

**extract** v. take out, select, remove, withdraw ★**insert**

**extraordinary** adj. unusual, incredible, strange, uncommon, marvellous ★**common**

**extravagant** adj. wasteful, reckless, prodigal, lavish ★**stingy**

**extreme** adj. ① excessive, outrageous, intense ★**moderate** ② farthest, final, remote

**extricate** v. loose, loosen, remove, retrieve, pull out

**exultant** adj. rejoicing, jubilant, joyous, triumphant ▷*elated* ★**depressed**

# F f

**fable** *n.* myth, legend, story, fantasy ★**fact**

**fabric** *n.* cloth, textile, material

**fabulous** *adj.* imaginary, legendary *Many tales have been passed down about the legendary deeds of Robin Hood,* mythical, marvellous ▷*wonderful*

**face** ① *n.* countenance, visage ② *n.* front, frontage, facade *The original facade was kept when the building was renovated* ③ *v.* confront, be opposite

**facetious** *adj.* frivolous, jocular, humorous, witty, comical ▷*funny* ★**serious**

**facility** *n.* ease, readiness, quickness, adroitness, knack

**facsimile** *n.* replica, copy, repro, photocopy

**fact** *n.* truth, deed, occurrence, event, reality, actuality ★**fiction**

**factory** *n.* plant, mill, works, shop

**factual** *adj.* true, actual, accurate, correct ▷*real* ★**false**

**fad** *n.* craze, fashion, passion, desire, mania *My sister has a mania for teddy bears,* vogue

**fade** *v.* discolour, bleach, dwindle, dim

**fail** *v.* collapse, fall, miss, trip, lose, flop ★**succeed**

**failing** *n.* frailty, weakness, fault, flaw ▷*defect*

**failure** *n.* collapse, crash, fiasco, downfall ★**success**

**faint** ① *adj.* indistinct *The writing was so indistinct that we could hardly read it,* soft, low, dim, feeble ② *v.* swoon, pass out, collapse FEINT

**fair** *adj.* ① just, equal, reasonable ★**unfair** ② mediocre *He was not a good piano player, just mediocre,* average, moderate ③ blonde, light-skinned, beautiful

**faith** *n.* trust, confidence, belief, fidelity, creed

**faithful** *adj.* ① loyal, constant, staunch, true ★**faithless** ② accurate, dependable *My watch is very dependable; it keeps accurate time,* exact, strict, close ★**inaccurate**

**faithless** *adj.* false, unfaithful, untrue ★**faithful**

**fake** *adj.* false, fictitious, pretended ▷*bogus* ★**genuine**

**fall** *v.* ① fall down, stumble, drop ② decline, dwindle *My mother's shares had dwindled and were worth much less,* lower ★**rise**

**fall down** *v.* stumble, lose one's balance

**fall through** *v.* collapse, fail, founder *The family business had foundered during the recession*

**fallacy** *n.* flaw, fault, mistake, illusion, deception

**false** *adj.* ① untrue, counterfeit, fake, inaccurate ② dishonest, disloyal ★**reliable**

**falsehood** *n.* lie, fiction, fable, fabrication, untruth, fib ★**truth**

**falter** *v.* reel, totter, stumble, waver, tremble

**fame** *n.* glory, distinction, honour, eminence, renown

**familiar** ① *adj.* common, frequent, well-known ② intimate *Joe and Mary are intimate friends of mine,* close, dear

**famine** *n.* scarcity, hunger, shortage, starvation

**famished** *adj.* hungry, starving, ravenous

**famous** *adj.* famed, well-known, celebrated, legendary *My grandmother was very attractive; her beauty was legendary,* notorious ★**unknown**

**fan** *v.* ventilate, cool, blow, stimulate

**fanatic** *n.* enthusiast, zealot, follower, fan

**fanciful** *adj.* romantic, fantastic, imaginary, unreal ★**ordinary**

**fancy** ① *adj.* decorative, beautiful, ornamental ② *v.* desire, hanker after *I had been hankering after a sea cruise all year,* yearn

**fantastic** *adj.* strange, bizarre, unfamiliar, romantic ▷*fanciful* ★**ordinary**

**far** *adj.* distant, faraway, remote ★**near**

**fare** ① *v.* manage *I managed quite well while my parents were abroad,* get along, happen ② *n.* charge, cost, fee, price ③ *n.* food, meals, menu, rations, provisions

**farewell** *interj.* goodbye, so long, adieu *We*

*bade our hosts adieu as we drove off*

**farm** ① *v.* cultivate, raise, grow ② *n.*
farmstead, homestead, ranch, holding *We
owned a small holding of land in the west*

**fascinate** *v.* bewitch, beguile, enthral,
engross ★**bore**

**fashion** ① *n.* style, fad, mode, manner ② *v.*
form, carve, sculpt, devise

**fast** ① *adj.* rapid, quick, speedy, brisk ② *v.*
starve, famish, go hungry

**fasten** *v.* fix, tie, attach, bind, hitch, truss
★**unfasten**

**fat** ① *adj.* stout, corpulent *Uncle Harry was
a corpulent old man* ▷*plump* ★**thin** ② *n.*
grease, oil, tallow

**fatal** *adj.* deadly, lethal, destructive, mortal
★**harmless**

**fate** *n.* fortune, destiny, future, lot, portion

**fathom** *v.* unravel, understand, follow,
comprehend

**fatigue** ① *n.* tiredness, weariness ② *v.* tire,
exhaust, languish *The survivors of the
shipwreck languished in an open boat*

**fault** *n.* ① defect, flaw, imperfection
② blame, responsibility, error

**faulty** *adj.* imperfect, defective, unreliable,
unsound, broken ★**perfect**

**favour** ① *n.* kindness, courtesy, benefit ② *v.*
indulge, prefer, approve ★**disapprove**

**favourite** ① *n.* choice, darling, preference
② *v.* best-liked, chosen, preferred

**fawn** *v.* crouch, crawl, grovel FAUN

**fear** ① *n.* fright, alarm, terror, panic, shock
★**courage** ② *v.* dread, be afraid, doubt

**fearful** *adj.* timid, anxious, alarmed, worried
▷*afraid* ★**courageous**

**fearless** *adj.* gallant, courageous, daring,
valiant *My ailing mother made a valiant
effort to keep working* ▷*brave* ★**timid**

**feast** *n.* banquet, repast, dinner

**feat** *n.* deed, exploit, achievement,
performance, stunt FEET

**feature** *n.* mark, peculiarity, distinction,
characteristic

**fee** *n.* charge, commission, cost

**feeble** *adj.* frail, faint, flimsy, puny ▷*weak*
★**strong**

**Feat**

**Feet**

**feed** *v.* nourish, sustain, foster, nurture
*These plants must be nurtured if they
are to survive*

**feel** *v.* touch, handle, perceive, comprehend,
know, suffer

**feign** *v.* fake, pretend, act, sham FAIN

**feint** *n.* bluff, pretence, dodge, deception
FAINT

**fellow** *n.* companion, comrade, associate,
colleague, mate

**female** *adj.* feminine, womanly, girlish,
maidenly ★**male**

**fence** ① *n.* barrier, paling, barricade ② *v*
dodge, evade, parry *The sudden attack was
parried by the defenders,* duel

**ferocious** *adj.* fierce, savage, brutal, grim,
vicious ★**gentle**

**fertile** *adj.* fruitful, productive, rich,
abundant ★**barren**

**fervent** *adj.* warm, passionate, enthusiastic, zealous ▷*ardent*

**festival** *n.* celebration, carnival, fête, jubilee

**festive** *adj.* convivial, jovial, sociable, gleeful, cordial ★**sombre**

**fetch** *v.* bear, bring, carry, deliver, convey

**fête** *n.* bazaar, carnival, fair, festival FATE

**fetter** *v.* manacle, handcuff, shackle, restrain

**feud** *n.* dispute, grudge, conflict, discord ★**harmony**

**fever** *n.* illness, infection, passion, excitement, heat ecstasy

**few** *adj.* scant, scanty, meagre, paltry, not many

**fiasco** *n.* washout, calamity, disaster, failure

**fib** *n.* lie, falsehood, untruth

**fickle** *adj.* unstable, changeable, faithless, disloyal ★**constant**

**fiction** *n.* stories, fable, myth, legend, invention ★**fact**

**fidelity** *n.* faithfulness, loyalty, allegiance *I owe allegiance to my family and my country* ★**treachery**

**fidget** *v.* be nervous, fret, fuss, jiggle, squirm

**field** *n.* farmland, grassland, green, verdure, meadow, prairie, paddock, pitch

**fiend** *n.* devil, demon, imp, beast, brute

**fiendish** *adj.* atrocious, cruel, devilish, diabolical

**fierce** *adj.* barbarous, cruel, brutal, merciless ▷*savage* ★**gentle**

**fiery** *adj.* passionate, inflamed, excitable, flaming ★**impassive**

**fight** *n.* & *v.* conflict, argument, encounter, combat, contest, battle

**figure** ① *n.* symbol, character, numeral ② *n.* form, shape, model ③ *v.* calculate, reckon *Bella has reckoned the amount correctly*

**filch** *v.* steal, thieve, sneak, purloin *Someone has purloined the letters from our mailbox*

**file** ① *v.* scrape, grind, grate, rasp ② *n.* binder, case, folder

**fill** *v.* load, pack, cram, replenish, occupy ★**empty**

**filter** *v.* sieve, sift, refine, clarify, screen, percolate PHILTRE

**filth** *n.* impurity, dirt, soil, slime, smut,
grime, muck, squalor, dung ★**purity**

**filthy** *adj.* unclean, impure, nasty, foul ▷*dirty* ★**pure**

**final** *adj.* terminal, closing, ultimate, conclusive ▷*last*

**find** *v.* discover, achieve, locate, obtain, perceive, meet with *Our plans met with the approval of the committee* ★**lose** FINED

**fine** ① *adj.* thin, minute, smooth, slender ② *adj.* excellent, sharp, keen, acute ③ *n.* forfeit, penalty

**finesse** *n.* skill, competence, deftness

**finger** ① *v.* feel, grope, handle, touch ② *n.* digit, thumb, pinkie

**finish** *v.* accomplish, complete, close, conclude ▷*end* ★**begin**

**fire** ① *n.* blaze, conflagration, heat ② *v.* ignite, light, discharge, shoot

**firm** ① *adj.* stable, steady, solid, substantial ② *n.* company, business

**first** *adj.* beginning, earliest, initial, chief, principal

**fishy** *adj.* suspicious, dubious, doubtful ★**honest**

**fissure** *n.* breach, cleft, crack, cranny FISHER

**fit** *adj.* ① suitable, fitting, able, apt, eligible ② trim, hale, healthy, sturdy,

**fitting** *adj.* proper, suitable, appropriate, correct ★**unsuitable**

**fix** ① *v.* repair, mend, attach, fasten ② *n.* predicament, jam, pickle, plight *After the earthquake, the town was in a desperate plight*

**flabby** *adj.* baggy, drooping, feeble, sagging, slack

**flag** ① *v.* droop, languish, dwindle, fail ② banner, ensign, colours *The regimental colours were flying at half-mast*

**flagrant** *adj.* blatant, bold, brazen, arrant ★**secret**

**flair** *n.* knack, talent, faculty, ability, gift FLARE

**flame** *n.* fire, blaze, radiance

**flap** *v.* agitate, flutter, wave, swing, dangle

**flare** ① *v.* blaze, burn, glare, flash, glow ② *n.* signal, beacon FLAIR

**flash** *v.* ① gleam, glimmer, sparkle, twinkle,

## Flags

Jack

Banner

Burgee

Signalling flags

Streamer

Standard

Ensign

Pennant

Jolly Roger

Bunting

scintillate, beam ② streak, dash

**flat** ① *adj.* level, smooth, even, horizontal ② *n.* apartment, chambers

**flatter** *v.* blandish, toady, soft-soap, butter up, curry favour *He gives me presents, but only to curry favour with me* ★**criticize**

**flavour** *n.* taste, savour, tang, aroma, quality

**flaw** *n.* fault, defect, blemish, mark, weakness

**flawless** *adj.* perfect, immaculate, faultless, sound ★**imperfect**

**flee** *v.* escape, abscond, run away, bolt, vanish ★**stay** FLEA

**fleet** ① *adj.* rapid, speedy, quick, nimble ▷ *swift* ★**slow** ② *n.* navy, armada, flotilla *A flotilla of yachts sailed up the river*

**fleeting** *adj.* passing, brief, momentary, temporary ★**lasting**

**flexible** *adj.* pliant, pliable, supple, elastic

**flicker** *v.* blaze, glitter, flare, burn, sparkle

**flimsy** *adj.* slight, meagre, fragile, trivial, rickety, weak, makeshift, feeble ★**sturdy**

**flinch** *v.* cower, cringe, shrink, wince *I had twisted my ankle, and winced with pain as I climbed the hill*

**fling** *v.* throw, pitch, cast, heave ▷ *hurl*

**flippant** *adj.* saucy, pert, brash, impudent, glib ★**earnest**

**float** *v.* drift, glide, hover, sail, swim

**flock** *n.* herd, drove, crush, group

**flog** *v.* beat, chastise, flay, lash, spank

**flood** *v.* deluge, engulf, inundate *The town was inundated when the river overflowed,* drown, swamp

**floor** *n.* deck, base, bottom, platform, level, storey

**flop** *v.* flap, fall, drop, droop, fall flat

**florid** *adj.* ruddy, flushed, red, ornate ★**pale**

**flounce** *v.* bounce, fling, jerk, spring, bob

**flounder** ① *v.* bungle, fail, falter, fumble ② *n.* flatfish

**flour** *n.* meal, bran, farina FLOWER

**Flower**

**Flour**

**flourish** v. ① shake, brandish, flaunt ② blossom, bloom, prosper ▷*thrive*

**flow** v. run, stream, glide, sweep, swirl ▷*gush* FLOE

**flower** n. & v. blossom, bloom, bud FLOUR

**fluent** adj. vocal, facile, articulate *Sally is very articulate and has a great command of language,* flowing, fluid

**fluid** adj. watery, flowing, liquid, runny ★**solid**

**flummox** v. baffle, confuse, fluster, confound ▷*bewilder* ★**enlighten**

**flush** ① v. glow, bloom, blush ② v. swab, drench, rinse ③ adj. level, even, flat

**fluster** v. bother, confuse, perturb, ruffle ▷*fuss* ★**calm**

**flutter** v. wave, flap, flop, flitter, hover, flit

**fly** ① v. take flight, glide, soar, float ② v. escape, hasten ③ n. winged insect

**foam** n. froth, scum, lather, suds, surf

**foe** n. enemy, opponent, rival, adversary ★**friend**

**fog** n. mist, vapour, haze, cloud

**foil** ① v. defeat, overcome, elude ② n. sheet metal, tinfoil, film, flake

**fold** n. & v. crease, hem, seam, crimp, pleat FOALED

**follow** v. ① pursue, succeed, come after ② understand, catch on to, comprehend

**folly** n. silliness, foolishness, absurdity, craziness ▷*nonsense* ★**wisdom**

**fond** adj. tender, loving, caring ▷*affectionate* ★**hostile**

**fondle** v. pet, stroke, cuddle, caress, coddle

**food** n. nourishment, nutriment, provender, provisions, fare, sustenance

**fool** ① n. idiot, dunce, clown, blockhead, simpleton ② v. deceive, trick, swindle

**foolhardy** adj. reckless, impetuous, madcap ▷*rash* ★**cautious**

**foolish** adj. absurd, ridiculous, daft ▷*silly* ★**wise**

**for** prep. on behalf of, towards, because of ★**against** fore, four

**forbid** v. bar, ban, prohibit, deter, hinder, prevent ★**allow**

**force** ① n. energy, strength, might, power ② v. make, compel, coerce *It's no use, you can't coerce me into flying home,* push

**fore** adj. first, front, leading FOR, FOUR

**forecast** v. foresee, predict, foretell, prophesy

**foreign** adj. alien, strange, remote, exotic, outlandish ★**domestic**

**foremost** adj. chief, leading, principal, uppermost

**forfeit** v. abandon, give up, lose, relinquish, sacrifice ★**reward**

**forge** v. ① counterfeit, falsify, copy, imitate ② construct, form, make, fashion

**forgery** n. fake, dud, counterfeit, imitation, phoney, sham, fraud

**forget** v. overlook, neglect, lose sight of, let slip ★**remember**

**forgive** v. pardon, absolve, reprieve, let off, overlook ★**blame**

**forlorn** *adj.* lonely, desolate, miserable, wretched ★**hopeful**

**form** ① *v.* make, fabricate, fashion, contrive, create ② *n.* manner, fashion, style ③ *n.* shape, figure *I made a clay figure of a pirate*

**formal** *adj.* stiff, solemn, ceremonial, ritualistic, aloof ★**informal**

**former** *adj.* earlier, previous, prior ★**later**

**formidable** *adj.* awful, terrible, alarming, terrifying, serious ★**trivial**

**forsake** *v.* abandon, give up, desert, discard, leave ▷*quit* ★**resume**

**forth** *adv.* ahead, forward, onward, outward

**forthright** *adj.* frank, candid, direct, bald, blunt ★**devious**

**forthwith** *adv.* immediately, directly, at once, instantly ★**soon**

**fortify** *v.* ① strengthen, confirm, corroborate, hearten ② garrison, protect, buttress *The old house was crumbling and the walls needed to be buttressed* ★**weaken**

**fortitude** *n.* courage, endurance, bravery, composure ▷*strength* ★**cowardice**

**fortunate** *adj.* happy, felicitous, auspicious, rosy ▷*lucky* ★**unfortunate**

**fortune** *n.* ① affluence, wealth, treasure ② chance, destiny, fate

**forward** ① *adv.* onward, forth, ahead, before ② *adj.* progressive, bold, audacious ★**modest** ③ *v.* advance, send, transmit

**foster** *v.* ① help, promote, aid ② care for, cherish, nurse

**foul** *adj.* mucky, nasty, filthy, dirty, murky ★**fair** FOWL

**found** *v.* create, build, erect, establish

**foundation** *n.* establishment, base, basis, groundwork *You will pick up Spanish easily, for you already have the groundwork*

**fountain** *n.* spring, well, reservoir, source

**fowl** *n.* bird, chicken, poultry FOUL

**foxy** *adj.* crafty, slick, cunning, tricky ▷*artful* ★**naive**

**fraction** *n.* portion, part, division ▷*fragment*

**fracture** *n.* break, cleft, crack, fissure, rupture, breach, opening ▷*split*

**fragile** *adj.* brittle, frail, delicate, dainty ▷*flimsy* ★**robust**

**fragment** *n.* portion, bit, chip, morsel, piece ▷*fracture*

**fragrance** *n.* aroma, smell, odour ▷*scent*

**frail** *adj.* weak, feeble, infirm ▷*fragile*

**frame** *n.* framework, casing, shape, mount, chassis

**frank** *adj.* sincere, candid, open, honest, blunt ▷*truthful* ★**insincere**

**frantic** *adj.* excited, furious, distracted, wild, mad ▷*frenzied* ★**calm**

**fraud** *n.* deceit, fake, extortion, swindle ▷*forgery*

**fraudulent** *adj.* sham, fake, counterfeit ▷*bogus* ★**genuine**

**fray** *n.* combat, contest, battle, brawl ▷*rumpus*

**freak** *adj.* abnormal, bizarre *A snowstorm in the tropics would be bizarre,* odd, unusual ★**common**

**free** ① *adj.* unhindered, at liberty, liberated, unrestricted ② *adj.* gratuitous, gratis, without cost ③ *v.* let loose, unleash, release, liberate, emancipate

**freeze** *n.* ice, frost, refrigerate FREES, FRIEZE

**frenzied** *adj.* agitated, excited, furious, hysterical *Lisa became hysterical when she saw the house on fire* ▷*frantic* ★**placid**

**frequent** *adj.* repeated, numerous, recurrent, common ▷*regular* ★**rare**

**frequently** *adv.* often, many times, commonly ★**rarely**

**fresh** *adj.* new, young, vigorous, blooming, recent, wholesome ★**stale**

**fret** *v.* worry, harass, irritate, torment ▷*vex* ★**calm**

**friction** *n.* ① rubbing, grating, contact, abrasion ② ill-feeling, discord, dispute

**friend** *n.* companion, associate, ally, crony *On Saturdays, my father plays golf with some of his cronies,* pal ▷*chum*

**friendly** *adj.* affable, amicable, kindly, cordial ▷*genial* ★**hostile**

**friendship** *n.* affection, fellowship, fondness, harmony ▷*concord* ★**enmity**

**fright** *n.* alarm, dread, dismay, terror ▷*fear* ★**calm**

**frighten** *v.* daunt, dismay, scare, alarm ▷*terrify* ★**reassure**

**frightful** *adj.* alarming, shocking, ghastly ▷*horrible* ★**pleasant**

**frigid** *adj.* cool, chilly, icy, frozen, wintry ★**warm**

**fringe** *n.* edge, border, limits, outskirts

**frisky** *adj.* lively, spirited, playful, active ★**quiet**

**frivolous** *adj.* frothy, facetious, flippant, foolish ▷*trivial* ★**serious**

**frock** *n.* robe, dress, gown, smock

**frolic** *v.* gambol, caper, frisk, sport

**front** *n.* fore, brow, forehead, face, facade, beginning ★**back**

**frontier** *n.* border, boundary, edge, limit

**frosty** *adj.* chilly, frigid, frozen, freezing ▷*cold* ★**warm**

**froth** *n.* scum, bubbles ▷*foam*

**frown** *v.* glower, grimace, glare ▷*scowl* ★**smile**

**frugal** *adj.* thrifty, economical, careful, sparing *We were poor in the old days and needed to be sparing with our money* ▷*meagre* ★**wasteful**

**fruitful** *adj.* fertile, productive, flourishing, plentiful, abundant, profitable ★**barren**

**fruitless** *adj.* unprofitable, sterile, barren, pointless ★**fruitful**

**frustrate** *v.* thwart, balk, foil, hinder, defeat ★**fulfil**

**fugitive** *n.* escapee, runaway, deserter

**fulfil** *v.* perform, render, please, accomplish, achieve ★**frustrate**

**full** *adj.* loaded, packed, laden, charged, abundant, complete ★**empty**

**fumble** *v.* grope, spoil, mismanage, flail ▷*bungle*

**fun** *n.* sport, frolic, gaiety, jollity, entertainment, amusement

**function** ① *n.* service, purpose, activity ② *n.* affair, party, gathering ③ *v.* act, operate, work

**fund** *n.* stock, supply, pool, store, treasury *The city treasury has a small surplus this year*, kitty, reserve

**fundamental** *adj.* basic, essential, primary, rudimentary ★**unimportant**

**funny** *adj.* comical, droll, amusing, ridiculous ▷*humorous* ★**solemn**

**furious** *adj.* agitated, angry, fierce, intense ▷*frantic* ★**calm**

**furnish** *v.* ① supply, provide, offer ② equip

**furrow** *n.* groove, channel, hollow, seam, rib

**further** ① *adj.* extra, more, other, supplementary, ② *v.* advanced, aid, hasten

**furtive** *adj.* secretive, sly, hidden ▷*stealthy* ★**open**

**fury** *n.* anger, frenzy, ferocity, passion ▷*rage* ★**calm**

**fuse** *v.* melt, smelt, combine, merge, solder, weld, integrate ▷*join*

**fuss** *n.* stir, excitement, tumult, bustle, bother, palaver, commotion ▷*ado* ★**calm**

**fussy** *adj.* busy, faddish, fastidious, finicky, exacting ★**plain**

**futile** *adj.* useless, in vain, hopeless *It was hopeless, the bear was too big for Zak to carry*, barren, forlorn, ineffective ★**effective**

**future** *adj.* forthcoming, coming, impending, eventual

**fuzzy** *adj.* murky, foggy, misty, unclear

**Futile**

*It was hopeless, the bear was too big for Zak to carry.*

# G g

**gain** *v.* get, win, acquire, attain, profit

**gale** *n.* storm, wind, hurricane, tornado, cyclone

**gallant** *adj.* courageous, noble, chivalrous ▷*brave*

**gallop** *v.* dash, run, career, rush

**gamble** *v.* bet, risk, wager, chance GAMBOL

**gambol** *v.* prance, romp, frisk, frolic ▷*jump* GAMBLE

**game** *n.* ① sport, pastime, contest, competition ★**work** ② quarry, prey

**gang** *n.* crew, team, troop, crowd, cluster, party

**gap** *n.* space, blank, hole, break, cranny, chink, opening, crack, interval

**gape** *v.* yawn, stare, gaze, gawk ▷*look*

**garbage,** *n.* trash, rubbish, refuse, waste, slops

**garden** *n.* flower bed, vegetable patch, patio, park, allotment

**garment** *n.* clothes, dress, attire, robe, costume ▷*clothing*

**garret** *n.* attic, loft, cupola

**gas** *n.* vapour, fume, mist, smoke

**gasp** *v.* gulp, pant, choke ▷*breathe*

**gate** *n.* door, portal, gateway GAIT

**gather** *v.* ① collect, pick up, pick, draw, amass, assemble, flock, hoard, acquire ★**disperse** ② understand *I understand that you have been elected treasurer of the club,* assume, judge

**gathering** *n.* meeting, assembly, function, affair, company, collection

**gaudy** *adj.* flashy, cheap, tawdry, loud, showy

**gaunt,** *adj.* thin, lean, skinny, spare ▷*haggard* ★**robust**

**gauge** ① *n.* measure, meter, rule ② *v.* judge, measure, estimate *We must estimate the number of beans in the jar,* probe

**gaze** *v.* stare, look, regard, contemplate

**gear** *n.* tackle, array, accessories, machinery, harness, equipment

**gem** *n.* jewel, stone, treasure

**general** *adj.* normal, usual, habitual, customary, total, whole ★**local**

**generous** *adj.* free, liberal, kind ★**selfish**

**genial** *adj.* cheerful, cheery, sunny, hearty, cordial, pleasant ▷*jolly* ★**cold**

**genius** *n.* brilliance, prowess, talent, power, skill, cleverness, brains ★**stupidity**

**genteel** *adj.* refined, polished, civil, courteous, well-bred, polite, elegant ★**boorish**

**gentle** *adj.* ① easy, mild, soft, kind, moderate, tender, humane ② gradual, faint, feeble, slight *The field had a slight slope as it came down to the river*

**genuine** *adj.* ① real, authentic, true, sound ② sincere, honest, candid, frank ★**false**

**germ** *n.* microbe, seed, embryo, nucleus

**gesture** *n.* sign, signal, motion, nod, shrug, movement

**get** *v.* ① acquire, obtain, gain, win, receive, secure, achieve, inherit ★**forfeit** ② understand, catch on *It took Johnny quite a while to catch on to what I meant,* fathom, figure out, learn

**get up** *v.* arise, awake, awaken

**get rid of** *v.* discard, reject, throw away, scrap

**ghastly** *adj.* shocking, hideous, horrible, fearful, terrible, frightful

**ghost** *n.* spook, spirit, spectre, banshee, phantom, apparition

**ghostly** *v.* uncanny, haunted, eerie, weird

**giant** *adj.* mammoth, huge, colossal, enormous, tremendous, immense ▷*big, gigantic* ★**tiny**

**gibber** *v.* gabble, prattle, jabber

**gibberish** *n.* nonsense, drivel, rubbish

**gibe** *v.* jeer, sneer, scoff, deride ▷*taunt*

**giddy** *adj.* dizzy, whirling, reeling, unsteady, wild, reckless

**gift** *n.* ① present, donation, bounty, boon ② talent, skill *Her skill was so great that I knew she must have been born with it,* ability, power

**gigantic** *adj.* stupendous, titanic, colossal ▷*giant* ★**minute**

**giggle** *v.* chuckle, chortle, cackle, snigger
▷ *laugh*

**gingerly** *adv.* carefully, daintily, warily,
cautiously

**girder** *n.* rafter, joist, beam

**girl** *n.* maid, maiden, miss, damsel, young
woman, lass, wench

**girlish** *adj.* maidenly, dainty, feminine

**girth** *n.* circumference, perimeter, fatness,
breadth

**gist** *n.* essence, substance, kernel,
nub, pith, significance

**give** *v.* ① donate, grant, distribute, bestow
② bend, yield *The wooden footbridge
suddenly yielded under his weight and
crashed into the stream,* relax, recede
③ produce, yield ④ pronounce, utter, emit
★**take**

**give back** *v.* return, restore

**give forth** *v.* emit, send out, radiate

**give in** *v.* surrender, quit, yield

**give off** *v.* belch, emit, exude

**give up** *v.* surrender, give in, relinquish,
hand over

**giver** *n.* donor, bestower, presenter

**glad** *adj.* joyful, joyous, delighted, pleased
▷ *happy* ★**sorry**

**gladden** *v.* make happy, gratify, delight,
elate ▷ *please* ★**grieve**

**gladly** *adv.* freely, readily, cheerfully,
willingly

**glamour** *n.* romance, interest, fascination,
attraction, enchantment

**glance** ① *n.* look, glimpse, peep ② *v.* peer,
notice ③ brush, shave, graze, *The bullet
merely grazed his head*

**glare** ① *v.* blaze, glow, flare, sparkle, dazzle
② frown, glower, stare

**glaring** *adj.* ① sparkling, dazzling ②
blatant, notorious, conspicuous

**glass** *n.* tumbler, goblet, beaker, mirror,
looking-glass

**glaze** *v.* polish, gloss, burnish, varnish

**gleam** *v.* sparkle, glitter, flash, glisten,
twinkle

**glee** *n.* jollity, gaiety, elation, triumph
▷ *happiness*

**glib** *adj.* fluent, slick, smooth, facile,
talkative, plausible

**glide** *v.* slide, slither, slip, soar, sail, skate,
skim

**glimmer** *v.* sparkle, scintillate, flicker, glow,
gleam

**glimpse** *v.* spy, spot, glance, view

**glisten** *v.* shine, glitter, glow, gleam

**glitter** *v.* gleam, sparkle, flash, glint, glisten,
scintillate

**gloat** *v.* whoop, exult, crow, revel, triumph

**globe** *n.* ball, sphere, planet, earth, world

**gloom** *n.* darkness, gloaming, dusk, shadow,
dimness, bleakness ★**light**

**gloomy** *adj.* cheerless, black, dark, bleak,
cloudy, overcast; dismal, dour, glum,
melancholy ▷ *dreary* ★**happy**

**glorious** *adj.* brilliant, lustrous, noble,
exalted, renowned ▷ *splendid*

**glory** *n.* brilliance, radiance, pride
▷ *splendour*

**gloss** *n.* lustre, sheen, shimmer, polish
▷ *glaze*

**glossy** *adj.* shiny, burnished, sleek, slick,
polished

**glow** *n. & v.* glare, glitter, bloom, blush,
flush, shine, gleam, twinkle

**glower** *v.* frown, stare, scowl, glare

**glue** ① *n.* paste, gum, cement, mucilage,
adhesive, size ② *v.* stick, fasten

**glum** *adj.* sullen, sulky, morose, miserable,
dejected, downcast ▷ *gloomy*

**glut** *n.* abundance, plenty, too much, surplus

**glutton** *n.* gorger, stuffer, crammer, pig,
gormandizer, gourmand

**gnash** *v.* grind, chomp, bite, crunch

**gnaw** *v.* chew, nibble, bite, consume

**go** *v.* ① walk, pass, move, travel, depart,
proceed ② stretch, reach, extend *The
prairie extended as far as the mountain
range*

**go after** *v.* pursue, chase, follow

**go ahead** *v.* progress, proceed, continue

**go away** *v.* leave, depart, vanish, disappear

**go back** *v.* return, resume, withdraw

**go by** *v.* pass, elapse, vanish

**go in** *v.* enter, advance, invade, penetrate

**go in for** *v.* enter, take part, participate, compete

**go off** *v.* explode, blow up, depart

**go on** *v.* continue, advance, proceed, move ahead, keep up

**go up** *v.* climb, mount, rise ▷ *ascend*

**goad** *v.* prod, incite, impel, drive, urge, sting, worry

**goal** *n.* target, ambition, aim, object, destination

**gobble** *v.* devour, gorge, swallow, gulp, bolt

**goblin** *n.* sprite, demon, gnome, elf

**God** *n.* the Creator, the Father, the Almighty, Jehovah, the Divinity, the Holy Spirit, King of Kings, the Supreme Being

**godless** *adj.* unholy, unclean, wicked, savage, profane ★**righteous**

**golden** *adj.* excellent, precious, brilliant, bright

**good** *adj.* ① excellent, admirable, fine ② favourable, *The calm weather provides favourable conditions for water-skiing,* advantageous, profitable ③ righteous, moral, true *A true friend can forgive your mistakes* ④ clever, skilful, expert ⑤ fit, proper, suited ★**bad**

**goodness** *n.* excellence, merit, worth, honesty, kindness ▷ *virtue* ★**evil**

**goods** *n.* wares, commodities, cargo, load, material, belongings

**gorge** ① *v.* swallow, gulp, devour ▷ *eat* ② *n.* canyon, glen, valley

**gorgeous** *adj.* beautiful, ravishing, stunning, superb, magnificent

**gossip** *v.* chat, chatter, prattle, tittle-tattle

**gouge** *v.* excavate, groove, dig out

**govern** *v.* rule, reign, manage, direct, guide, control, conduct, command

**government** *n.* rule, administration, supervision, parliament, council

**governor** *n.* director, manager, leader, chief, overseer, head of state

**gown** *n.* robe, dress, frock

**grace** *n.* elegance, refinement, polish, symmetry ▷ *beauty*

**graceful** *adj.* beautiful, lovely, shapely, refined ▷ *elegant*

Great

Grate

**gracious** *adj.* amiable, kind, suave, urbane, affable, elegant ★**churlish**

**grade** *n.* ① class, rank, degree ② slope, gradient, incline, slant

**gradual** *adj.* by degrees, step-by-step, continuous, little by little ★**sudden**

**graft** ① *v.* splice, insert, bud, plant ② *n.* bribery, corruption

**grain** *n.* fibre, crumb, seed, particle, atom, bit, drop

**grand** *adj.* splendid, impressive, stately, magnificent, wonderful, superb

**grandeur** *n.* magnificence, splendour, majesty, lordliness

**grant** ① *n.* bounty, award, subsidy ② *v.* bestow, donate *We all donated some money to help the earthquake victims,* confer, give

**grapple** *v.* struggle, tussle, wrestle, seize, grasp, clutch

**grasp** *v.* ① grip, seize, take, grab, hold ② understand, comprehend

**grasping** *adj.* greedy, avaricious, covetous, miserly ★**generous**

**grate** ① *v.* rasp, file, jar, clash, rub, grind

② annoy, irritate, vex ③ *n.* fireplace GREAT

**grateful** *adj.* thankful, appreciative, obliged, indebted

**gratify** *v.* delight, satisfy, please, content, enchant, indulge, favour ★**displease**

**gratitude** *n.* thankfulness, appreciation, obligation

**grave** ① *adj.* solemn, sober, momentous, dignified, majestic ② essential, important *I have important news to tell* ③ *n.* tomb, vault, shrine

**gravity** *n.* ① seriousness, solemnity, importance, significance ② force, gravitation, weight

**graze** *v.* ① scrape, brush, shave, glance ② browse, crop, bite GREYS

**grease** *n.* fat, suet, tallow, oil

**great** *adj.* ① large, considerable, bulky, huge, ample ② important, elevated, noted *Here is a list of noted citizens of this town* ③ main, chief, principal GRATE

**greedy** *adj.* gluttonish, voracious, grasping, selfish, acquisitive ★**unselfish**

**green** *adj.* ① emerald, jade, turquoise ② ungrown, immature, raw *During the war, many raw recruits were drafted into the army,* untrained ★**expert**

**greet** *v.* welcome, accost, hail, salute, salaam, address

**grief** *n.* woe, sadness, regret, distress, anguish ▷*sorrow* ★**joy**

**grievance** *n.* injury, hardship, complaint, wrong, trial ★**boon**

**grieve** *v.* lament, deplore, mourn, sorrow, be sad, afflict, hurt ★**rejoice**

**grievous** *adj.* lamentable, deplorable, grave, critical, severe, mortal

**grill** ① *v.* fry, broil ② *n.* grating, grid

**grim** *adj.* ① serious, stern, harsh, solemn, dour, forbidding ② horrid, dreadful, terrible ▷*sombre* ★**mild**

**grime** *n.* filth, soil, dust, soot ▷*dirt*

**grin** *n.* & *v.* smile, beam, smirk, simper

**grind** *v.* ① scrape, file, crush, powder ② sharpen, whet, grate

**grip** *v.* grasp, grab, snatch, clasp, seize ▷*hold* ★**loosen**

**Groups of Animals**

a drove of cattle
a flock of birds
a herd of elephants
a mob of kangaroos
a pack of wolves
a pride of lions
a school of porpoises
a sloth of bears
a swarm of bees
a troop of monkeys
a colony of seals
a cete of badgers
a skulk of foxes

**grisly** *adj.* horrid, horrible, dreadful, ghastly ▷*grim*

**grit** *n.* ① powder, dust, sand, gravel ② nerve, mettle, pluck ▷*courage*

**groan** *v.* moan, complain, grumble, creak GROWN

**groom** ① *n.* husband, bridegroom ② *n.* stable-boy, servant, ostler ③ *v.* spruce, tidy, preen

**groove** *n.* furrow, ridge, corrugation, channel, rut, score

**grope** *v.* feel, handle, finger, manipulate, touch, pick

**gross** *adj.* ① large, bulky, unwieldy, massive ② coarse, vulgar, crude ③ outrageous,

### Growls, grunts, and other animal noises

| | |
|---|---|
| Bees buzz | Horses neigh |
| Cats meow | Lions roar |
| Cockerels crow | Mice squeak |
| Cows moo | Owls hoot |
| Dogs bark | Pigs grunt |
| Dogs also growl | Snakes hiss |
| Ducks quack | Wolves howl |

glaring, flagrant *The driver was arrested for a flagrant disregard of the speed limit*

**grotesque** *adj.* deformed, malformed, misshapen, freakish, abnormal, bizarre

**ground** *n.* ① dry land, soil, earth, dust ② bottom, base, foundation

**grounds** *n.* ① foundation, cause, basis, excuse ② dregs, sediment, silt ③ gardens, parkland, estate

**group** *n.* ① division, section, branch ② gang, throng, cluster, bunch, class, set

**grovel** *v.* fawn, crouch, crawl, toady, cringe, wallow, cower

**grow** *v.* ① increase, advance, expand, extend, develop, raise ② sprout, germinate, shoot

**growl** *v.* snarl, snap, threaten, thunder

**growth** *n.* expansion, development, advance ▷*increase*

**grow up** *v.* mature, develop, ripen

**grubby** *adj.* messy, dirty, mucky

**grudge** *n. & v.* hate, envy, dislike, spite

**gruesome** *adj.* frightful, hideous, ghastly ▷*grisly*

**gruff** *adj.* husky, throaty, croaky, blunt, churlish, crusty, curt ★**affable**

**grumble** *v.* complain, snivel, murmur, growl, protest

**grumpy** *adj.* disgruntled, dissatisfied, surly, sour, irritable, sullen ★**affable**

**grunt** *n. & v.* snort, groan ★**growl**

**guarantee** *n.* warranty, assurance, security, pledge

**guard** ① *n.* protector, sentry, guardian, watchman ② *v.* protect, defend, watch over, shelter, shield

**guess** *v.* surmise, conjecture, judge, think, suspect, suppose

**guest** *n.* visitor, caller GUESSED

**guide** ① *n.* pilot, director, leader, controller ② *v.* steer, navigate, lead, direct, manage, conduct *Our teacher conducted us to the bus and we all climbed aboard*

**guild** *n.* club, trade union, association, federation, fellowship, band, society

**guile** *n.* knavery, foul play, trickery, deceit, cunning, fraud ★**honesty**

**guilty** *adj.* blameworthy, sinful, wicked, wrong ★**innocent**

**guise** *n.* garb, pose, posture, role, aspect *The motel manager's aspect was a little too friendly; we did not trust him,* appearance GUYS

**gulch** *n.* valley, gully, ravine

**gulf** *n.* ① bay, basin, inlet ② chasm, opening, abyss, depths

**gullible** *adj.* credulous, innocent, naive, trusting, suggestible

**gully** *n.* trench, ditch, channel, ravine

**gulp** *v.* swallow, consume, guzzle, devour

**gun** *n.* rifle, cannon, revolver, pistol, automatic, shotgun

**gurgle** *v.* ripple, murmur, purl, babble

**gush** *v.* stream, spurt, spout, flow, run, pour out

**gust** *n.* blast, blow, squall, wind

**gusto** *n.* relish, zest, eagerness, zeal, pleasure

**gutter** *n.* moat, ditch, dike, drain, gully, channel, groove

**guzzle** *v.* gulp, imbibe, drink, swill, quaff

# H h

**habit** *n.* ① custom, practice, routine, way, rule ② mannerism *One of his annoying mannerisms is drumming his fingers on the table,* addiction, trait

**hack** *v.* chop, mangle, gash, slash

**hackneyed** *adj.* stale, trite, commonplace, tired ★**new**

**hag** *n.* crone, harridan, witch, virago *I know I have a temper, but Julia is a real virago*

**haggard** *adj.* drawn, wan, pinched, thin ▷*gaunt* ★**hale**

**haggle** *v.* bargain, barter, bicker, dispute ★**yield**

**hail** ① *v.* salute, call to, accost, welcome, greet ② *n.* sleet, frozen rain, ice storm HALE

**hair** *n.* locks, mane, tresses, strand

**hale** *adj.* hearty, robust, sound, fit ▷*healthy* ★**ill** HAIL

**half** *n.* division, fraction, segment, share

**hall** *n.* entrance, foyer, corridor, lobby, vestibule *There is a coat rack and an umbrella stand in the vestibule of her house* HAUL

**hallow** *v.* sanctify, consecrate, bless, dedicate, make holy

**hallucination** *n.* illusion, fantasy, delusion, mirage, dream ★**reality**

**halt** *v.* end, pause, rest, cease ▷*stop* ★**start**

**halting** *adj.* faltering, hestitating, wavering, awkward ★**fluent**

**hammer** ① *v.* beat, pound, bang ② *n.* mallet, gavel *The leader banged his gavel on the desk and called for order*

**hamper** ① *v.* hinder, interfere, impede, curb ★**aid** ② *n.* basket, creel, *The fisherman carried a creel to put his catch in*

**hand** ① *v.* give, pass, present, yield ② *n.* fist, palm, paw, mitt

**handicap** *n.* defect, disability, drawback, restriction ★**advantage**

**handicraft** *n.* skill, hobby, art, workmanship, craft, occupation

**handle** ① *n.* shaft, holder, grip ② *v.* feel,

## Habitations

| | |
|---|---|
| Apartment | Igloo |
| Bungalow | Lodge |
| Cabin | Mansion |
| Castle | Palace |
| Chalet | Ranch |
| Chateau | Shack |
| Cottage | Shanty |
| Duplex | Villa |
| Estate | |
| Flat | |
| Hacienda | |
| Hut | |

touch, finger, work, wield, grasp, fondle

**handsome** *adj.* ① good-looking, graceful, attractive ② generous, lavish *Aunt Betsy is always lavish with presents for the children* HANSOM

**handy** *adj.* ready, convenient, deft, skilled ★**clumsy**

**hang** *v.* dangle, suspend, sag, droop, swing

**hanker for** *v.* long for, yearn for, crave, desire ★**dislike**

**haphazard** *adj.* accidental, random, aimless, casual ▷*chance* ★**deliberate**

**hapless** *adj.* ill-fated, luckless, unlucky ▷*miserable* ★**lucky**

**happen** *v.* occur, take place, come about, result, transpire

**happening** *n.* event, incident, occurrence, occasion, phenomenon

**happiness** *n.* delight, ecstasy, gaiety, joy, enjoyment ▷*bliss* ★**unhappiness**

**happy** *adj.* cheerful, blithe, content, joyous, jubilant ▷*merry* ★**unhappy**

**harass** *v.* beset, annoy, upset, bother, pester,

badger, hassle ▷*distress* ★**assist**

**harbour** ① *n.* port, anchorage, mooring ② *n.* refuge, shelter, safety *At last we were back in the safety of our home* ③ *v.* give shelter to

**hard** *adj.* ① firm, stony, rocky, solid ★**soft** ② difficult, tough *I had a very tough problem to solve,* perplexing ★**easy** ③ stern, severe, callous, ruthless

**hardly** *adv.* seldom, rarely, scarcely, slightly

**hardship** *n.* trouble, suffering, want ▷*difficulty* ★**ease**

**hardy** *adj.* rugged, sturdy, tough, healthy, sound ▷*robust* ★**weak**

**hark** *v.* listen, hear ▷*listen*

**harm** ① *n.* damage, mischief, ruin, wrong, abuse, sin ② *v.* abuse, blemish, hurt *I'm sorry, I didn't mean to hurt you,* injure ★**benefit**

**harmful** *adj.* injurious, evil, wicked, damaging ★**harmless**

**harmless** *adj.* safe, gentle, innocuous, innocent ★**harmful**

**harmony** *n.* agreement, conformity, accord, unity, goodwill ★**discord**

**harp** ① *n.* lyre, stringed instrument ② *v.* harp on, dwell on *I tried to forget our quarrel, but Carol continued to dwell on it,* allude to

**harrow** *v.* agonize, taunt, distress, torture, harry ▷*harass* ★**hearten**

**harsh** *adj.* ① jarring, coarse, rasping, rough ② severe, strict, ruthless ★**mild**

**harvest** *v.* plough, harrow, reap, pluck

**hash** *n.* ① mess, confusion, muddle ② stew, goulash, hotpot

**hassle** *n.* argument, bother, difficulty, squabble, struggle

**haste** *n.* rush, bustle, dispatch, urgency, swiftness ▷*hurry* ★**delay**

**hasten** *v.* hurry, hustle, quicken, accelerate, speed up ★**dawdle**

**hasty** *adj.* hurried, rushed, abrupt, indiscreet ★**deliberate**

**hate** *v.* abhor, detest, loathe ▷*despise* ★**love**

**hateful** *adj.* abominable, loathsome, odious, despicable ★**pleasing**

**haughty** *adj.* arrogant, disdainful, scornful, snobbish ★**humble**

**haul** *v.* pull, draw, tug, drag, heave HALL

**have** *v.* possess, occupy, own, receive, take in

**haven** *n.* harbour, port, refuge, retreat, sanctum, shelter

**havoc** *n.* wreckage, ruin, destruction, disorder, mayhem

**hay** *n.* pasture, silage, grass, straw HEY

**haze** *n.* cloud, vapour, fog, mist HAYS

**hazy** *adj.* foggy, misty, murky, vague, uncertain ★**clear**

**head** ① *n.* visage, skull, cranium, pate ② *adj.* chief, main, principal

**heading** *n.* caption, headline, title, inscription

**headlong** *adj.* rough, dangerous, reckless ▷*rash*

**heal** *v.* soothe, treat, cure, mend, restore HEEL, HE'LL

**healthy** *adj.* fine, fit, hearty, sound, vigorous ▷*hale* ★**sick**

**heap** *n.* pile, mass, mound, collection

**hear** *v.* listen to, hearken, overhear HERE

**hearten** *v.* assure, encourage, embolden, inspire ★**dishearten**

**heartless** *adj.* brutal, callous, cold ▷*unkind* ★**kind**

**hearty** *adj.* cordial, sincere, earnest, honest, jovial ★**cold**

**heat** *n.* ① warmth, temperature ② passion, ardour, fervour *She spoke with great fervour about what she believed*

**heave** *v.* fling, cast, hurl, hoist, pull, tug

**heavenly** *adj.* beautiful, blessed, divine, lovely ★**hellish**

**heavy** *adj.* weighty, hefty, ponderous, loaded ★**light**

**hectic** *adj.* excited, fast, frenzied, wild ▷*frantic* ★**leisurely**

**heed** *v.* listen, pay attention, follow, respect, obey ★**ignore**

**heedless** *adj.* thoughtless, reckless, unwary, rash ▷*careless*

**height** ① *n.* altitude, stature ② top, apex, peak, zenith, climax ★**depth**

**Headgear**

| | | |
|---|---|---|
| Balaclava | Helmet | Stetson |
| Beret | Homburg | Tam-o'-shanter |
| Boater | Hood | Top hat |
| Bonnet | Kepi | Toque |
| Cap | Panama | Trilby |
| Glengarry | Shako | Turban |
| Fedora | Sombrero | Tyrolean hat |
| Fez | Sou'wester | Yarmulke |

**hellish** *adj.* abominable, awful, inhuman, fiendish ★**heavenly**

**help** ① *n.* aid, support, assistance ② *v.* lend a hand *We all lent a hand in building the hut,* aid, assist ★**hinder**

**helpful** *adj.* caring, considerate ▷*useful* ★**useless**

**helping** *n.* ration, portion, piece, serving, helping *Mike would like a second helping. He's still hungry,* share, dollop

**helpless** *adj.* incapable, powerless, unfit, forlorn ▷*weak* ★**strong**

**hem** *n.* edge, border, fringe, margin

**hence** *adv.* accordingly, thus, therefore, henceforward

**herd** *n.* crowd, crush, flock, group, mass, mob, horde HEARD

**here** *adv.* present, attending, hereabouts, in this place HEAR

**heritage** *n.* inheritance, legacy, birthright, tradition

**hermit** *n.* recluse, solitary, monk

**hero** *n.* champion, daredevil, star, idol, conqueror, celebrity, superstar ★**villain**

**heroic** *adj.* bold, fearless, lion-hearted, gallant ▷*brave* ★**cowardly**

**heroine** *n.* celebrity, goddess *Marilyn Monroe was a goddess of the screen,* idol, star, lead

**hesitate** *v.* falter, dither, doubt, wait

**hew** *v.* chop, cut, fashion, carve, sculpt HUE

**hidden** *adj.* concealed, covered, veiled, unseen ★**open**

**hide** *v.* conceal, cover, obscure, bury, cloak ★**reveal** HIED

**hideous** *adj.* repulsive, unsightly, gruesome, horrible ▷*ugly* ★**beautiful**

**hiding** *n.* beating, thrashing, caning

**high** ① *adj.* tall, towering, lofty, elevated ② shrill *The referee blew a shrill blast on his whistle,* treble, strident ③ expensive, costly, exorbitant, excessive ★**low**

**highbrow** *adj.* brainy, educated, intellectual

**hijack** *v.* raid, kidnap, seize, snatch, steal

**hike** *v.* walk, ramble, tramp

**hilarious** *adj.* amusing, gleeful, jocular,

entertaining ▷*funny* ★**serious**

**hill** *n.* hummock, rise, climb, height, elevation, slope

**hinder** *v.* hamper, impede, obstruct, retard, frustrate ▷*handicap* ★**help**

**hindrance** *n.* impediment, obstruction, check, barrier ★**aid**

**hint** *n.* clue, inkling *We had just an inkling of what was in store,* whisper, tip, suggestion, pointer

**hire** *v.* charter, rent, lease, retain, engage ★**dismiss** HIGHER

**hiss** *v.* boo, hoot, jeer, deride, whistle ▷*ridicule* ★**applaud**

**history** *n.* narration, account, saga, story, chronicle *The new book is a chronicle of the progress of equal rights*

**hit** ① *v.* strike, slap, beat, batter, whack ② *v.* collide, strike, clash ★**miss** ③ *n.* stroke, collision, blow ④ success, triumph

**hitch** ① *v.* attach, connect, fasten ② *n.* delay, hold-up, problem, snag *The work went smoothly for hours, until we hit a snag*

**hoard** *v.* accumulate, save, collect, treasure ★**squander** HORDE

**hoarse** *adj.* raucous, croaky, husky, throaty ★**mellow** HORSE

**hoax** *n.* trick, deception, fraud, joke, spoof, lie, cheat, swindle

**hobble** *v.* dodder, falter, shuffle, stagger

**hobby** *n.* pastime, amusement, recreation, interest, pursiut

**hoist** *v.* lift, raise, erect, heave, winch up

**hold** ① *v.* have, possess, own, retain, keep, grasp ② *v.* contain, accommodate *This cabin can accommodate four people* ③ *v.* stop, arrest ④ *n.* fortress, keep, storeplace HOLED

**hole** *n.* aperture, slot, perforation, opening, cavity, gap WHOLE

**hollow** ① *adj.* concave, empty, vacant ② *adj.* insincere, artificial ③ *n.* basin, depression *Water had accumulated in a small depression,* crater, channel

**holy** *adj.* sacred, pure, consecrated, blessed, hallowed ★**wicked** WHOLLY

**home** *n.* house, dwelling, homestead

**homely** *adj.* ① humble, unpretentious, comfortable, modest ② ordinary, plain, simple, unpretentious

**honest** *adj.* upright, fair, sincere, honourable ★**devious**

**honesty** *n.* integrity, honour, sincerity, morality ★**dishonesty**

**honour** *n.* morality, honesty, reputation, integrity, uprightness ★**disgrace**

**honourable** *adj.* honest, respectable, high-minded, virtuous ★**dishonest**

**hook** *n.* clasp, link, catch, fastener, barb *The fishhook ended in a number of small barbs*

**hoop** *n.* loop, ring, band, circle

**hoot** *v.* call, cry, howl, shout, shriek, yell

**hop** *v.* jump, leap, skip, spring, vault, caper

**hope** *v.* anticipate, envision, envisage, desire, expect, foresee ★**despair**

**hopeful** *adj.* expectant, confident, optimistic ★**pessimistic**

**hopeless** *adj.* despairing, desperate, downhearted, unattainable ★**hopeful**

**horde** *n.* crowd, gang, band, throng, swarm *We were suddenly attacked by a swarm of hornets,* HOARD

**horrible** *adj.* awful, atrocious, frightful, ghastly ▷*horrid* ★**agreeable**

**horrid** *adj.* beastly, bloodcurdling, dreadful, frightening ▷*horrible* ★**pleasant**

**horror** *n.* dread, fear, fright, outrage, panic, loathing ★**attraction**

**horse** *n.* mount, charger, hack, stallion, mare, filly, colt, foal HOARSE

**hose** *n.* ① tubing, pipe ② socks, stockings HOES

**hospitable** *adj.* sociable, neighbourly, charitable, welcoming ★**hostile**

**host** *n.* ① entertainer, master-of-ceremonies, landlord ② army, band, legion, horde

**hostile** *adj.* unfriendly, antagonistic, alien, malevolent ★**friendly**

**hot** ① *adj.* warm, fiery, scalding, roasting, heated ★**cold** ② pungent, peppery, sharp

**hotel** *n.* inn, hostelry *The stagecoach pulled in to a local hostelry for refreshment,* tavern, motel, resort, public house

**house** *n.* home, residence, dwelling, abode

**Hue**

*A hue is a tint or variety of a colour.*
**Blue:** aquamarine beryl turquoise indigo azure sapphire ultramarine
**Brown:** amber chocolate dun fawn beige khaki auburn chestnut
**Green:** apple emerald jade moss olive pea sea
**Purple:** violet lilac heliotrope amethyst mauve magenta
**Orange:** carrot tangerine sandy
**Red:** crimson scarlet cherry cerise terracotta salmon pink cardinal
**Yellow:** sulphur primrose apricot saffron citron canary lemon

**hovel** *n.* cabin, shed, den, shack, shanty

**hover** *v.* fly, float, hang, dally, linger

**howl** *v.* hoot, cry, bellow, shriek ▷*scream*

**hub** *n.* centre, axis, focal point, pivot

**hubbub** *n.* racket, bedlam, chaos, clamour, uproar ▷*row* ★**calm**

**huddle** *v.* cluster, flock, gather, herd, nestle ★**separate**

**hue** *n.* colour, dye, shade, tinge, tint HEW

**huff** *n.* anger, passion, mood, pique *My cousin stormed off in a fit of pique* ▷*sulk*

**hug** *v.* clasp, embrace, enfold ▷*cuddle*

**huge** *adj.* enormous, monstrous, colossal, immense ▷*vast* ★**tiny**

**hum** *v.* drone, croon, buzz, pulsate, throb

**human** *adj.* reasonable, understandable, mortal ▷*humane* ★**inhuman**

**humane** *adj.* benign, forgiving, gentle, lenient, kind ★**inhumane**

**humble** *adj.* low, lowly, meek, unassuming, respectful, servile ▷*modest* ★**arrogant**

**humbug** *n.* bluff, bunkum, claptrap *The salesman's goods were cheap and he talked a lot of claptrap about them,* quackery, trickery, eye-wash, bluff

**humdrum** *adj.* monotonous, commonplace, everyday, boring ▷*dreary* ★**exceptional**

**humid** *adj.* clammy, damp, moist, wet, vaporous ★**dry**

**humiliate** *v.* embarrass, humble, abash, degrade, deflate ★**boost**

**humorous** *adj.* amusing, droll, comical, whimsical ▷*funny* ★**serious** HUMERUS

**humour** ① *n.* comedy, fun, banter, whimsy ② *v.* flatter, coax, pamper, spoil

**hunch** ① *n.* feeling, guess, idea, inkling ② *v.* crouch, curl up, squat *We squatted in the long grass, where we were out of sight*

**hunger** ① *n.* craving, desire, starvation ② *v.* crave, desire, hanker

**hungry** *adj.* famished, starving, voracious

**hunt** *v.* chase, seek, scour, search, stalk, trail

**hurdle** *n.* barrier, fence, hedge, obstruction

**hurl** *v.* cast, fling, heave, pitch, throw, propel, toss

**hurry** *v.* dash, hustle, quicken, accelerate ▷*hasten* ★**dally**

**hurt** ① *v.* harm, wound, pain, sting, suffer ② *v.* upset, annoy, distress ③ *adj.* rueful, sad, offended

**hurtful** *adj.* cutting, cruel, distressing, wounding ★**kind**

**hurtle** *v.* chase, charge, dash, rush, speed, tear, race, fly

**hush** *v.* calm, quiet down, soothe ★**disturb**

**husky** *adj.* croaking, gruff, harsh ▷*hoarse*

**hustle** *v.* bustle, speed, hasten ▷*hurry*

**hut** *n.* cabin, shelter, shanty, shack

**hymn** *n.* anthem, chant, carol, psalm HIM

**hypnotize** *v.* mesmerize, fascinate, spellbind *We stood spellbound as we watched the trapeze artist,* bewitch

**hypocrite** *n.* fraud, deceiver, impostor, mountebank

**hysterical** *adj.* ① distraught, mad, delirious, beside oneself ② comical, hilarious, farcical ★**calm**

# I i

**icy** *adj.* freezing, frozen, cold, frigid, frosty

**idea** *n.* notion, thought, belief, fancy, impression, image

**ideal** *adj.* perfect, absolute, supreme, best, model, complete

**identical** *adj.* same, alike, twin, duplicate, equal ★**different**

**identify** *v.* detect, recognize, know, distinguish, spot

**identity** *n.* existence, self, singularity, individuality

**idiot** *n.* imbecile, moron, fool, dimwit, dolt

**idiotic** *adj.* crazy, stupid, simple, fatuous ▷*foolish* ★**sane**

**idle** *adj.* ① unoccupied, unemployed, unused ② lazy, frivolous, sluggish ★**active** IDOL

**idol** *n.* ① image, icon, god, fetish ② hero, favourite, star *Buster Keaton was a star of the silent films* IDLE

**ignite** *v.* kindle, set light to, spark off, catch fire, burn

**ignorant** *adj.* unknowing, ill-informed, unread, stupid, thick ★**wise**

**ignore** *v.* disregard, neglect, omit, overlook, pass over ★**note**

**ill** *adj.* ① ailing, diseased, frail, infirm, sick, poorly ★**well** ② hostile, malicious *Cinderella's sisters were cruel and malicious,* evil, harmful

**ill-mannered** *adj.* coarse, crude, boorish, uncivil ▷*rude* ★**polite**

**ill-tempered** *adj.* bad-tempered, curt, irritable ★**good-tempered**

**ill-treat** *v.* abuse, harm, injure, neglect, oppress ★**care for**

**ill will** *n.* animosity, hard feelings, dislike, hatred, hostility ▷*malice* ★**good will**

**illegal** *adj.* unlawful, wrong, villainous, illicit, contraband ★**legal**

**illegible** *adj.* unreadable, indecipherable, obscure, indistinct ★**legible**

**illegitimate** *adj.* illegal, unlawful, improper, wrong ★**legitimate**

**illiterate** *adj.* uneducated, unlearned, unlettered, unread, untaught ★**literate**

**illness** *n.* ailment, attack, complaint, disease, disorder

**illuminate** *v.* brighten, clarify, enlighten, light up ★**darken**

**illusion** *n.* apparition, fancy, fantasy, mirage, deception ★**reality**

**illustration** *n.* picture, drawing, explanation, sketch

**image** *n.* likeness, effigy, portrait, replica, reflection, double

**imaginary** *adj.* unreal, fanciful, fictitious, visionary ★**real**

**imagination** *n.* idea, notion, thought, illusion, conception, fancy, vision, impression ★**reality**

**imagine** *v.* assume, believe, invent, pretend, think up ▷*visualize*

**imbecile** *n.* blockhead, fool, idiot, bungler, dolt

**imitate** *v.* emulate, follow, reproduce, simulate, mock ▷*copy*

**immaculate** *adj.* clean, spotless, faultless, stainless ▷*pure* ★**soiled**

**immature** *adj.* callow, raw, crude, childish, unripe, green ★**mature**

**immediate** *adj.* ① instant, instantaneous, prompt ② nearest, next, neighbouring *As children, my mother and father lived in neighbouring houses* ★**distant**

**immediately** *adv.* at once, directly, without delay, forthwith

**immense** *adj.* tremendous, enormous, vast ▷*huge* ★**tiny**

**immerse** *v.* plunge, dip, douse, submerge, duck ▷*sink*

**imminent** *adj.* impending, approaching, looming, close, forthcoming

**immobile** *adj.* at rest, at a standstill, motionless ★**moving**

**immodest** *adj.* shameless, barefaced, indelicate, improper ★**modest**

**immoral** *adj.* evil, unscrupulous, vicious, vile, depraved ▷*wicked* ★**moral**

**immortal** *adj.* undying, eternal, everlasting, constant ★**mortal**

**immune** *adj.* exempt, resistant, safe, protected ★**susceptible**

**imp** *n.* rascal, urchin, elf

**impact** *n.* blow, shock, stroke, collision, crash, knock

**impair** *v.* damage, spoil, devalue, cheapen, harm ▷*hinder* ★**enhance**

**impart** *v.* communicate, render, bestow, disclose *I am unable to disclose where I heard that story* ▷*tell*

**impartial** *adj.* unbiased, candid, fair-minded, impersonal ★**biased**

**impatient** *adj.* intolerant, irritable, hasty, curt ★**patient**

**impede** *v.* hamper, interfere with, obstruct ▷*hinder* ★**aid**

**impel** *v.* goad, incite, urge, actuate, push ▷*drive* ★**dissuade**

**impending** *adj.* approaching, coming, forthcoming, looming ★**remote**

**imperfect** *adj.* defective, unsound, blemished, flawed ▷*faulty* ★**perfect**

**imperial** *adj.* august, majestic, lofty, regal, royal, sovereign, grand

**imperious** *adj.* arrogant, domineering, overbearing ★**humble**

**impersonal** *adj.* aloof, detached, remote, neutral, cold ★**friendly**

**impersonate** *v.* imitate, mimic, masquerade as, pose as, portray

**impertinent** *adj.* insolent, impudent, discourteous ▷*cheeky* ★**polite**

**impetuous** *adj.* sudden, unexpected, impulsive, spontaneous ▷*hasty* ★**careful**

**implement** ① *v.* accomplish, bring about, fulfil *I was able to fulfil my dream of going to Japan* ② *n.* instrument, tool, gadget

**implicate** *v.* connect, entangle, involve, throw suspicion on ★**absolve**

**implicit** *adj.* implied, indicated, understood, tacit, insinuated

**implore** *v.* beseech, entreat, beg, crave, plead

**imply** *v.* hint at, intimate, insinuate ▷*suggest* ★**declare**

**impolite** *adj.* discourteous, ill-mannered ▷*rude* ★**polite**

**import** ① *v.* bring in, carry in ② *n.* meaning, purport *When I grew old enough I realized the purport of my mother's advice,* sense

**important** *adj.* significant, essential, serious, substantial ▷*great* ★**trivial**

**imposing** *adj.* impressive, massive, magnificent ▷*stately* ★**modest**

**impossible** *adj.* hopeless, not possible, unworkable, unacceptable ★**possible**

**impostor** *n.* impersonator, masquerader, deceiver, fraud, pretender, bluffer

**impoverish** *v.* bankrupt, diminish, weaken, ruin, beggar ★**enrich**

**impractical** *adj.* impossible, unworkable, idealistic, unusable ★**practical**

**impress** *v.* ① influence, affect, sway, inspire ② emboss *She wore a crown of gold embossed with diamonds,* engrave, indent

**impression** *n.* ① belief, concept, fancy, effect ② dent, imprint, stamp, printing *The book had sold 5,000 copies, and a new printing was planned*

**imprison** *v.* jail, lock up, confine ★**free**

**improbable** *adj.* doubtful, unlikely, implausible ▷*dubious* ★**probable**

**impromptu** *adj.* improvised, spontaneous, ad lib, unrehearsed ★**planned**

**improper** *adj.* ① erroneous, false, unsuitable ② immoral *My parents always taught me that lying and cheating were immoral,* indecent ▷*wrong* ★**proper**

**improve** *v.* make better, repair, restore, improve upon, refine ★**diminish**

**impudent** *adj.* impertinent, audacious, brazen, disrespectful ▷*rude* ★**polite**

**impulse** *n.* motive, drive, force, inclination, urge, notion, wish

**impulsive** *adj.* sudden, unexpected, reckless ▷*impetuous* ★**cautious**

**impure** *adj.* contaminated, corrupted, foul, corrupt ★**pure**

**inaccessible** *adj.* remote, isolated, unattainable ★**accessible**

**inaccurate** *adj.* erroneous, incorrect, imprecise ▷*faulty* ★**accurate**

**inactive** *adj.* inert, static, dormant, quiet, unoccupied ★**active**

**inadequate** *adj.* deficient, unequal, incapable ▷*unfit* ★**adequate**

**inane** *adj.* absurd, ridiculous, stupid, senseless ▷*silly* ★**sensible**

**inappropriate** *adj.* improper, wrong, incorrect, unsuitable, unfitting ★**appropriate**

**inattentive** *adj.* unheeding, indifferent, careless, neglectful ★**attentive**

**incapable** *adj.* helpless, inadequate, unable, unfit, weak ★**capable**

**incense** ① *v.* (in-*cense*) enrage, infuriate, annoy ② *n.* (*in*-cense) fragrance *We walked through fields where the fragrance of wild flowers was wonderful,* aroma, perfume

**incentive** *n.* motive, impulse, drive, spur, lure

**incident** *n.* event, happening, episode, circumstance, occurrence

**incidental** *adj.* casual, chance, accidental, random, minor

**incite** *v.* encourage, urge, drive, goad, impel, provoke ▷*prompt* ★**restrain**

**incline** ① *n.* (*in*-cline) slant, slope, grade, gradient ② *v.* (in-*cline*) tend, verge, lean to, bias, favour

**inclined** *adj.* liable, prone, disposed, favourable

**include** *v.* contain, cover, incorporate, embody, comprise ★**exclude**

**inclusive** *adj.* comprehensive, all-embracing ★**exclusive**

**income** *n.* earnings, royalty, revenue, receipts, profits ★**expenses**

**incomparable** *adj.* brilliant, first-class, superb ▷*unrivalled* ★**ordinary**

**incompetent** *adj.* incapable, inadequate, inept, helpless ▷*clumsy* ★**competent**

**incomplete** *adj.* unfinished, partial, imperfect, wanting ★**complete**

**incomprehensible** *adj.* unintelligible, perplexing, puzzling ★**comprehensible**

**inconceivable** *adj.* incredible, unlikely, strange, unthinkable, unheard of ▷*extraordinary* ★**comprehensible**

**inconsiderate** *adj.* tactless, careless, insensitive ▷*thoughtless* ★**considerate**

**inconsistent** *adj.* incongruous, unstable, unpredictable ★**consistent**

**inconspicuous** *adj.* indistinct, faint, hidden, ordinary ★**conspicuous**

**inconvenient** *adj.* annoying, awkward, difficult, troublesome ★**convenient**

**incorrect** *adj.* erroneous, imprecise, mistaken ▷*wrong* ★**correct**

**increase** ① *v.* add to, boost, magnify, heighten ② *n.* addition *We heard the news today that Emily has had an addition to her family,* rise, enhancement ★**decrease**

**incredible** *adj.* unbelievable, amazing, far fetched, wonderful ★**ordinary**

**incriminate** *v.* implicate, accuse, indict ▷*blame* ★**acquit**

**indecent** *adj.* immodest, improper, impure, coarse ★**decent**

**indeed** *adv.* actually, truly, really, very much, positively

**indefinite** *adj.* uncertain, unsure, unreliable, dubious ▷*vague* ★**certain**

**indelicate** *adj.* coarse, immodest, indecent ▷*unseemly* ★**delicate**

**independent** *adj.* free, self-reliant, separate, self-governing ★**dependent**

**indicate** *v.* show, point out, denote, suggest, symbolize, specify, signal

**indifference** *n.* disinterest, unconcern, apathy, coldness ★**interest**

**indifferent** *adj.* uninterested, cold, casual, apathetic, listless ★**interested**

**indignant** *adj.* annoyed, resentful, wrathful ▷*angry* ★**pleased**

**indirect** *adj.* devious, roundabout, incidental ★**direct**

**indiscreet** *adj.* incautious, thoughtless, ill-advised ▷*hasty* ★**discreet**

**indiscriminate** *adj.* confused, bewildered, careless ▷*random* ★**deliberate**

**indispensable** *adj.* necessary, crucial, vital ▷*essential* ★**unnecessary**

**indistinct** *adj.* faint, dim, unclear, obscure, murky ▷*vague* ★**distinct**

**individual** ① *adj.* single, odd, special, exclusive ② *n.* person, being *Sharon enjoys the company of other human beings,*

creature, body, soul, fellow

**indulge** *v.* gratify, humour, pamper, satisfy, spoil

**industrious** *adj.* busy, hard-working, diligent, conscientious ★**lazy**

**inedible** *adj.* deadly, poisonous, harmful, uneatable ★**edible**

**inefficient** *adj.* negligent, incapable ▷*incompetent* ★**efficient**

**inelegant** *adj.* awkward, ungainly, crude, coarse ▷*clumsy* ★**elegant**

**inept** *adj.* awkward, absurd, unskilled ▷*clumsy* ★**skilful**

**inert** *adj.* inactive, passive, static, sluggish, listless, dead ★**alive**

**inevitable** *adj.* unavoidable, certain, sure, necessary ★**uncertain**

**inexact** *adj.* imprecise, inaccurate ▷*erroneous* ★**exact**

**inexpensive** *adj.* low-priced, reasonable, economical ▷*cheap* ★**expensive**

**inexperienced** *adj.* inexpert, unskilled, untrained ▷*inept* ★**experienced**

**infallible** *adj.* perfect, unerring, faultless ▷*reliable* ★**faulty**

**infamous** *adj.* notorious, shady, scandalous, shameful, disgraceful ★**glorious**

**infant** *n.* baby, child, little one, toddler

**infatuated** *adj.* in love, beguiled, charmed, fascinated, smitten

**infect** *v.* contaminate, blight, defile, pollute

**infectious** *adj.* catching, contagious

**infer** *v.* reason, conclude, judge, understand

**inferior** *adj.* second-rate, lesser, lower, poor, mediocre, imperfect ★**superior**

**infinite** *adj.* eternal, unending, endless, immense, unbounded

**infirm** *adj.* weak, feeble, frail, senile, decrepit ★**healthy**

**inflame** *v.* inspire, provoke, excite, stimulate, arouse ★**cool**

**inflate** *v.* expand, dilate, swell, pump up, blow up ★**deflate**

**inflict** *v.* apply, burden, deal, deliver, force

**influence** ① *n.* authority, control, guidance, force ② *v.* affect, impress, inspire *After Annie visited the old city, she was inspired to write a poem,* prejudice

**inform** *v.* tell, let know, acquaint, warn, enlighten

**informal** *adj.* casual, easy, familiar, relaxed, simple ★**formal**

**information** *n.* knowledge, news, intelligence, advice

**infrequent** *adj.* unusual, uncommon, occasional ▷*rare* ★**frequent**

**infringe** *v.* disobey, violate, encroach, trespass, flout

**infuriate** *v.* anger, enrage, madden, incense, vex ▷*annoy* ★**calm**

**ingenious** *adj.* clever, resourceful, shrewd, adroit, inventive ★**clumsy**

**ingenuous** *adj.* honest, open, simple, trusting, sincere ★**artful**

**ingratiate** *v.* curry favour, flatter, grovel, toady *We distrusted Tim, as he was always trying to ingratiate himself with the teacher*

### Ingratiate

*We distrusted Tim, as he was always trying to ingratiate himself with the teacher.*

**ingredient** *n.* component, element, part, factor, constituent

**inhabit** *v.* live in, dwell in, reside in, dwell, occupy, stay

**inhale** *v.* breathe in, inspire, sniff, suck in ★**exhale**

**inherit** *v.* succeed to, acquire, take over, receive, come into

**inhospitable** *adj.* unfriendly, desolate, unkind, unsociable ★**hospitable**

**inhuman** *adj.* barbaric, brutal, beastly, heartless, savage

**inhumane** *adj.* callous, cruel, pitiless, ruthless ▷*inhuman* ★**humane**

**initiate** *v.* start, launch, teach, instruct, train ▷*begin*

**initiative** *n.* ambition, drive, enterprise, resourcefulness

**inject** *v.* inoculate, infuse, vaccinate

**injure** *v.* hurt, mar, spoil, wound, blemish, deform, disfigure

**inkling** *n.* suspicion, impression, notion, clue

**inlet** *n.* bay, gulf, basin, bight, estuary, harbour, fjord

**inn** *n.* hotel, motel, lodge, tavern IN

**innocent** *adj.* guiltless, faultless, stainless, virtuous, blameless ★**guilty**

**inoffensive** *adj.* harmless, safe, gentle, quiet ▷*innocent* ★**malicious**

**inquire** *v.* ask, examine, inspect, check, question, look into, probe

**inquisitive** *adj.* nosy, snooping, eager, inquiring, ▷*curious*

**insane** *adj.* demented, mad, frenzied, crazy, wild, lunatic ★**sane**

**inscribe** *v.* write, stamp, cut, carve, etch

**inscription** *n.* heading, caption, legend, epitaph, label

**insecure** *adj.* perilous, unsafe, hazardous, dangerous, unconfident, uncertain ★**secure**

**insensible** *adj.* ① unconscious, stunned, knocked out *The reigning champion was knocked out in the third round* ② insensitive, numb, stupefied

**insensitive** *adj.* impassive, indifferent, thick-skinned, unruffled, insensible ★**sensitive**

**inseparable** *adj.* indivisible, devoted, intimate, close

**insert** *v.* put in, inset, introduce, place, interleave ★**remove**

**inside** *adv.* indoors, inner, inward, within, core, middle ★**outside**

**insight** *n.* awareness, intelligence, judgement, knowledge ▷*wisdom*

**insignificant** *adj.* unimportant, non-essential, meagre, irrelevant ▷*humble* ★**important**

**insincere** *adj.* pretended, deceptive, dishonest, two-faced, false ★**sincere**

**insinuate** *v.* suggest, imply, signify, get at, intimate, indicate

**insipid** *adj.* tasteless, flat, flavourless, bland, banal ★**tasty**

**insist** *v.* assert, maintain, request, require, demand, persist ★**waive**

**insolent** *adj.* impudent, impertinent, discourteous, insulting, fresh, rude, cheeky ★**respectful**

**inspect** *v.* examine, check, oversee, supervise, superintend

**inspiration** *n.* motive, stimulus, brain wave, revelation ▷*encouragement*

**inspire** *v.* hearten, prompt, provoke, excite ▷*encourage* ★**deter**

**instal** *v.* establish, plant, set, position, fix, introduce, locate

**instance** *n.* example, case, occasion, occurrence INSTANTS

**instant** ① *adj.* immediate, instantaneous *I pressed the button, and there was an instantaneous explosion,* rapid ② *n.* moment, minute, flash, jiffy

**instantly** *adv.* at once, right away, immediately, now ▷*forthwith* ★**later**

**instead** *adv.* alternatively, preferably, rather

**instead of** *adv.* in place of, in one's place, on behalf of, preferably

**instinct** *n.* ability, knack, intuition, feeling, sixth sense

**institute** ① *n.* association, college, establishment, organization ② *v.* begin, start *The people raised enough money to start a new programme to help the poor,* found

**Musical Instruments**

Accordion
Bagpipes
Balalaika
Banjo
Bassoon
Bells
Bugle
Castanets
Cello
Clarinet
Cornet
Cymbals
Didgeridoo
Double bass
Drum
Dulcimer
Electric
  guitar

Fiddle
Fife
Flute
French horn
Glockenspiel
Guitar
Harmonica
Harp
Harpsichord
Hurdy-gurdy
Kazoo
Kettledrum
Lute
Lyre
Mandolin
Maraca
Oboe

Organ
Piano
Piccolo
Recorder
Saxophone
Synthesizer
Tambourine
Triangle
Trombone
Trumpet
Tuba
Ukulele
Viola
Violin
Whistle
Xylophone
Zither

**instruct** *v.* teach, direct, order, educate, coach, drill, train

**instrument** *n.* device, gadget, implement, contraption, tool, utensil

**insufferable** *adj.* unbearable, intolerable, impossible ★**tolerable**

**insufficient** *adj.* inadequate, lacking, scanty, wanting ▷*sparse* ★**sufficient**

**insulate** *v.* protect, shield, isolate, set apart

**insult** *n.* & *v.* slander, slight, snub, abuse, outrage ★**compliment**

**insure** *v.* guarantee, protect, warrant, assure

**intact** *adj.* whole, unharmed, uncut, complete, in one piece, sound ★**damaged**

**integrity** *n.* honour, uprightness, honesty, goodness, purity ★**dishonesty**

**intellectual** *adj.* scholarly, studious, thoughtful ▷*intelligent* ★**foolish**

**intelligent** *adj.* acute, astute, brainy, brilliant, intellectual ▷*clever* ★**stupid**

**intend** *v.* mean, aim, determine, ordain, plan, project, resolve

**intense** *adj.* extreme, ardent, earnest, forcible, passionate ▷*keen* ★**mild** INTENTS

**intention** *n.* aim, intent, project, design, notion, end, goal

**intercept** *v.* stop, arrest, confiscate, delay, obstruct ▷*thwart*

**interest** *n.* appeal, fascination, zest, activity, concern ★**boredom**

**interesting** *adj.* appealing, fascinating, absorbing, entertaining ★**boring**

**interfere** *v.* meddle, intrude, interrupt, butt in, tamper ★**assist**

**interior** *adj.* internal, inner, inside, inward ★**exterior**

**interlude** *n.* pause, interval, intermission, spell, recess

**internal** *adj.* inner, inward ▷*interior* ★**external**

**interpret** *adj.* explain, define, construe

**interrogate** *v.* question, examine, ask, inquire, quiz ▷*investigate*

**interrupt** *adj.* break in, butt in, interject, disturb, hold up, suspend

**interval** *n.* space, period, term, intermission ▷*interlude*

**intervene** *v.* break in, interrupt, intrude, mediate, arbitrate ▷*interfere*

**interview** *n.* conference, inquiry, meeting, consultation, talk

**intimate** ① *adj.* near, close, familiar, private, secret ★**distant** ② *v.* hint at, suggest *The evidence suggests that the defendant has not been telling the truth* ▷*insinuate*

**intimidate** *v.* daunt, overawe, cow, bully, frighten, browbeat ★**persuade**

**intolerant** *adj.* bigoted, unfair, small-minded, dogmatic ★**tolerant**

**intoxicated** *adj.* drunk, inebriated, tipsy

**intrepid** *adj.* daring, heroic, unafraid, bold, gallant ▷*fearless*

**intricate** *adj.* complex, complicated, elaborate, tricky ★**simple**

**intrigue** ① *n.* plot, scheme, affair, liaison ② *v.* attract, enchant *The old man enchanted us with his stories,* captivate, scheme

**introduce** *v.* ① put in, insert, inject ② acquaint, present ③ propose, offer

**intrude** *v.* interrupt, interfere, invade, trespass ★**withdraw**

**inundate** *v.* flood, deluge, engulf, immerse, submerge, swamp *We advertised for a new assistant and were swamped with replies*

**invade** *v.* break in, penetrate, assault, assail ▷*enter* ★**withdraw** INVEIGHED

**invalid** ① *adj.* (in-*val*-id) null, void *These*

*tickets are void, for they are more than a year old,* useless ② *n.* (*in*-val-id) patient, sufferer, sick person, disabled person

**invaluable** *adj.* precious, costly, priceless, valuable ★**worthless**

**invent** *v.* fabricate, conceive, devise, make up, originate, concoct

**invention** *n.* creation, gadget, contrivance, discovery

**investigate** *v.* explore, examine, research, inquire, search, study

**invisible** *adj.* hidden, concealed, out of sight, unseen, masked ★**visible**

**invite** *v.* ask, beckon, attract, summon, urge, encourage ★**force**

**involve** *v.* comprise, complicate, entangle, include, take in, entail

**inward** *adj.* hidden, inner, internal, secret, inside ★**outward**

**irate** *adj.* incensed, cross, annoyed, furious, infuriated ▷*angry* ★**calm**

**irksome** *adj.* annoying, irritating, disagreeable ★**pleasing**

**ironic** *adj.* satirical, derisive, mocking, scornful

**irregular** *adj.* uncertain, unsettled, disordered, singular ▷*odd* ★**regular**

**irrelevant** *adj.* immaterial, unnecessary, unrelated ★**relevant**

**irresistible** *adj.* charming, compelling, overpowering, fascinating ★**resistible**

**irresponsible** *adj.* undependable, unreliable, feckless, flighty ★**responsible**

**irritable** *adj.* bad-tempered, edgy, fretful, peevish ▷*cross* ★**cheerful**

**irritate** *v.* annoy, vex, irk, offend, provoke ▷*bother* ★**please**

**island** *n.* isle, islet, key, atoll, cay

**issue** ① *v.* flow, ooze, bring out, circulate, publish ② *n.* edition, printing, publication *My book of poems was ready for publication,* impression ③ problem, question, affair, concern

**itch** ① *v.* prickle, tingle, irritate ② *n.* impulse, motive, desire *I have always had a strong desire to work in a hospital*

**item** *n.* point, particular, thing, object, article

# J j

**jab** *v.* poke, prod, push, stab, dig

**jabber** *v.* chatter, gabble, mumble, babble

**jacket** *n.* coat, jerkin, cover, case, sheath

**jagged** *adj.* rough, broken, snagged, notched, uneven ★**smooth**

**jail** *n.* prison, penitentiary, lock-up, brig

**jam** ① *n.* jelly, preserves, conserve, marmalade ② *v.* crowd, pack *All the buses were full, and we were packed in like sardines,* crush, squeeze JAMB

**jar** ① *n.* jug, beaker, ewer, vase, pitcher, pot ② *v.* jog, rattle, grate *That singer's voice really grates on me,* grind

**jaunt** *n.* & *v.* trip, journey, cruise, travel, tour

**jaunty** *adj.* light-hearted, showy, dapper, spruce, debonair, perky

**jealous** *adj.* envious, covetous, grudging

**jealousy** *n.* envy, covetousness, distrust, spite

**jeer** *v.* laugh at, deride, mock, ridicule, insult ▷*taunt*

**jeopardy** *n.* peril, risk, hazard, plight ▷*danger* ★**safety**

**jerk** *n.* & *v.* yank, pull, drag, jog, jolt, tug

**jersey** *n.* pullover, sweater, jumper

### Jewels

Agate
Amethyst
Aquamarine
Bloodstone
Carbuncle
Carnelian
Coral
Diamond
Emerald
Garnet
Jasper
Moonstone
Onyx

Opal
Ruby
Sapphire
Topaz
Turquoise
Zircon

**jest** *n.* joke, jape, spoof, banter, chaff

**jester** *n.* clown, buffoon, merry-andrew, prankster, comedian

**jet** *n.* & *v.* spurt, squirt, flow, gush

**jetty** *n.* wharf, dock, quay, pier

**jewel** *n.* gem, stone, trinket, charm, locket

**jibe** *v.* mock, scoff, scorn, sneer, taunt ▷*jeer*

**jiffy** *n.* instant, flash, minute, moment

**jilt** *v.* abandon, brush off, desert, drop, forsake

**jingle** *v.* tinkle, clink, chink, ring, jangle

**job** *n.* task, work, chore, place, office, post, position, situation, profession, trade

**jocular** *adj.* gleeful, hilarious, witty, humorous, jolly ▷*funny* ★**serious**

**jog** *v.* ① prod, nudge, shove, shake ② run, sprint, canter, trot, exercise

**join** *v.* ① unite, link, combine, connect, attach ★**separate** ② enlist, sign up *Gaby and Bill have signed up for tennis lessons*

**joint** ① *n.* junction, knot, union, connection ② *adj.* shared, united, mutual *It's in our mutual interest to keep expenses down*

**joke** *n.* gag, trick, frolic, lark, jape, game, prank ▷*jest*

**jolly** *adj.* jovial, cheerful, blithe, frisky ▷*merry* ★**sad**

**jolt** *n.* & *v.* jar, shock, shove, rock, jerk, bump

**jostle** *v.* push, shove, shoulder, thrust, elbow

**jot** ① *n.* atom, bit, grain, particle ② *v.* note, scribble, take down

**journal** *n.* ① ledger, account book ② diary, newspaper, magazine *I've just become editor of the natural history society's magazine*

**journey** *n.* excursion, trip, tour, jaunt, ramble

**jovial** *adj.* jolly, festive, cordial, affable, cheerful ▷*merry* ★**sad**

**joy** *n.* rapture, enchantment, delight, pleasure, charm ▷*bliss* ★**sorrow**

**joyful** *adj.* joyous, enjoyable, pleasurable, happy, jovial, delighted ★**sorrowful**

**jubilant** *adj.* exultant, gleeful, happy, overjoyed, excited ★**depressed**

**judge** ① *n.* justice, magistrate, referee, umpire ② *v.* assess *We can ask the jeweller to assess the value of these pearls,* decide, find, appraise, estimate

**judgement** *n.* ① decision, opinion, verdict *The*

# K k

**Key**

**Keys**

*jury gave a verdict of 'not guilty',* decree, finding ② intelligence, understanding, valuation

**judicious** *adj.* prudent, shrewd, discreet, expedient, wise ★**indiscreet**

**jug** *n.* beaker, ewer, urn, vase ▷*jar*

**juggle** *v.* conjure, manipulate

**juice** *n.* essence, extract, sap, fluid, nectar

**jumble** *n.* medley, mixture, muddle, tangle, clutter, hotch-potch

**jump** *v.* spring, bound, hop, skip, vault, ▷*leap*

**junction** *n.* ① union, combination, joint, connection ② crossroads, intersection, juncture, crossing

**jungle** *n.* forest, bush, wilderness

**junior** *adj.* lesser, lower, younger, subordinate ★**senior**

**junk** *n.* trash, debris, rubbish, waste, clutter, litter, scrap, garbage, refuse

**just** ① *adj.* sound, regular, orderly, exact, fair, honest, impartial ② *adv.* exactly, precisely ③ *adv.* only, merely, simply

**justice** *n.* equity, impartiality, fairness, right ★**injustice**

**justify** *v.* vindicate, acquit, condone, uphold, legalize

**jut** *v.* bulge, extend, stick out, overhang, project *We took shelter where the cliff projects over the path* ★**recede**

**juvenile** ① *adj.* adolescent, youthful, young, childish ★**mature** ② *n.* boy, girl, child, youngster, youth

**keen** ① *adj.* eager, ardent, earnest, diligent ② sharp *Her wit is as sharp as a razor*, acute, fine ★**dull**

**keep** ① *v.* hold, retain, collect, possess ★**abandon** ② *v.* care for, maintain, shelter *We have arranged to shelter the refugees* ③ *n.* tower, dungeon, castle, fort, stronghold

**keeper** *n.* jailer, warden, attendant, caretaker, janitor, curator, guardian

**keeping** *n.* compliance, obedience, accord

**keep on** *v.* continue, go on, endure, persist ★**give up**

**keepsake** *n.* souvenir, token, memento, reminder, relic

**keg** *n.* barrel, cask, tub, drum, container

**ken** *n.* grasp, grip, understanding, mastery, knowledge

**kerchief** *n.* scarf, headscarf, shawl, neckcloth

**kernel** *n.* core, heart, hub, centre, gist, nub COLONEL

**kettle** *n.* boiler, cauldron, cooking pot, tea-kettle

**key** ① *n.* opener ② *n.* solution, clue, answer ③ *n.* cay, isle, inlet, atoll ④ *adj.* essential, fundamental, vital, crucial QUAY

**kick** *v.* ① boot, strike with the foot, punt, hit ② complain, grumble, rebel *The people rebelled against the harsh rule of the new king,* resist

**kidnap** *v.* abduct, capture, seize, snatch, steal, hijack

**kill** *v.* slay, assassinate, destroy, massacre, slaughter ▷*murder*

**killjoy** *n.* spoil-sport, wet blanket *I don't want to be a wet blanket, but I'm too tired to play,* grouch, complainer ★**optimist**

**kin** *n.* race, kindred, offspring, kind, family, relation

**kind** ① *adj.* gentle, kindly, genial, good-natured, amiable ★**unkind** ② *n.* style, character, sort, variety

**kindle** *v.* ① light, ignite, set fire to ② inflame

## A Little Knowledge is a Dangerous Thing – and Other Misquotes

Many of the familiar quotations we use from literature, history or the world of entertainment are incorrect adaptations of the original. Greta Garbo did not say 'I want to be alone'. Her true words were: 'I like to be alone', Shakespeare did not say 'Discretion is the better part of valour'. The correct quotation is: 'The better part of valour is discretion'. Here are some more, with the correct original version printed in italic type:

**From Shakespeare**
Alas, poor Yorick: I knew him well.
*Alas, poor Yorick; I knew him,*
*Horatio: a fellow of infinite jest.*
(Hamlet)

O Romeo. Romeo! wherefore art thou, Romeo?
*O Romeo. Romeo! wherefore art thou*
*Romeo?* (Romeo and Juliet)
(Note the position of the comma.
'Wherefore' means 'why' not 'where'.)

To gild the lily . . .
*to gild refined gold, to paint the lily . . .*
(King John)
Screw your courage to the sticking-point
*But screw your courage to the sticking-*
*place* (Macbeth)

All that glitters is not gold
*All that glisters is not gold*
(The Merchant of Venice)

Discretion is the better part of valour.
*The better part of valour is discretion.*
(King Henry IV, part I)

**From the King James Bible**
Pride goes before a fall
*Pride goeth before destruction and an*
*haughty spirit before a fall* (Proverbs)

Money is the root of all evil
*For the love of money is the root of*
*all evil* (Timothy)

To go the way of all flesh
*And, behold, this day I am going the*
*way of all the earth* (Joshua)

---

*The mayor's words only inflamed the*
*people even more,* excite, provoke, rouse
**kindness** *n.* good nature, charity, amiability, affection, tenderness ★**cruelty**
**king** *n.* monarch, sovereign, majesty, ruler, emperor
**kink** *n.* ① knot, loop, bend, coil ② freak, eccentricity, whim *This strange tower was built as the result of a whim by the eccentric designer*
**kiss** *v.* salute, embrace, buss, smooch
**kit** *n.* set, outfit, baggage, effects, gear, rig
**knack** *n.* flair, talent, ability, genius, gift ▷*skill*

**knave** *n.* cheat, rascal, villain, scamp, scoundrel ▷*rogue* NAVE
**knead** *v.* form, squeeze, mould, shape, press NEED
**kneel** *v.* bend the knee, genuflect *The nun genuflected before the altar, then said her rosary,* bow down, worship
**knife** *n.* scalpel, blade, dagger, cutter
**knight** *n.* cavalier, champion, soldier, warrior, baronet NIGHT
**knit** *v.* weave, crochet, spin, twill, link, loop
**knob** *n.* boss, bump, handle, opener, button
**knock** *v.* hit, slap, punch, bang, smite, strike
**knock out** ① *v.* stun, make insensible,

# L l

**Other sources**
Water, water, everywhere, and not a drop
to drink
*Water, water, everywhere, Nor any drop to
drink* (The Rime of the Ancient Mariner)

A little knowledge is a dangerous thing *A
little learning is a dang'rous thing*
(Alexander Pope)

Tomorrow to fresh fields and pastures new
*Tomorrow to fresh woods, and pastures
new* (Paradise Lost)

They shall not grow old as we that are left
grow old
*They shall grow not old, as we that are left
grow old* (Laurence Binyon)

Play it again, Sam (Humphrey Bogart,
in the film *Casablanca*)

*Play it, Sam. Play* "As Time Goes By"
(Ingrid Bergman, in the film *Casablanca*)

render unconscious ② *n.* success, hit
**knoll** *n.* barrow, hill, mound, hillock
**knot** *n.* ① tie, bond, join, loop, kink,
② cluster, group NOT
**know** *v.* perceive, discern, notice, identify
▷*understand* NO
**know-how** *n.* skill, knowledge, talent
**knowing** *adj.* astute, knowledgeable,
intelligent, perceptive ★**ignorant**
**knowledge** *n.* understanding, acquaintance,
learning, wisdom, scholarship, information,
sapience ★**ignorance**
**kudos** *n.* prestige, distinction, fame, glory,
recognition

**label** *n.* badge, tag, ticket, sticker, docket,
slip
**laborious** *adj.* ① hard-working, diligent
② strenuous, arduous *Digging potatoes is
arduous work,* hard ★**easy**
**labour** *n.* & *v.* toil, work, drudge, strain,
struggle, slog, sweat
**lack** ① *n.* need, want, absence, deficiency,
scarcity *During the hot weather there was
a scarcity of water* ② *v.* need, require, want,
miss
**laconic** *adj.* terse, curt, brief, concise
★**wordy**
**lad** *n.* boy, fellow, kid, youth, chap
**laden** *adj.* loaded, burdened, hampered,
weighed down ★**empty**
**ladle** *v.* dip, scoop, dish, shovel
**lady** *n.* woman, female, dame, damsel,
matron, mistress
**lag** *v.* dawdle, loiter, tarry, saunter ▷*linger*
★**lead**
**lagoon** *n.* pool, pond, lake, basin
**lair** *n.* den, nest, retreat, hideout, hole
**lake** *n.* lagoon, loch, pond, spring, reservoir
**lam** *v.* beat, hit, clout, knock ▷*strike*
**lame** *adj.* ① crippled, hobbled, disabled
② weak, feeble *That's a feeble excuse for
missing school,* inadequate, unconvincing
**lament** *v.* deplore, mourn, grieve, sorrow
▷*regret* ★**rejoice**
**lamp** *n.* lantern, light, flare, torch
**lance** ① *n.* spear, pike, javelin, shaft ② *v.*
puncture, pierce, cut
**land** ① *n.* country, district, tract, area,
nation, region ② *v.* alight, arrive, carry,
touch down *We had engine trouble, so the
aircraft touched down in the desert*
**landlord** *n.* host, hotelier, innkeeper, owner
**landmark** *n.* milestone, milepost, beacon,
monument, signpost
**landscape** *n.* scenery, view, prospect,
countryside, panorama
**lane** *n.* alley, drive, passage, way LAIN

**language** *n.* tongue, speech, utterance, dialect, jargon

**languid** *adj.* leisurely, unhurried, sluggish, slow, easy ★**lively**

**languish** *v.* decline, droop, flag, pine, suffer, yearn ★**flourish**

**lanky** *adj.* tall, rangy, gangling, scrawny, weedy ★**squat**

**lantern** *n.* lamp, flashlight, torch

**lap** ① *v.* lick, drink, sip, sup ② *n.* circuit, course, distance ③ *n.* thighs, knees

**lapse** *v.* expire, die, pass, elapse, go by, deteriorate LAPS

**larder** *n.* pantry, storeroom, cellar

**large** *adj.* big, ample, substantial, great, broad ▷ *huge* ★**small**

**lark** *n.* adventure, escapade, spree, joke, frolic, gambol

**lash** ① *v.* beat, cane, whip, flay, flog ② *n.* prod, goad, drive, whip

**lass** *n.* girl, maiden, maid, young woman

**last** ① *adj.* final, concluding, latest, utmost, aftermost ★**first** ② *v.* remain, linger *The foggy weather lingered for most of the morning,* endure, stay

**latch** *n.* bolt, bar, padlock, fastener

**late** *adj.* tardy, behindhand, departed, slow ★**early**

**lately** *adv.* recently, latterly, formerly

**lather** *n.* suds, foam, bubbles, froth

**latter** *adj.* final, last, latest, recent, closing ★**former**

**laud** *v.* compliment, praise, applaud, glorify ★**blame**

**laugh** *v.* chuckle, giggle, guffaw, snigger, titter, fall about ★**cry**

**launch** ① *v.* start, begin, commence, establish, initiate ② *n.* motorboat

**lavish** ① *adj.* abundant, generous, liberal, extravagant ② *v.* waste, squander *My parents left me a small fortune, but I squandered it all,* give

**law** *n.* rule, ordinance, regulation, edict, decree

**lawful** *adj.* legal, legitimate, rightful ★**illegal**

**lawyer** *n.* attorney, counsel, jurist, barrister, solicitor, advocate, QC

**lax** *adj.* careless, casual, slack, relaxed, vague ★**strict** LACKS

**lay** ① *v.* put, set *It's time for dinner; let's set the table,* deposit, place, spread ② *v.* impute, charge ③ *adj.* non-professional, amateur; *amateur actors*

**layer** *n.* seam, sheet, thickness, tier

**lazy** *adj.* idle, inactive, slothful, slow, sluggish ★**active**

**lead** *v.* conduct, guide, escort, direct, command ★**follow**

**leader** *n.* guide, pilot, conductor, chief, head, master, captain, boss

**leaf** *n.* frond, blade, sheet LIEF

**league** *n.* band, association, society, guild, group, federation, coalition

**leak** *v.* trickle, ooze, seep, exude, flow out, percolate LEEK

**lean** ① *adj.* spare, slim, thin, skinny *Lina has no flesh on her; she is very skinny,* ② *v.* bend, curve, tilt, incline LIEN

**leap** *v.* spring, bound, jump, hop, skip

**learn** *v.* find out, ascertain, determine, acquire knowledge, understand

**learned** *adj.* cultured, educated, scholarly, literate ★**ignorant**

**learning** *n.* scholarship, education, knowledge ▷ *wisdom* ★**ignorance**

**least** *adj.* fewest, smallest, slightest, lowest, tiniest ★**most** LEASED

**leave** ① *v.* abandon, desert, forsake, quit, go ② bequeath, bestow ③ *n.* vacation, furlough *Jack is on a furlough from the army,* permission

**lecture** *n.* talk, speech, address, sermon

**ledge** *n.* shelf, ridge, step

**legacy** *n.* bequest, inheritance, gift

**legal** *adj.* legitimate, lawful, valid, sound, authorized, rightful ★**illegal**

**legend** *n.* ① fable, myth, tale, fiction ② inscription *The box bore a brass plate with an inscription,* heading, caption

**legible** *adj.* clear, readable, understandable, distinct ★**illegible**

**legitimate** *adj.* legal, lawful, proper, rightful ▷ *genuine* ★**illegal**

## Lights

Arc lamp
Candle
Chandelier
Desk lamp
Electric light
Flashlight
Fluorescent lamp
Footlights
Gaslight
Headlight
Lantern
Nightlight
Reading light
Spotlight
Sunlamp
Table lamp
Torch

**leisurely** *adj.* unhurried, slow, easy, carefree, tranquil ★**hectic**

**lend** *v.* loan, advance, provide, supply, grant, lease ★**borrow**

**lengthen** *v.* extend, elongate, stretch, draw out, prolong ★**shorten**

**lengthy** *adj.* long, drawn out, long-winded ▷*tedious* ★**short**

**lenient** *adj.* tolerant, merciful, sparing, forbearing, indulgent ★**severe**

**less** *adj.* lesser, smaller, inferior, lower

**lessen** *v.* reduce, cut, become smaller, diminish, decrease ★**increase** LESSON

**lesson** *n.* instruction, lecture, information, teaching, exercise LESSEN

**let** ① *v.* allow, permit, suffer, authorize *The mayor authorized our school to hold the celebrations in the park,* grant ② lease

**let down** *v.* ① lower, take down ② betray, abandon, disappoint ★**satisfy**

**letter** *n.* ① dispatch, communication, epistle, message ② character *The book was printed in Hebrew characters,* sign, symbol

**level** ① *n.* plane, grade ② *adj.* even, flat, smooth ★**uneven** ③ *v.* aim, direct, point ④ *v.* demolish *Many houses were demolished during the earthquake,* destroy

**liable** ① *adj.* answerable, accountable, responsible ② apt *My parents are apt to be annoyed if I play loud music,* prone, inclined

**liar** *n.* deceiver, fibber, teller of tales LYRE

**libel** *v.* slander, malign, blacken, defame, slur ★**praise**

**liberal** *adj.* open-handed, generous, open-hearted, free, lavish

**liberate** *v.* set free, save, release, ★**restrict**

**liberty** *n.* freedom, independence ★**slavery**

**license** *v.* allow, permit, entitle ★**ban**

**lie** ① *n.* untruth, falsehood ② *v.* recline *I shall recline on the sofa for the afternoon,* lounge, repose ▷*loll* ③ *v.* tell a lie, fib, invent LYE

**life** *n.* being, existence, activity, energy, ★**death**

**lift** *v.* raise, erect, hoist, elevate, hold up ★**lower**

**light** ① *n.* radiance, glow, shine, glare, brightness ② *n.* lamp, beacon, flame ② *v.* ignite, illuminate, kindle *The scouts kindled a fire to cook their food* ③ *adj.* fair, light-coloured, sunny ★**dark** ④ lightweight, buoyant, airy ★**heavy**

**like** ①*adj.* similar, resembling, akin ★**unlike**

② v. admire, love, adore, cherish, prize ★**dislike**

**likely** adj. probable, expected, possible

**likeness** n. ① resemblance, appearance ② photograph *That's a wonderful photograph of my grandmother,* portrait

**likewise** adv. also, too, furthermore, further

**limb** n. leg, arm, extension, branch, shoot, bough

**limit** ① n. barrier, boundary, border, edge, end, restraint ② v. reduce, restrict *The heavy rain was restricted to the hilly country,* confine ★**free**

**limited** adj. restricted, reduced, narrow, confined ★**unrestricted**

**limp** ① adj. flabby, flimsy, flexible ② v. hobble, falter, shuffle

**line** n. ① stripe, streak, dash, bar ② cord, thread ③ row, queue, file ④ calling *Being an opera singer is a noble calling but a difficult one,* occupation

**linger** v. loiter, lag, dally, tarry, delay ▷*dawdle* ★**speed**

**link** ① n. bond, tie, connection, joint ② v. unite, join, couple, bracket ★**separate**

**liquefy** v. liquidize, melt

**liquid** n. fluid, liquor, solution, juice, sap

**list** ① n. schedule, table, catalogue, register ② v. tilt, lean, heel *The yacht heeled over as it turned into the wind,* careen, slope

**listen** v. hear, hearken, hark, heed

**listless** adj. languid, dull, lethargic, lifeless ▷*sluggish* ★**lively**

**literally** adv. actually, faithfully, precisely, really ★**loosely**

**literate** adj. educated, well-educated, learned, lettered ★**illiterate**

**lithe** adj. agile, nimble, flexible, supple ★**stiff**

**litter** n. clutter, jumble, rubbish, mess, refuse

**little** ① adj. small, tiny, short, slight, trivial, petty ▷*small* ★**large** ② adv. hardly, rarely, seldom

**live** ① adj. alive, living, existing, active, alert ★**dead** ② v. be, subsist, breathe, exist

**lively** adj. active, brisk, vivacious, animated, agile ★**listless**

**livid** adj. ① angry, enraged, furious, mad ② ashen *We were really scared, and Bob's face was ashen,* greyish, pale, leaden

**living** ① adj. alive, existing ② n. job, occupation, work, livelihood

**load** ① n. freight, cargo, goods, burden ② v. fill, pack, burden, pile up, stack LODE, LOWED

**loaf** ① v. waste time, idle, dally, dawdle ② n. block, cube, lump, cake

**loan** ① n. credit, advance, allowance ② v. allow, lend, advance *The bank advanced me the money to pay the mortgage* LONE

**loath** or **loth** adj. reluctant, disinclined, opposed

**loathe** v. abhor, detest, despise, dislike ▷*hate* ★**like**

**lobby** n. hallway, entrance, vestibule, foyer

**local** adj. regional, district, provincial

**locate** v. find, discover, detect, unearth

**lock** ① n. bolt, fastener, latch, clasp ② v. bolt, fasten, secure ③ n. floodgate, weir ④ n. curl, braid, tress *I kept a tress of her hair in a locket*

**lodge** ① v. stay at, put up, shelter, get stuck *A fishbone got stuck in his throat,* remain ② n. inn, hotel

**lofty** adj. ① tall, high, noble, great ② proud, exalted, arrogant ★**modest**

**logical** adj. fair, justifiable, reasonable, sound ★**illogical**

**loiter** v. lag, trail, linger, dally, dawdle, hang around, dilly dally

**loll** v. recline, sprawl, lounge, lie, rest, flop

**lone** adj. single, sole, lonely, separate, unaccompanied LOAN

**lonely** v. alone, forsaken, friendless, remote, forlorn, lonesome

**long** ① adj. lengthy, extended, expanded ★**short** ② v. crave, hanker, yearn, desire

**look** ① v. appear, seem ② v. peer, glance, watch, behold ③ n. appearance, glance, gaze *Her gaze fell upon me, and I had to answer the next question*

**loom** v. menace, portend, rise, emerge, appear

**loop** n. bend, circle, coil, noose, twist

**loophole** n. escape, way out, excuse, get-out

**loose** *adj.* ① slack, separate, apart, flimsy, flabby, baggy ② free, relaxed, ③ vague, indefinite

**loosely** *adv.* freely, separately, vaguely

**loosen** *v.* slacken, relax, undo, detach, release, unfasten ★**tighten**

Loot          Lute

**loot** *n.* booty, haul, swag, spoils, prize, plunder LUTE

**lord** *n.* noble, ruler, duke, marquess, earl, viscount, baron

**lose** *v.* ① mislay, misplace, miss ★**find** ② be defeated, suffer defeat *The rebels suffered defeat at the hands of the army,* fail ★**win**

**loser** *n.* failure, dud, flop ★**winner**

**loss** *n.* damage, harm, forfeit, ruin, misfortune ★**gain**

**lost** *adj.* mislaid, missing, gone, vanished, strayed, ruined ★**found**

**lot** *n.* ① group, batch, assortment ② fate, portion, fortune ③ plot, patch, land

**lotion** *n.* balm, salve, ointment, cream, liniment

**loud** *adj.* ① noisy, blatant, shrill, blaring, deafening ② gaudy, vulgar, tasteless ★**quiet**

**lounge** ① *v.* recline, lie, loll, sprawl, laze ② *n.* parlour *Step into my parlour said the spider to the fly,* reception room, sitting room

**lout** *n.* oaf, clod, boor, lummox

**lovable** *adj.* winsome, charming, attractive, fascinating ★**hateful**

**love** ① *v.* adore, idolize, worship, dote on, cherish, treasure ② *n.* affection, passion, devotion, ardour ★**hate**

**lovely** *adj.* charming, delightful, beautiful, adorable ★**hideous**

**low** *adj.* ① base, vulgar, crude, improper ② not high, flat, level ③ soft, faint, muffled, deep ④ humble, modest, lowly ⑤ cheap, inexpensive ★**high** LO

**lower** ① *v.* let down, fall, descend ② *v.* debase, disgrace, degrade ③ *adj.* inferior, lesser, smaller, minor

**loyal** *adj.* constant, staunch *Bill was Kathy's staunch friend for years,* true ▷*faithful* ★**disloyal**

**lucid** *adj.* clear, obvious, intelligible, bright ▷*transparent* ★**murky**

**luck** *n.* chance, fortune, success, windfall ★**misfortune**

**lucky** *adj.* fortunate, successful, blessed, charmed, favoured ★**unlucky**

**ludicrous** *adj.* absurd, foolish, silly, outlandish, ▷*ridiculous*

**lug** *v.* pull, draw, drag, haul, tow, heave

**luggage** *n.* baggage, suitcases, trunks, boxes

**lull** ① *v.* calm, dwindle, cease, slacken, subside ② *n.* calm, hush, respite

**lumber** ① *n.* timber, wood, boards, logs ② *v.* plod, shuffle, clump ③ clutter, jumble

**luminous** *adj.* shining, radiant, bright

**lump** *n.* bit, piece, chunk, block, knob, swelling *I noticed a rather mysterious swelling on my arm*

**lunatic** *n.* insane person, maniac, psychopath

**lunge** *v.* push, thrust, plunge, charge, pounce

**lurch** *v.* lean, list, reel, rock, stagger, stumble

**lure** *v.* attract, draw, decoy, ensnare, invite ▷*tempt* ★**repulse**

**lurid** *adj.* ghastly, disgusting, grim, grisly, melodramatic, sensational

**lurk** *v.* slink, skulk, crouch, hide, prowl, snoop

**luscious** *adj.* juicy, succulent, mellow, delicious, scrumptious ★**nauseous**

**lush** *adj.* wild, luxuriant, green, rich, abundant

**lust** *n.* desire, passion, craving, greed

**lustre** *n.* brightness, brilliance, gleam, sheen

**lusty** *adj.* hale, hearty, vigorous, energetic, rugged, tough ★**weak**

**luxury** *n.* affluence, wealth, richness, comfort, bliss

**lyre** *n.* harp, zither LIAR

# M m

**macabre** *adj.* ghastly, grisly, hideous, horrible ▷*ghostly*

**machine** *n.* engine, contrivance, device

**mad** *adj.* ① angry, furious ② lunatic, crazy ▷*insane* ★**sane**

**madcap** *adj.* flighty, reckless, thoughtless, impulsive

**magazine** *n.* ① periodical, publication ② storehouse, depot, arsenal

**magic** ① *n.* wizardry, witchcraft, sorcery, conjuring ② *adj.* bewitching *She greeted me with a bewitching smile,* fascinating, miraculous

**magician** *n.* conjuror, wizard, witch, sorcerer, juggler

**magistrate** *n.* judge, justice, bailiff

**magnanimous** *adj.* forgiving, generous, charitable, liberal ★**paltry**

**magnate** *n.* industrialist, merchant, tycoon, VIP, leader MAGNET

**magnet** *n.* lodestone, attraction, bait, draw MAGNATE

**magnetic** *adj.* attracting, attractive, absorbing, entrancing, alluring, mesmerizing ▷*charming* ★**repulsive**

**magnificent** *adj.* majestic, noble, grand, brilliant, superb ▷*splendid* ★**modest**

**magnify** *v.* enlarge, increase, exaggerate ▷*enhance* ★**diminish**

**maid** *n.* ① maiden, virgin, miss, damsel ② maidservant, domestic help, waitress MADE

**mail** *n.* ① letters, post, correspondence, epistles ② armour *The knight's armour was made of breastplates and chain mail,* shield MALE

**maim** *v.* mutilate, injure, mangle, crush ▷*disable* ★**heal**

**main** ① *adj.* leading, principal, central, chief, head *Such important matters are dealt with at our head office,* ② *n.* channel, duct, line, pipe

**mainly** *adv.* chiefly, generally, mostly, on the whole, usually

**Mail**

**Mail**

**maintain** *v.* ① sustain, keep, support, provide for ② affirm, advocate *The chairman advocated an increase in charges,* assert

**majestic** *adj.* dignified, grand, noble, august, elevated ▷*magnificent* ★**unimportant**

**major** ① *adj.* senior, chief, leading, more important, greater ★**minor** ② *n.* officer, soldier

**majority** *n.* greater number, most part, bulk, mass ★**minority**

**make** *v.* ① build, construct, fabricate, fashion ② compel, drive, coerce ③ designate *Two days after her boss retired Liz was designated as the new head of the department,* appoint

**make up** *v.* ① invent, fabricate, create ② forgive and forget, bury the hatchet *At last, my brother and sister stopped arguing and decided to bury the hatchet*

**makeshift** *adj.* improvised, temporary, stop-gap *I fixed the car engine, but it was only a stop-gap repair* ★**permanent**

**malady** *n.* illness, sickness, ailment, affliction, disease

**malevolent** *adj.* malign, baleful, venomous, malicious ▷*hostile* ★**benevolent**

**malice** *n.* bitterness, rancour, spite, enmity ▷*hatred* ★**kindness**

**malicious** *adj.* malignant, spiteful, resentful, bitter ▷*hateful* ★**kind**

**maltreat** *v.* bully, harm, abuse, injure ▷*hurt* ★**assist**

**mammoth** *adj.* giant, colossal, massive, enormous ▷*huge* ★**small**

**man** ① *n.* male, sir, mankind, gentleman ② *n.* valet, manservant ③ *v.* equip, fit out, arm, crew

**manage** *v.* ① direct, control, administer ② get along *I get along quite well on my own,* fare, cope with ★**fail**

**manager** *n.* director, superintendent, overseer, supervisor, boss

**mandate** *n.* authority, command, instruction, warrant

**mangle** *v.* crush, deform, destroy, maul ▷*maim*

**mania** *n.* madness, delirium, craze, fad, enthusiasm, passion, craziness

**manifest** *v.* signify, suggest, demonstrate, display ▷*show* ★**hide**

**manipulate** *v.* work, handle, wield, use conduct, control ▷*operate*

**manly** *adj.* male, masculine, brave, bold, strong, ▷*fearless*

**manner** *n.* fashion, style, form, mode, demeanour, bearing, way MANOR

**manoeuvre** *v.* direct, drive, guide, handle ▷*manipulate*

**manor** *n.* estate, country house, château, hall MANNER

**mansion** *n.* house, castle, residence ▷*manor*

**mantle** *n.* canopy, cape, covering, hood, shroud, cloak MANTEL

**mantel** *n.* fireplace shelf, mantelpiece MANTLE

**manual** ① *adj.* hand-operated, physical *We found the electric typewriter easier to use than the manual typewriter* ② *n.* guide, guidebook, handbook

**manufacture** *v.* make, build, fabricate, create, produce ▷*construct*

**manuscript** *n.* ① script, article, essay, theme ② handwriting, autograph

**many** *adj.* numerous, varied, various, frequent, countless ★**few**

**map** *n.* chart, plan, diagram, outline

**mar** *v.* deface, disfigure, injure, blemish, damage ▷*spoil* ★**enhance**

**march** *v.* stride, walk, pace, step, file, trek

**margin** *n.* edge, border, rim, side, boundary, brim, brink ★**centre**

**mariner** *n.* seaman, sailor, seafarer, deckhand, tar, seadog

**mark** ① *n.* feature, emblem, impression *The letter had a hand-stamped impression on it,* blemish ② *v.* scratch, blemish, stain ③ *v.* take notice of, observe

**marked** *adj.* noticeable, conspicuous, apparent, clear, striking ★**slight**

**market** *n.* supermarket, bazaar, fair, mart

**maroon** *v.* desert, beach, strand, abandon, cast away ★**rescue**

**marry** *v.* wed, get married, espouse, mate, unite ★**separate**

**marsh** *n.* swamp, mire, moor, morass, bog

**marshal** *v.* gather, group, deploy, assemble MARTIAL

**martial** *adj.* military, militant, hostile, warlike ★**peaceful** MARSHAL

**marvel** *n.* miracle, wonder, spectacle, sensation

**marvellous** *adj.* wonderful, wondrous, fabulous, spectacular, superb, astounding ▷*remarkable* ★**ordinary**

**masculine** *adj.* manlike, manly, strong, robust, strapping ▷*male* ★**feminine**

**mash** *v.* crush, squash, pulverize, grind

**mask** ① *n.* camouflage, veil, domino ② *v.* conceal, disguise *Aladdin went to the market-place disguised as a beggar,* shield ★**uncover**

**mass** *n.* batch, combination, hunk, load, quantity, lump

**massacre** *v.* exterminate, butcher, murder, slaughter, kill

**massive** *adj.* big, large, bulky, enormous ▷*huge* ★**small**

**master** ① *n.* controller, director, leader, captain, champion ② *v.* tame *Our job on* *ranch was to tame the wild horses,* control, defeat, subdue

**match** ① *n.* light, fuse, taper, lucifer ② *v.* copy, pair, equal, tone with

**mate** ① *n.* spouse, husband, wife, companion, chum, comrade ② *v.* breed, join, wed, yoke

**material** ① *n.* fabric, textile, cloth, stuff, matter ② *adj.* actual, real, concrete *There was concrete evidence of the prisoner's innocence*

**maternal** *adj.* motherly, parental, kind, affectionate, protective

**matter** ① *n.* affair, concern, subject, topic ② *n.* stuff, material, substance *This rock contains some sort of mineral substance* ③ *n.* trouble, distress ④ *v.* signify, count, affect *What does it matter?*

**mature** *adj.* ripe, mellowed, seasoned, developed, grown-up, adult ★**immature**

**maul** *v.* batter, beat, molest, paw ▷*mangle*

**maxim** *n.* saying, motto, axiom, proverb

**maximum** *adj.* supreme, highest, most, greatest, top, largest ★**minimum**

**maybe** *adv.* possibly, perhaps, perchance

**maze** *n.* labyrinth, puzzle, tangle, confusion ▷*muddle* MAIZE

**meadow** *n.* grassland, field, mead, pasture

**meagre** *adj.* thin, spare, slight, flimsy, sparse ▷*scanty* ★**substantial**

**meal** *n.* repast, dinner, lunch, breakfast, supper ▷*feast*

**mean** ① *v.* signify, denote, express, suggest ② *adj.* cruel, base, low, paltry, miserly ★**generous** ③ average, medium mien

**meaning** *n.* significance, explanation, sense

**means** *n.* ① resources, money, wealth ② technique, ability *She has the ability to become a professional player,* method

**measure** ① *n.* meter, gauge, rule ② *n.* limit, extent, amount ③ *v.* estimate, value, quantify *It is hard to quantify how much damage has been done*

**meat** *n.* flesh, viands, victuals, food MEET

**Measurements**

Inch
Foot
Yard
Mile
Pint
Quart
Gallon
Ounce
Pound
Ton

Millimetre
Centimetre
Metre
Kilometre
Millilitre
Litre
Milligram
Gram
Kilogram
Tonne

Measuring jug

Ruler

Callipers

Bathroom scales

**mechanical** *adj.* ① automatic, machine-driven ② routine, unthinking

**medal** *n.* award, decoration, ribbon, prize, trophy MEDDLE

**meddle** *v.* interfere, intervene, intrude, tamper, butt in MEDAL

**medicine** *n.* remedy, cure, physic, medicament, nostrum, drug, prescription

**mediocre** *adj.* average, common, inferior, middling ▷*ordinary* ★**excellent**

**meditate** *v.* ponder, puzzle over, think, reflect, contemplate

**medium** ① *n.* means, agency, centre ② *n.* conditions, setting, atmosphere *I like school because it has such a wonderful atmosphere of learning* ③ *adj.* average, fair ▷*mediocre*

**medley** *n.* assortment, jumble, collection, hotchpotch

**meek** *adj.* docile, humble, quiet, patient, uncomplaining ▷*mild* ★**arrogant**

**meet** *v.* come together, converge, join, flock, assemble, encounter MEAT, METE

**meeting** *n.* gathering, assembly, convention

**melancholy** *adj.* glum, gloomy, unhappy, sad ▷*miserable* ★**cheerful**

**mellow** *adj.* ① ripe, rich, full-flavoured ★**unripe** ② jovial, cheerful ③ smooth, soothing, delicate *The wine had a smooth, delicate flavour*

**melodious** *adj.* sweet, mellow, silver-toned, rich, resonant ★**harsh**

**melody** *n.* tune, air, lay, song, chant, theme

**melt** *v.* dissolve, liquefy, soften, thaw ★**solidify**

**member** *n.* ① fellow, associate, comrade, fellow, representative ② limb, part, portion, leg, arm

**memorable** *adj.* unforgettable, fresh, indelible, noticeable, striking, noteworthy ▷*conspicuous*

**memorial** *n.* monument, memento, relic, mausoleum *The emperor was buried in the state mausoleum*

**memorize** *v.* learn, commit to memory, remember, learn by heart

**memory** *n.* recall, recapture, recollection, remembrance, renown ▷*fame*

**menace** *v.* threaten, intimidate, frighten, alarm ▷*bully*

**mend** *v.* restore, correct, promote, improve, rectify, heal ▷*repair* ★**damage**

**menial** ① *adj.* servile, ignoble, base ② *n.* skivvy, dog's body, underling, lackey

**mental** *adj.* intellectual, theoretical *Edward's knowledge of music is purely theoretical; he can't play or sing,* abstract ★**physical**

**mention** *v.* declare, announce, observe, disclose, speak of, say

**mercenary** ① *adj.* acquisitive, grasping, greedy ▷*selfish* ② *n.* soldier of fortune *The men who were killed were not patriots, but soldiers of fortune,* freelance, hireling

**merchandise** *n.* wares, goods, commodities, cargo, freight, stock

**merchant** *n.* dealer, trader, marketeer, vender, retailer, tradesman

**merciful** *adj.* humane, clement, lenient, compassionate, sparing, forgiving ★**merciless**

**merciless** *adj.* callous, cruel, pitiless, unrelenting, inhuman ★**merciful**

**mercy** *n.* compassion, clemency, forgiveness, forbearance, grace ▷*pity* ★**cruelty**

### Metals

Aluminium
Brass
Bronze
Chromium
Copper
Gold
Iron and Steel
Lead
Manganese
Mercury
Nickel
Platinum
Silver
Tin
Zinc

Trophy

Girder

**mere** *adj.* pure, unmixed, absolute, unaffected, simple, paltry

**merge** *v.* mix, mingle, combine, fuse, blend, weld ▷*unite*

**merit** ① *n.* excellence, quality, virtue, worth, calibre ▷*talent* ★**failing** ② *v.* deserve, be worthy of

**merry** *adj.* jolly, gleeful, cheerful, mirthful, sunny ▷*happy* ★**melancholy**

**mesh** *n.* net, lattice, snare, netting, tangle, trap, web

**mess** ① *n.* muddle, confusion, clutter, jumble, chaos ▷*plight* ★**order** ② dining hall, mess hall, dining-hall

**message** *n.* communication, letter, missive, notice, note, dispatch *The reporter sent a dispatch to her paper in Lisbon*

**messenger** *n.* courier, runner, agent, bearer, carrier, herald

**mete** *v.* measure, apportion, distribute, divide, deal MEAT, MEET

**method** *n.* routine, usage, way, means, system, rule, manner ▷*mode*

**metre** *n.* ① measure, gauge, rule ② cadence *He recited some of his poems, which had a peculiar cadence to them,* rhythm, lilt, swing

**mettle** *n.* spirit, life, fire, animation, ardour, boldness ▷*courage*

**middle** ① *n.* centre, heart, midst ② *adj.* medium, average, normal

**midget** ① *n.* dwarf, gnome, pygmy ② *adj.* little, miniature, small ▷*tiny* ★**giant**

**mien** *n.* appearance, air, look, manner, expression MEAN

**miffed** *adj.* annoyed, nettled, offended, hurt ▷*upset* ★**delighted**

**might** ① *n.* strength, ability, power, force, energy ② *v. past tense of* **may** *She might not have gone had she known it would snow* MITE

**mighty** *adj.* strong, powerful, potent, stupendous ▷*hefty* ★**weak**

**mild** *adj.* moderate, calm, gentle, genial, docile ▷*meek* ★**harsh**

**military** *adj.* martial, soldierly, warlike

**mill** ① *n.* grinder, works, factory, plant ② *v.* crush, grind, pulverize *The rock was pulverized to make roads,* pound, grate

**mimic** *v.* impersonate, copy, simulate, imitate

**mince** *v.* shred, chop, crumble, grind, hash, dice MINTS

**mind** ① *n.* brain, intellect, soul, spirit ② *v.* listen to, obey, follow orders ③ *v.* take care of, look after ④ *v.* be careful, watch out for

**mine** ① *n.* quarry, colliery, shaft, deposit, tunnel ② *n.* bomb, explosive ③ *v.* excavate, dig out ④ *pron.* belonging to me *This shop is mine*

**mingle** *v.* mix, blend, combine ▷*merge*

**miniature** ① *adj.* tiny, small, dwarf, midget, minute ② *n.* small portrait

**minimum** *adj.* least, smallest, lowest, slightest ★**maximum**

**minister** ① *n.* clergyman, vicar, priest ② *n.* ambassador, diplomat *My aunt was a diplomat working in the Brazilian embassy* ③ *n.* secretary, cabinet member ④ serve, give aid

**minor** *adj.* lesser, smaller, lower, junior, trivial, trifling ★**major** MINER

**mint** ① *v.* stamp, forge, cast ② *adj.* new, perfect, untarnished ③ *n.* peppermint, plant

**minute** ① *n.* (*min*-it) flash, instant, moment ② *adj.* (my-*nyute*) slight, tiny, small ▷*miniature* ★**huge**

**miracle** *n.* marvel, wonder, phenomenon

**miraculous** *adj.* supernatural, amazing, wondrous, prodigious ★**ordinary**

**mire** *n.* slime, muck, ooze, mud

**mirror** ① *n.* looking glass, reflector ② *v.* imitate, simulate, reflect *The essay reflected my feelings about my old home,* copy

**mirth** *n.* hilarity, laughter, jocularity, fun, frolic, jollity ★**melancholy**

**misbehave** *v.* do wrong, disobey, offend, be naughty ★**behave**

**miscellaneous** *adj.* various, varied, divers, sundry, mixed, jumbled

**mischief** *n.* roguery, pranks, damage, hurt, annoyance, harm

**mischievous** *adj.* rascally, villainous, naughty, destructive, spiteful ★**good**

**misconduct** *n.* misbehaviour, wrong-doing, naughtiness, rudeness

**miser** *n.* niggard, skinflint, scrooge, penny-pincher, tightwad ★**spendthrift**

**miserable** *adj.* forlorn, wretched, pitiable, desolate, suffering ★**cheerful**

**misery** *n.* sorrow, woe, grief, anguish, distress ▷*unhappiness* ★**happiness**

**misfit** *n.* eccentric *Professor Jones is something of an eccentric and comes to lectures in her slippers,* drop-out, oddball, nonconformist

**misfortune** *n.* adversity, bad luck, hardship, evil, calamity ▷*disaster* ★**luck**

**misgiving** *n.* distrust, mistrust, doubt, apprehension, anxiety ▷*qualm* ★**confidence**

**mishap** *n.* misadventure, blow, accident, setback ▷*misfortune*

**misjudge** *v.* underestimate, overestimate, overrate, underrate ▷*mistake*

**mislay** *v.* lose, misplace, miss

**mislead** *v.* deceive, lead astray, hoodwink, take in, outwit, fool ▷*bluff*

**miss** ① *v.* fail, fall short of, skip, pass over, mistake ② *v.* grieve over, yearn for, lament ③ *n.* girl, young woman, damsel

**missile** *n.* projectile, arrow, dart, pellet, shot, rocket, torpedo

**mission** *n.* errand, task, assignment, object, objective, end, aim ▷*quest*

**mist** *n.* moisture, dew, vapour, fog, cloud, smog, haze MISSED

**mistake** ① *n.* error, fault, lapse, blunder, oversight ② *v.* slip up, misunderstand, confuse, confound, blunder

**mistaken** *adj.* erroneous, untrue, false, fallacious ▷*wrong* ★**correct**

**mistrust** *v.* disbelieve, distrust, doubt, fear ▷*suspect* ★**trust**

**misunderstand** *v.* mistake, misinterpret, take wrongly ★**grasp**

**misuse** *v.* exploit, abuse, corrupt, harm

**mite** *n.* ① grain, atom, morsel, particle ② bug, parasite *The plants were infested with parasites* MIGHT

**mitigate** *v.* allay, ease, abate, moderate, justify, vindicate ★**aggravate**

**mix** *v.* blend, whip, mingle, combine ▷*stir*

**mix up** *v.* confuse, confound, muddle, jumble ▷*bewilder*

**mixture** *n.* miscellany, medley, jumble, blend

**moan** *v.* wail, groan, grouse, grumble, grieve, whinge

**mob** *n.* crowd, mass, gang, flock, rabble, company, throng

**mobile** *adj.* active, portable, wandering, movable ★**immobile**

**mock** ① *v.* mimic, imitate, jeer at, laugh at, ridicule ▷*flatter* ② *adj.* pretended, artificial, sham, false, fake

**mode** *n.* fashion, style, vogue, manner, way, form ▷*method* MOWED

**model** *n.* ① pattern, original, prototype *This car is a prototype, and we will produce many like it* ② mannequin ③ replica, representation

**moderate** *adj.* reasonable, medium, gentle, mild, quiet, modest ▷*fair*

**modern** *adj.* new, up-to-date, modish, stylish, recent, current, contemporary, state-of-the art, trendy ANTIQUATED

**modest** *adj.* bashful, demure, diffident, unassuming, humble ★**vain**

**modesty** *n.* humility, diffidence, reserve, shyness, decency ★**vanity**

**modify** *v.* transform, convert, change, alter, revise, redesign

**moist** *adj.* damp, humid, watery, clammy, dank ▷*wet* ★**dry**

**moisture** *n.* damp, dampness, liquid, wetness, dew, dankness

**molest** *v.* annoy, bother, pursue, attack, pester, plague, tease, torment ▷*harry*

**moment** *n.* ① second, instant, twinkling ② importance, worth, weight *I think your argument has some weight, and I agree with you*

**momentous** *adj.* notable, outstanding, decisive, important, significant, weighty, grave ★**insignificant**

**monarch** *n.* king, sovereign, ruler, emperor, prince *The head of state in Monaco is a prince*

## World Money

| | |
| --- | --- |
| afghani | Afghanistan |
| balboa | Panama |
| bolivar | Venezuela |
| cedi | Ghana |
| colón | Costa Rica, El Salvador |
| cruzeiro | Brazil |
| dinar | Algeria, Bahrain, Iraq, Jordan, Kuwait |
| dollar | Australia, Bahamas, Canada, USA, etc |
| drachma | Greece |
| escudo | Portugal |
| forint | Hungary |
| franc | Belgium, France, etc |
| guarani | Paraguay |
| guilder | Netherlands |
| kip | Laos |
| krona | Iceland, Sweden |
| krone | Denmark, Norway |
| lek | Albania |
| leu | Romania |
| lev | Bulgaria |
| lira | Italy, Turkey |
| mark | Germany |
| markka | Finland |
| naira | Nigeria |
| peseta | Spain |
| peso | Argentina, Chile, Cuba |
| pound | United Kingdom |
| rand | South Africa |
| rial | Iran, Oman, Yemen |
| rouble | Russia |
| rupee | India |
| schilling | Austria |
| sol | Peru |
| sucre | Ecuador |
| yen | Japan |
| yuan | China |
| zloty | Poland |

**money** *n.* wealth, cash, coin, legal tender

**mongrel** *n.* hybrid, mixed, crossbreed, dog

**monitor** ① *n.* listener, auditor, watchdog, prefect ② *v.* check, supervise, oversee

**monologue** *n.* lecture, oration, speech, recitation, sermon

**monopolize** *v.* control, take over, appropriate ▷ *dominate* ★**share**

**monotonous** *adj.* tedious, uninteresting, dull, prosaic *His speech was so prosaic that I almost dropped off to sleep,* repetitive ▷ *tiresome*

**monstrous** *adj.* hideous, frightful, dreadful, terrible, criminal ▷ *wicked*

**mood** *n.* state of mind, humour, temper, disposition *My grandmother's gentle disposition won her many friends*

**moody** *adj.* morose, sulky, sullen, peevish, cantankerous *I didn't like Uncle Harry; he was a cantankerous old man* ★**cheerful**

**moor** ① *v.* tether, picket, tie, chain, anchor, secure ② *n.* heath, moorland MORE

**mop** *n.* ① sponge, swab, towel ② hair, tresses, locks, mane

**mope** *v.* grieve, moon, pine, sulk

**moral** *adj.* virtuous, good, honest, honourable ▷ *upright* ★**immoral**

**morbid** *adj.* gruesome, macabre, melancholy, grisly, putrid

**more** ① *adj.* in addition, also, beyond, extra, further ② *adv.* better, again, longer

**morning** *n.* dawn, daybreak, daylight, cockcrow *I rose at cockcrow, saddled my horse, and was off to Richmond,* sunrise ★**evening** MOURNING

**morose** *adj.* glum, sullen, sulky, broody, taciturn ▷ *moody* ★**cheerful**

**morsel** *n.* bit, bite, piece, scrap, nibble

**mortal** *adj.* ① human, feeble, ephemeral ② fatal, final, deadly, severe

**most** ① *adj.* greatest nearly all ② *adv.* mostly, chiefly, mainly, utmost

**mostly** *adv.* as a rule, principally, usually, normally

**mother** ① *n.* female parent, ma, mummy, mama ② *v.* nurse, protect, rear, care for

**motherly** *adj.* caring, comforting, loving, maternal, gentle

**motion** *n.* ① movement, locomotion, action, passage ② proposal *I vote that we accept the proposal,* suggestion

**motionless** *adj.* stationary, still, transfixed, stable, inert ★**moving**

**motive** *n.* reason, purpose, occasion, impulse, cause ▷*spur*

**mottled** *adj.* speckled, spotted, pied, piebald

**motto** *n.* saying, slogan, watchword, maxim *My mother's maxim was 'Always look on the bright side'.* proverb

**mould** ① *v.* form, shape, fashion, cast, create ② *n.* pattern, matrix ③ *n.* earth, loam

**mouldy** *adj.* mildewed, putrid, bad

**mound** *n.* hillock, pile, knoll, rise, mount

**mount** *v.* ascend, climb, rise, vault

**mourn** *v.* lament, deplore, sorrow, regret, weep ▷*grieve* ★**rejoice**

**mournful** *adj.* doleful, sombre, cheerless, sorrowful ▷*melancholy* ★**joyful**

**mouth** *n.* aperture, opening, entrance, orifice, inlet, jaws

**mouthful** *n.* bite, morsel, sample, taste, titbit

**move** *v.* ① march, proceed, walk, go ② propose, suggest, recommend ③ propel, drive, impel

**moving** *adj.* touching, affecting, stirring *The band played a stirring rendition of 'Amazing Grace',* emotional

**much** ① *adj.* abundant, considerable, ample ② *adv.* considerably, greatly, often ③ *n.* lots, loads, heaps, plenty

**muck** *n.* dirt, filth, mire, ooze, mud, scum

**muddle** ① *n.* confusion, clutter, jumble, mix-up ② *v.* bungle, tangle, confound ▷*bewilder*

**muff** *v.* botch, mismanage, miss, spoil ▷*muddle*

**muffle** *v.* ① deaden, mute, muzzle, silence

② wrap, envelop, wind, swaddle

**mug** ① *n.* innocent, simpleton ② *n.* cup, beaker, tankard ③ *v.* attack, beat up, rob

**muggy** *adj.* clammy, dank, damp, humid, close ★**dry**

**mull** *v.* meditate *I meditated over the weekend before deciding what to do,* consider, study, think about

**multiply** *v.* increase, spread, grow, extend, intensify ★**decrease**

**multitude** *n.* crowd, legion, throng, swarm, horde ★**handful**

**munch** *v.* crunch, chew, bit, nibble ▷*eat*

**murder** *v.* slay, assassinate, butcher, destroy, slaughter ▷*kill*

**murky** *adj.* foggy, cloudy, dark, gloomy, dull, misty ★**bright**

**murmur** *n.* & *v.* whisper, mutter, mumble, drone

**muscular** *adj.* brawny, athletic, burly, beefy, powerful ▷*robust* ★**puny**

**muse** *v.* meditate, ponder, puzzle over, brood, deliberate

**must** ① *v.* ought to, should, be obliged to ② *n.* duty, necessity, requirement

**muster** *v.* marshal, collect, assemble, rally *The troops rallied and prepared to attack again,* enrol

**musty** *adj.* mouldy, rank, mildewy, decayed

**mute** *adj.* silent, speechless, voiceless, soundless ★**loud**

**mutilate** *v.* injure, hurt, cut, damage ▷*maim*

**mutiny** *n.* & *v.* protest, revolt, strike, riot

**mutter** *v.* mumble, grouse, grumble ▷*murmur* ★**exclaim**

**mutual** *adj.* common, reciprocal, interchangeable ▷*joint* ★**one-sided**

**mysterious** *adj.* obscure, unrevealed, unexplained, secret ▷*hidden* ★**clear**

**mystery** *n.* puzzle, enigma, secrecy, riddle, problem

**mystify** *v.* confuse, bamboozle, hoodwink, puzzle, mislead ▷*baffle* ★**enlighten**

**myth** *n.* fable, legend, supposition, fabrication, tradition, fantasy ★**fact**

**mythical** *adj.* fabulous, fabled, legendary, traditional, imaginary ★**true**

# N n

**nab** *v.* arrest, apprehend, seize, catch, capture, grab

**nag** ① *v.* pester, hector, heckle, badger, annoy, henpeck, scold *My parents scolded me for coming home late* ② *n.* horse, pony

**nail** ① *n.* pin, peg, pin, spike, tack ② *v.* hammer, fix, tack, peg

**naive** *adj.* innocent, unworldly, unsophisticated, simple, trusting, artless, natural, childlike, unaffected, ingenuous, credulous ★**cunning, sophisticated**

**naked** *adj.* nude, bare, unclothed, undressed ★**clothed**

**name** ① *n.* title, description, designation ② *n.* character, reputation *A good reputation is very important to me,* distinction ③ *v.* christen, style, term, entitle

**nap** ① *v.* sleep, doze, drowse, rest ② *n.* down, fibre, fuzz *Velvet is a cloth with a kind of fuzz on the surface*

**narrate** *v.* describe, tell, recite, relate

**narrow** *adj.* slender, fine, small ▷*thin* ★**wide**

**nasty** *adj.* dirty, mucky, foul, offensive, unpleasant ▷*squalid* ★**nice**

**national** *adj.* civil, governmental, public, general, nationwide

**native** *adj.* natural, inborn, aboriginal, domestic, local

**natural** *adj.* frank, genuine, innate, instinctive, ordinary, usual

**naturally** *adj.* absolutely, certainly, frankly, normally

**nature** *n.* ① temper, personality, disposition ② the world, the outdoors, landscape

**naughty** *adj.* mischievous, rascally, wicked, disobedient ▷*bad* ★**well-behaved**

**nauseous** *adj.* disgusting, sickening, repulsive, revolting ★**pleasant**

**nautical** *adj.* maritime *Ancient Greece was a great maritime nation,* seamanlike, naval, sailing, seafaring

**navigate** *v.* voyage, cruise, sail, guide, pilot

**navy** *n.* ships, fleet, armada, flotilla

**near** *adj.* close, nearby, adjacent, bordering, neighbouring, beside ▷*nigh* ★**remote**

**nearly** *adv.* about, almost, all but, thereabouts, roughly

**neat** *adj.* ① tidy, spruce, smart, stylish ★**untidy** ② skilful, clever, adroit *I admire your adroit handling of that tricky situation,* ingenious

**necessary** *adj.* needed, essential, basic, required, compulsory ★**optional**

**need** ① *v.* require, want, crave ▷*demand* ★**have** ② *n.* distress, want, necessity, deprivation *During the long war, the people suffered many deprivations* KNEAD

**needed** *adj.* wanted, desired, lacking ▷*necessary* ★**unnecessary**

**needless** *adj.* pointless, unnecessary, superfluous, useless ★**necessary**

**needy** *adj.* destitute, down-and-out, deprived ▷*poor* ★**well-off**

**neglect** *v.* overlook, ignore, scorn, slight, disregard ▷*spurn* ★**cherish**

**neglected** *adj.* unkempt, abandoned, dilapidated, uncared for ★**cherished**

**negligent** *adj.* neglectful, forgetful, slack, indifferent ▷*careless* ★**careful**

**negotiate** *v.* bargain, deal, treat, haggle, mediate, transact

**neighbourhood** *n.* vicinity, surroundings, district, area, locality *There are many fine houses in this locality*

**neighbourly** *adj.* hospitable, friendly, kind, obliging ▷*helpful*

**nerve** *n.* ① mettle, guts, pluck, courage ② audacity, impudence *Mr Thompson already owes us money and yet he has the impudence to ask for more*

**nervous** *adj.* tense, taut, jumpy, flustered, jittery, anxious, timid ★**confident**

**nest** *n.* den, burrow, haunt, refuge, resort

**nestle** *adj.* cuddle, snuggle, huddle, nuzzle

**net** ① *v.* catch, trap, lasso, capture ② *n.* mesh, lattice, trap, web, lace *I have some new lace curtains* ③ *adj.* clear *I made a clear £15,000 after taxes,* final, lowest

**nettle** *v.* exasperate, annoy, ruffle ▷VEX

**National and Religious Holidays**

Advent, All Saints' Day, Anzac Day, Ascension Day, Ash Wednesday, Australia Day, Bastille Day, Boxing Day, Canada Day, Candlemas, Carnival, Christmas, Commonwealth Day, Diwali, Day of the Dead, Easter, Father's Day, Gandhi's Birthday, Good Friday, Guy Fawkes Day, Halloween, Hanukkah, Independence Day, Kwanzaa, Labour Day, Lent, Mardi Gras, Martin Luther King Day, Memorial Day, Mother's Day, Muhammad's Birthday, New Year's Day, Palm Sunday, Passover, Pentecost, Purim, Ramadan, Rosh Hashanah, Saint Patrick's Day, Shavuot, Sukkot, Thanksgiving Day, Valentine's Day, Yom Kippur

*A puppet from the Mexican Day of the Dead Festival.*

**neutral** *adj.* impartial, unbiased, fair-minded, unprejudiced ★**biased**

**never** *adv.* at no time, not at all, under no circumstances ★**always**

**new** *adj.* recent, just out, current, latest, fresh, unused ▷*novel* ★**old** GNU, KNEW

**news** *n.* information, intelligence, tidings, account, bulletin, rumour

**next** *adj.* ① following, succeeding, after, later ② adjacent, adjoining *I live on Park Street, and my friend lives on the adjoining street,* beside

**nibble** *v.* bite, peck, gnaw, munch ▷*eat*

**nice** *adj.* ① pleasant, agreeable, amiable, charming, delightful ★**nasty** ② precise, accurate, fine, subtle

**niche** *n.* compartment, hole, corner, recess, place

**nick** *v.* ① dent, score, mill, cut, scratch ② prison, gaol, police station

**nigh** *adj.* next, close, adjacent, adjoining ▷*near* ★**distant**

**night** *n.* dark, darkness, dusk, evening ★**day** KNIGHT

**nimble** *adj.* active, agile, spry, lithe, skilfull ▷*deft* ★**clumsy**

**nip** *v.* cut, snip, pinch, twinge, bite

**no** ① *adj.* not any, not one, none ② *adv.* nay, not at all KNOW

**noble** *adj.* ① dignified, lofty *My aunt is very important and has a lofty position on the council,* generous, grand, stately, elevated ★**base** ② aristocrat, peer

**nod** *v.* ① beckon, signal, indicate, salute ② sleep, doze, nap

**noise** *n.* din, discord, clamour, clatter, hubbub, tumult, uproar ★**silence**

**noisy** *adj.* loud, boisterous, turbulent, rowdy, clamorous ★**quiet**

**nominate** *v.* appoint, assign, elect, choose, propose, suggest

**nonchalant** *adj.* casual, unperturbed, calm, blasé *We enjoyed the new musical, but Sue has been to so many shows she was very blasé about it,* cool, detached ★**anxious**

**nondescript** *adj.* commonplace, colourless, dull, ordinary ▷*plain* ★**unusual**

**none** *pron.* not one, not any, not a part, nil, nobody NUN

**nonsense** *n.* absurdity, balderdash, drivel, rot, garbage, twaddle ★**sense**

**nook** *n.* compartment, hole, corner, alcove,

crevice, cranny, cavity, hide-out ▷*niche*
**noose** *n.* loop, bight, snare, rope, lasso
**normal** *adj.* usual, general, average, sane, lucid, rational, standard ★**abnormal**
**nose** *n.* ① beak, bill, neb, snout ② prow, stem, bow, front
**nosy** *adj.* inquisitive, curious, prying, snooping, intrusive
**nostalgia** *n.* homesickness, longing, pining, regret, remembrance, yearning
**notable** *adj.* eventful, momentous, marked, outstanding, great, celebrated, eminent ▷*famous* ★**commonplace**
**notch** *n.* dent, nick, score, cut, cleft, indentation
**note** *n.* ① letter, message, communication ② remark, record, report ③ fame, renown, distinction ④ banknote, bill
**noted** *adj.* eminent, renowned, celebrated, great ▷*famous* ★**obscure**
**nothing** *n.* zero, naught, null, nil, zilch ★**something**
**notice** ① *n.* announcement, advice, sign, poster ② *v.* note, remark, observe *After observing that his bike had a flat tyre, Jo knew he would have to walk to school,* perceive, make out, see ★**ignore**
**notify** *v.* inform, tell, intimate, announce, declare ★**withhold**

**Notice**

*After observing that his bike had a flat tyre, Jo knew he would have to walk to school.*

**notion** *n.* idea, conception, opinion, belief, view, judgement
**notorious** *adj.* infamous, questionable, scandalous, blatant
**notwithstanding** *adv.* nevertheless, nonetheless, however, despite
**nourish** *v.* feed, sustain, nurture, comfort, cherish, support ★**starve**
**nourishing** *adj.* beneficial, healthful, nutritious, wholesome
**novel** ① *adj.* fresh, unusual, original, unique, rare, uncommon ② *n.* fiction, story, book, romance, tale
**novice** *n.* beginner, learner, apprentice, tiro, pupil, trainee ★**expert**
**now** *adv.* at this moment, at present, at once, instantly, right away
**now and then** *adv.* from time to time, sometimes, occasionally
**nude** *adj.* bare, naked, unclothed, stripped, undressed
**nudge** *v.* poke, push, prod, jog, shove, dig
**nuisance** *n.* offence, annoyance, plague, trouble, bore, pest, irritation
**nullify** *v.* annul, invalidate, cancel, quash ▷*abolish* ★**establish**
**numb** *adj.* deadened, insensible, dazed, stunned, unfeeling ★**sensitive**
**number** ① *n.* figure, amount, volume, quantity, sum ② *n.* crowd, throng, multitude *The new president's visit to the town was watched by a multitude of people* ③ *n.* figure, symbol ▷*numeral* ④ *v.* count, reckon, tally
**numeral** *n.* symbol, figure, character, cipher
**numerous** *adj.* many, divers, several, plentiful ▷*abundant* ★**few**
**nun** *n.* sister, abbess, prioress NONE
**nurse** ① *v.* attend, care for, foster, support, sustain ② *n.* hospital sister, matron, nanny
**nursery** *n.* ① children's room, creche ② greenhouse, hothouse, garden
**nurture** *v.* feed, nourish, cherish, foster, tend, care for ▷*nurse*
**nutritious** *adj.* healthful, substantial, health-giving ▷*nourishing* ★**bad**

# O o

**oaf** *n.* brute, lout, blockhead, dolt, ruffian,

**obedient** *adj.* respectful, obliging, law-abiding, servile, dutiful, deferential, yielding ★**rebellious**

**obey** *v.* comply, conform, submit, heed, mind, behave ★**disobey**

**object** ① *v.* (ob-*ject*) protest, complain, argue, oppose, refuse ★**agree** ② *n.* (*ob*-ject) thing, article, commodity, item ③ *n.* mission, purpose *The purpose of my visit is to end this conflict,* end,

**objectionable** *adj.* displeasing, distasteful, disagreeable, repugnant ★**pleasant**

**obligation** *n.* responsibility, liability, commitment ★**choice**

**oblige** *v.* ① require, compel, force, make ② gratify, please, help ▷*assist* ★**displease**

**obliging** *adj.* helpful, polite, agreeable, courteous ▷*willing* ★**unkind**

**obliterate** *v.* blot out, efface, erase, wipe out, destroy, annihilate

**oblivious** *adj.* unmindful, absent-minded, heedless, unaware ★**aware**

**obnoxious** *adj.* repulsive, revolting, offensive ▷*unpleasant* ★**pleasant**

**obscene** *adj.* dirty, unclean, vile, filthy, nasty, immoral, indecent ★**decent**

**obscure** ① *adj.* indistinct, dim, vague, hidden, confusing *The language of a legal document can be very confusing* ▷*doubtful* ★**clear** ② *v.* conceal, hide, cloud, darken, cover ▷*hide* ★**clarify**

**observant** *adj.* attentive, watchful, heedful ▷*alert* ★**inattentive**

**observation** *n.* ① attention, study, supervision ② utterance, comment, remark, statement *The police issued a statement*

**observe** *v.* ① abide by *I intend to abide by the laws of this country,* adhere to, carry out, keep up ② note, notice, perceive, watch ▷*see* ③ utter, remark, mention

**obsolete** *adj.* dated, outmoded, unfashionable, out-of-date ★**current**

**obstacle** *n.* obstruction, barrier, bar, hindrance ▷*drawback* ★**advantage**

**obstinate** *adj.* determined, dogged, unyielding, perverse *As a child I upset my parents by my perverse behaviour* ▷*stubborn* ★**docile**

**obstruct** *v.* hinder, impede, block, bar, choke ▷*restrain* ★**help**

**obstruction** *n.* hindrance, restraint, impediment, snag

**obtain** *v.* acquire, achieve, gain, procure, attain ▷*get* ★**lose**

**obtuse** *adj.* dull, stupid, unintelligent, stolid, thick, blunt ★**bright**

**obvious** *adj.* plain, evident, self-evident, explicit, apparent ▷*clear* ★**obscure**

**occasion** *n.* ① affair, episode, occurrence, circumstance ② reason, purpose, motive

**occasional** *adj.* casual, rare, infrequent, periodic ★**frequent**

**occult** *adj.* hidden, unrevealed, secret, mysterious, supernatural *Edgar Allan Poe wrote tales of the supernatural* ★**open**

**occupant** *n.* owner, resident, proprietor, tenant, inmate, inhabitant

**occupation** *n.* ① activity, employment, calling, job ② possession, tenancy, residence

**occupied** *adj.* ① busy, employed, active ② settled, populated, peopled ★**unoccupied**

**occupy** *v.* ① inhabit, live in, reside, dwell in, own, possess, hold ② invade, overrun

**occur** *v.* take place, befall, turn out, come to pass, result ▷*happen*

**occurrence** *n.* happening, affair, circumstance, incident, occasion ▷*event*

**ocean** *n.* sea, main *The pirates of the Spanish Main were the curse of shipping,* deep, tide

**odd** *adj.* ① single, unmatched ② singular,

### Oceans and Waters

| | | |
|---|---|---|
| Antarctic | Bay | Sound |
| Arctic | Fjord | Straits |
| Atlantic | Gulf | |
| Indian | Lagoon | |
| Pacific | Loch | |

peculiar, quaint, queer ★**ordinary**
③ surplus, left over, remaining

**odds and ends** *n.* leavings, debris *The police found the debris of the crashed aircraft,* leftovers, oddments, remains

**odious** *adj.* hateful, offensive, detestable ▷*abominable* ★**pleasant**

**odorous** *adj.* fragrant, perfumed, aromatic, sweet-smelling

**odour** *n.* ① scent, aroma ▷*fragrance* ② stink, stench, reek ▷*smell*

**off** ① *adv.* away from, over, done ② *prep.* along, against, opposite, distant ★**on** ③ *adj.* bad, mouldy, rotten

**offence** *n.* insult, outrage, attack, crime, hurt

**offend** *v.* ① insult, hurt, wound, outrage, displease ② transgress, sin ★**please**

**offensive** *adj.* insulting, offending, rude, repugnant, hurtful, distasteful

**offer** ① *v.* propose, proffer, present, tender, attempt ② *n.* bid, endeavour, proposal

**offering** *n.* sacrifice, donation, gift, present

**offhand** *adj.* ① brusque, casual, curt, informal, abrupt ② informal, improvised, impromptu *My sister, who is a singer, gave an impromptu performance* ★**planned**

**office** ① *n.* bureau, department, room ② position, appointment, post

**officer** *n.* ① official, administrator, functionary, executive ② military rank, policeman, minister *A minister from the French Embassy called*

**official** ① *adj.* authorized, authentic, proper, formal ★**unofficial** ② *n.* executive, office-holder, bureaucrat *The city bureaucrats take months to get a job done*

**officious** *adj.* interfering, meddlesome, self-important

**offspring** *n.* child, children, descendant, heir, family, issue, progeny

**often** *adv.* frequently, regularly, recurrently, time after time, repeatedly ★**seldom**

**ointment** *n.* lotion, salve, cream, balm, embrocation, liniment

**old** *adj.* ① ancient, antique, aged, antiquated ② crumbling, decayed *Beneath the ivy were the decayed remains of the castle wall,*

decrepit ★**new** ③ out-of-date, old-fashioned, passé ④ aged, mature, elderly ★**young**

**ominous** *adj.* menacing, threatening, foreboding, sinister

**omit** *v.* leave out, neglect, let go, overlook, miss out, skip ★**include**

**once** *adv.* formerly, at one time, previously

**one** ① *adj.* sole, alone, lone, whole ② *n.* unit, single thing

**one-sided** *adj.* unequal, unfair, unjust, biased

**only** ① *adj.* exclusive, single, sole, lone, solitary ② *adv.* solely, barely, exclusively

**onset** *n.* start, outbreak, assault, attack, onslaught, onrush

**onslaught** *n.* charge, attack, bombardment

**ooze** ① *n.* mire, muck, slime ② *v.* bleed, discharge, emit, exude, leak

**open** ① *v.* uncover, unlock, unfasten ② *v.* start, commence, begin ③ *adj.* uncovered, clear, evident, apparent ★**closed** ④ *adj.* frank, honest, candid, fair

**opening** *n.* ① aperture, mouth, crevice, recess, hole ② commencement, beginning

**openly** *adv.* candidly, frankly, plainly, sincerely ★**secretly**

**operate** *v.* function *Despite its age, the old millwheel continued to function,* work, manipulate, drive, ▷*perform*

**operation** *n.* performance, movement, action, motion, proceeding

**opinion** *n.* view, concept, judgement, belief, point of view, stance

**opponent** *n.* antagonist, rival, competitor, contestant, foe ▷*enemy* ★**ally**

**opportune** *adj.* timely *It had started to rain, thus the timely arrival of the bus was welcome,* convenient, fortunate, suitable ★**untimely**

**opportunity** *n.* occasion, chance, opening, scope, moment

**oppose** *v.* withstand, resist, obstruct, confront, hinder ▷*defy* ★**support**

**opposite** *adj.* ① facing, fronting ② conflicting, opposing, contrary, adverse ★**same**

**opposition** *n.* antagonism, defiance, hostility, difference ▷*resistance* ★**co-operation**

**oppress** *v.* crush, depress, harass, overpower, overwhelm, subdue

**optimist** *n.* hopeful person, perfectionist ★**pessimist**

**optimistic** *adj.* hopeful, cheerful, confident, positive ★**pessimistic**

**option** *n.* preference, choice, alternative

**optional** *adj.* possible, voluntary, unforced, open ★**compulsory**

**opulent** *adj.* rich, affluent, prosperous, well-to-do ▷*wealthy* ★**poor**

**oration** *n.* sermon, lecture, speech, discourse

**orb** *n.* globe, ball, sphere

**orbit** *n.* ① path, passage, trajectory ② province, realm, domain *The river, the forest, and the castle were all within her domain*

**ordeal** *n.* trial, nightmare, torment, agony

**order** ① *n.* arrangement, pattern, grouping, organization ② *n.* command, law, rule, decree *A decree was issued forbidding the killing of deer* ③ *n.* shipment, consignment ④ *v.* direct, instruct, command ⑤ *v.* arrange, control, conduct

**orderly** *adj.* regular, methodical, trim, neat, well-mannered ★**messy**

**ordinary** *adj.* common, usual, commonplace, general, customary ★**extraordinary**

**organization** *n.* ① association, group, institute, establishment ② structure, arrangement, system

**organize** *v.* arrange, form, structure, establish, classify ★**disorganize**

**origin** *n.* beginning, start, basis, foundation, root, source ★**end**

**original** *adj.* ① first, aboriginal, ancient, former, primary ② fresh, new, novel *Travelling by camel was a novel experience*

**originate** ① *v.* create, conceive, compose ② arise, begin ▷*start* ★**end**

**ornament** ① *n.* decoration, adornment, tracery, pattern ② trinket, curio, knick-knack

**ornate** *adj.* decorated, adorned, flowery,

**Original**

*Travelling by camel was a novel experience.*

embellished, showy, garish ★**plain**

**oust** *v.* expel, eject, evict, dismiss, throw out ▷*overthrow*

**out** ① *adj.* away, outside, absent ★**in** ② *adj.* open, revealed, uncovered ③ *adv.* loudly, aloud, audibly

**out of order** *adj.* broken, not working

**out of sorts** *adj.* sick, ill, poorly, gloomy, fed up

**outbreak** *n.* epidemic *An epidemic of cholera had hit the village,* rebellion, eruption, explosion, flare-up

**outburst** *n.* eruption, explosion ▷*outbreak*

**outcast** *n.* exile, castaway *Robinson Crusoe was a castaway on a desert island,* derelict, refugee, reject

**outcome** *n.* effect, consequence, conclusion, result, upshot

**outcry** *n.* commotion, row, uproar, tumult, shouting, hue and cry ▷*clamour*

**outdated** *adj.* old, antique, old-fashioned, unfashionable, obsolete ★**modern**

**outdo** *v.* surpass, excel, beat, outclass, eclipse, exceed, outshine

**outfit** *n.* ensemble, set *My mother bought a new set of dishes in the sale for half price,* rig, equipment, gear

**outing** *n.* excursion, picnic, expedition, trip, ramble

**outlandish** *adj.* strange, erratic, odd, queer, quaint, bizarre ★**ordinary**

**outlaw** *n.* bandit, highwayman, hooligan, desperado *Billy the Kid was a desperado in the Wild West,* robber

**outlet** *n.* exit, egress, way out, vent, spout, nozzle, opening ★**inlet**

**outline** ① *n.* diagram, plan, blueprint, sketch, framework, summary ② *v.* draw, sketch, describe

**outlook** *n.* view, prospect, forecast, attitude, aspect, prognosis

**output** *n.* yield, product, produce, achievement, manufacture

**outrage** ① *n.* disgrace, injury, offence, affront ② *v.* offend, insult, shock, violate

**outrageous** *adj.* insulting, offensive, exorbitant, monstrous ★**acceptable**

**outright** ① *adj.* complete, thorough, absolute, wholesale ② *adv.* at once, completely, entirely, altogether

**outset** *n.* first, opening, beginning, inauguration, kick-off ▷*start* ★**finish**

**outside** ① *n.* exterior, surface, front ② *adj.* exterior, external, outward, surface

**outsider** *n.* stranger, foreigner, alien, misfit *Gulliver was something of a misfit in the land of the tiny Lilliputians*

**outskirts** *n.* limits, bounds, boundary, outpost, suburb

**outspoken** *adj.* frank, open, straightforward, blunt, direct ▷*candid* ★**tactful**

**outstanding** *adj.* striking, pronounced, conspicuous, notable ▷*exceptional* ★**ordinary**

**outward** *adj.* exterior, outside, outer, superficial *From a distance, my father and Bill Jones look alike, but it's really just superficial*

**outwit** *v.* get the better of, swindle, defraud, dupe ▷*cheat*

**over** ① *adj.* concluded, ended, done with, settled ② *prep.* above, more than, exceeding ③ *adv.* aloft, above, beyond, extra

**overall** ① *adj.* complete, inclusive, total, broad ② *adv.* by and large, on the whole

**overbearing** *adj.* domineering, dictatorial, haughty, pompous ▷*arrogant* ★**modest**

**overcast** *adj.* cloudy, heavy, dark, murky, dull ★**bright**

**overcome** *adj.* overwhelm, conquer, crush, defeat, vanquish ▷*subdue*

**overdo** *v.* overwork, exaggerate, go too far *I didn't mind your eating one of my apples, but taking all four was going too far*

**overdue** *adj.* delayed, belated, late, behindhand ★**early**

**overflow** *v.* swamp, deluge, inundate, submerge, soak, spill

**overhaul** *v.* ① repair, mend, fix, inspect, examine ② overtake, pass, gain on

**overhead** *adv.* above, upward, aloft, on high ★**below**

**overhear** *v.* listen, eavesdrop, snoop, spy

**overjoyed** *adj.* elated, jubilant, rapturous ▷*delighted* ★**disappointed**

**overlap** *v.* overrun, go beyond, coincide, overlay

**overlook** *v.* ① disregard, pardon, condone, ignore ② neglect, miss, pass over ③ inspect, check, examine

**overpower** *v.* conquer, crush, master, subdue, vanquish ▷*defeat*

**overseas** *adj.* abroad, foreign ★**domestic**

**overseer** *n.* inspector, supervisor, boss, manager, master, mistress

**oversight** *n.* omission, blunder, error, fault, lapse ▷*mistake*

**overtake** *v.* catch up, pass, outdo, outstrip, pass ▷*overhaul*

**overthrow** *v.* defeat, beat, topple ▷*overpower*

**overture** *n.* ① (in music) prelude, opening, introduction ② offer, proposal, invitation

**overwhelm** *v.* overcome, stun, shock, overpower, deluge, inundate *The reply to our advertisement was huge; we were inundated with letters*

**overwhelming** *adj.* all-powerful, formidable, breathtaking, shattering ★**insignificant**

**owe** *v.* be in debt, incur, be due

**own** ① *v.* possess, occupy, hold ② *v.* admit, confess, grant ③ *adj.* individual, personal, private

**owner** *n.* proprietor, possessor, landlord

# P p

**pace** ① *n. & v.* step, tread, stride ② *n.* speed, rate, velocity, tempo

**pacify** *v.* appease, calm, moderate, tranquilize ▷*soothe* ★**aggravate**

**pack** ① *n.* bundle, bunch, swarm, crowd, group ② *v.* cram, load, fill, throng

**package** *n.* parcel, packet, bundle, box, carton, bale, consignment

**packet** *n.* bag, pack, container, parcel ▷*package*

**pact** *n.* contract, treaty, agreement, arrangement, deal, understanding PACKED

**pad** ① *n.* tablet, notepad, jotter ② *n.* foot, paw ③ *v.* fill, pack, shape, stuff, cushion

**paddle** ① *n.* oar, sweep, scull ② *v.* row, steer, propel ③ *v.* wade, splash, swim

**pagan** *n.* heathen, idol-worshipper, infidel

**page** *n.* ① sheet, leaf, paper ② boy, attendant, bell-boy, messenger

**pageant** *n.* fair, parade, procession, exhibition, masque ▷*show*

**pail** *n.* bucket, churn, tub, container PALE

**pain** ① *n.* ache, pang, throb, twinge, spasm, cramp ② *v.* hurt, sting, ache ▷*ail* PANE

**painful** *adj.* aching, throbbing, sore, agonizing ★**painless**

**painstaking** *adj.* scrupulous *Carly kept a scrupulous record of all she spent,* careful, diligent, particular ★**negligent**

**paint** *v.* colour, draw, daub, varnish, stain

**painting** *n.* drawing, illustration, picture, mural, design, fresco

**pair** *n.* couple, brace, two, twins, twosome, duo PARE, PEAR

**pal** *n.* chum, friend, mate, buddy, crony ▷*comrade* ★**enemy**

**palace** *n.* castle, château, stately home *In Britain you can visit stately homes belonging to the aristocracy,* mansion

**pale** *adj.* pallid, ashen, pasty, colourless, faint, feeble, white ★**ruddy** PAIL

**pallid** *adj.* ashen, colourless, livid *The man had a livid scar across his forehead,*

**Paper**

| | |
|---|---|
| Blotting paper | Parchment |
| Carbon paper | Rice paper |
| Cardboard | Stationery |
| Crepe paper | Tissue paper |
| Manila paper | Toilet paper |
| Newsprint | Vellum |
| Notepaper | Wallpaper |
| Papyrus | Writing paper |

waxen, chalky, wan, sallow ▷*pale*

**paltry** *adj.* petty, mean, shabby, trifling, pitiable, trashy ★**significant**

**pamper** *v.* humour, indulge, coddle, fondle ▷*spoil* ★**neglect**

**pan** *n.* container, saucepan, casserole ▷*pot*

**pandemonium** *n.* uproar, clatter, row, turmoil, bedlam, rumpus, din, chaos *The ice storm reduced the airline schedule to total chaos* ▷*noise* ★**calm**

**pander** *v.* indulge, pamper, please, give in to

**pane** *n.* panel, glass, window PAIN

**panel** *n.* ① pane, rectangle, insert ② jury, group, committee, forum *There will be a forum of all the candidates before the election*

**pang** *n.* ache, throe, twinge, throb ▷*pain*

**panic** ① *n.* fright, alarm, fear, terror ② *v.* scare, frighten, startle, stampede ★**relax**

**pant** *v.* puff, snort, blow, gasp, heave

**pantry** *n.* larder, buttery, storeroom, cupboard

**paper** *n.* stationery, document, deed, article, dossier *The police have a dossier on all known criminals in this town*

**parade** ① *n.* procession, march, display ▷*pageant* ② *v.* display, exhibit, flaunt, show off

**paralyse** *v.* cripple, disable, incapacitate, deaden, stun

**paramount** *adj.* leading, chief, supreme, outstanding ▷*foremost* ★**minor**

**paraphernalia** *n.* baggage, equipment, gear

**parasite** *n.* sponger, hanger-on, leech, scrounger

**parcel** *n.* batch, bundle, lot ▷*package*

**parched** *v.* arid, scorched, withered, dry, thirsty, dehydrated

**pardon** *v.* excuse, forgive, acquit, condone, absolve ★**condemn**

**pare** *v.* skin, peel, uncover, strip, scrape, shave PAIR, PEAR

**parent** *n.* father, mother, guardian, begetter

**park** ① *n.* garden, green, grounds, pleasureground, woodland ② *v.* leave *You can leave your car outside our house,* position, station

**parlour** *n.* drawing-room, living-room, sitting room

**parody** *n.* caricature, burlesque, satire, imitation, lampoon, skit

**parry** *v.* avoid, avert, fend off, rebuff, repel

**parsimonious** *adj.* niggardly *The factory workers received a niggardly sum for their work,* sparing, miserly, stingy ▷*frugal* ★**generous**

**part** ① *n.* piece, fragment, portion, scrap ② *n.* character, role *My sister has a leading role in the play,* duty ③ *v.* separate, divide, detach ④ *v.* depart, quit, leave

**partial** *adj.* ① imperfect, limited, part, unfinished ② biased, favourable to, inclined

**partially** *adv.* incompletely, somewhat, in part

**participate** *v.* take part, share, co-operate

**particle** *n.* morsel, atom, bit, seed, crumb, grain, scrap, sliver

**particular** *adj.* ① choosy, fastidious, scrupulous ② strange, odd, peculiar ③ special, distinct, notable *Old John Cotton was one of the notable citizens of our city*

**partly** *adv.* in part, incompletely, to some degree, up to a point ★**totally**

**partner** *n.* colleague, associate, ally, helper

**party** *n.* ① function, celebration, festivity, rave-up, social ② group, faction *A small faction on the committee wanted the park to be closed,* body, rave-up

**pass** ① *v.* exceed, overstep, outstrip ② *v.* go by, elapse, proceed, flow, run, move, vanish ③ *v.* neglect, ignore ④ *n.* permit, ticket, passport ⑤ *n.* defile, gap, notch, passage

**passage** *n.* ① corridor, pathway, alley ② journey, cruise, voyage ③ sentence, paragraph, clause

**passenger** *n.* traveller, commuter, wayfarer

**passing** *adj.* casual, fleeting, hasty, temporary, brief ★**permanent**

**passion** *n.* desire, ardour, warmth, excitement, zeal ▷*emotion* ★**calm**

**passionate** *adj.* ardent, impetuous, fiery, earnest, enthusiastic ★**indifferent**

**past** ① *adj.* finished, ended, former, gone ★**present** ② *prep.* after, exceeding, beyond ③ *n.* history, yesterday ★**future** PASSED

**paste** *n.* glue, cement, gum, adhesive

**pastime** *n.* recreation, sport, fun, hobby, amusement, distraction, activity

**pasture** *n.* grass, field, meadow, mead

**pat** ① *v.* tap, caress, fondle, stroke, touch ② *adv.* timely, exactly *Celia arrived at exactly the right moment,* precisely

**patch** *v.* mend, repair, sew, darn, cobble

**path** *n.* way, track, road, route, course, footway, lane, bridleway

**pathetic** *adj.* pitiable, sad, wretched, miserable, poor, puny *We picked out the*

### Paths and Passageways

| | | |
|---|---|---|
| Alley | Highway | Path |
| Avenue | Lane | Pavement |
| Boulevard | Mountain | Road |
| Drive | pass | Street |
| | Passage | Thoroughfare |

*puniest pup in the litter for a pet*

**patience** *n.* endurance, perseverance, composure, calmness, restraint, fortitude ★**impatience** PATIENTS

**patient** *adj.* forbearing, long-suffering, persevering, understanding ★**impatient**

**patriotic** *adj.* loyal, nationalistic, public-spirited, jingoistic

**patrol** *v.* police, watch, guard, protect, tour

**patronize** *v.* ① assist, encourage, foster, buy from ② talk down to, condescend

**pattern** *n.* ① model, standard, prototype ② arrangement, decoration, ornament

**pause** ① *v.* halt, cease, suspend, stop, delay ② *n.* lull, intermission, break, interruption, breathless, stoppage PAWS

**pay** ① *v.* reward, award, support, compensate, discharge ② *n.* payment, salary, wages, compensation

**peace** *n.* harmony, calm, concord, serenity, quiet, tranquillity *We spent the day in total tranquillity down by the lake* ★**tumult** PIECE

**peaceful** *adj.* serene, quiet, restful, harmonious ▷*tranquil* ★**disturbed**

**peak** *n.* summit, apex, top, crown, pinnacle

**peal** *v.* ring, strike, toll, knell, clang, chime, resound PEEL

**peasant** *n.* farmer, rustic, bumkin, countryman, yokel

**peculiar** *adj.* ① singular, odd, curious, unusual, uncommon, strange ② unique, private, special, distinctive

**peddle** *v.* sell, hawk, canvas, trade, vend, retail, tout

**pedestal** *n.* base, stand, plinth, support

**pedlar** *n.* hawker, street-trader

**peel** ① *v.* skin, strip, pare, scale ② *n.* skin, covering, rind, coat PEAL

**peep** *n. & v.* glimpse, blink, look ▷*peer*

**peer** ① *v.* peep, stare, look, gaze ② *n.* aristocrat, lord, noble ③ *n.* equal, fellow, counterpart PIER

**peerless** *adj.* unequalled, unique, beyond compare, unbeatable

**peevish** *adj.* cross, childish, grumpy, crusty, irritable ▷*testy* ★**good-tempered**

**peg** *n.* hook, knob, pin, post, hanger, fastener

**pelt** ① *v.* beat, bombard, thrash, throw ② *v.* rain cats and dogs, teem, pour ③ *n.* skin, hide, fleece, fur

**pen** ① *n.* quill, ballpoint ② *n.* cage, coop, hutch, stall ③ *v.* write, autograph, scribble

**penalty** *n.* fine, forfeit, punishment, price ★**reward**

**pending** *adj.* awaiting, unfinished, doubtful, uncertain, undecided, in the balance

**penetrate** *v.* ① pierce, perforate, stab, permeate *The aroma of lilacs and roses permeated the house* ② discern, see through, comprehend

**penetrating** *adj.* ① sharp, perceptive, understanding ② shrill, stinging

**pennant** *n.* flag, streamer, bunting, banner

**penniless** *adj.* destitute, needy, poverty-striken ▷*poor* ★**wealthy**

**pensive** *adj.* thoughtful, reflective, wistful, preoccupied, meditative

**people** ① *n.* folk, society, the public, populace, inhabitants ② *v.* populate, inhabit, settle

**pep** *n.* punch, energy, high spirits, vigour ▷*vitality*

**peppery** *adj.* ① biting, caustic *I'm afraid your essay wasn't very good; the teacher made some very caustic comments*, hot-tempered, angry ② hot, pungent, sharp

**perceive** *v.* feel, sense, observe, notice, make out, understand ▷*see*

**perch** ① *v.* alight, settle, sit, squat, roost ② *n.* rod, pole, staff, roost ③ *n.* fish

**perfect** ① *adj.* (*per*-fect) absolute, ideal, sublime, excellent, splendid, faultless ★**imperfect** ② *v.* (per-*fect*) complete, finish, fulfil, refine

**perforate** *v.* puncture, drill, punch, penetrate

**perform** *v.* ① carry out, do, fulfil, accomplish ② play, act, stage, present *The local drama group will present a new play next week*

**performer** *n.* actor, player, singer, entertainer, artist

**perfume** *n.* scent, essence, aroma, odour

**perhaps** *adv.* possibly, perchance, maybe, conceivably

**peril** *n.* hazard, jeopardy, menace, risk, insecurity ▷*danger* ★**safety**

**period** *n.* spell, time, duration, term, interval, course, span, age

**periodical** ① *n.* magazine, publication, journal, gazette, review ② *adj.* regular, routine, recurring, repeated

**perish** *v.* die, pass away, wither, disintegrate, expire, shrivel

**perky** *adj.* bouncy, bright, cheerful, lively ▷*sprightly* ★**dull**

**permanent** *adj.* endless, ageless, timeless, constant ▷*durable* ★**fleeting**

**permission** *n.* authorization, sanction, privilege, warrant *The police have a warrant for your arrest* ★**prohibition**

**permit** ① *v.* (per-*mit*) allow, grant, agree, empower ② *n.* (*per*-mit) warrant, licence, pass

**perpendicular** *adj.* upright, erect, sheer, steep, vertical ★**horizontal**

**perpetrate** *v.* commit, do, inflict, perform, practise, execute, carry out

**perpetual** *adj.* everlasting, ceaseless, eternal, never ending ▷*endless* ★**fleeting**

**perplex** *v.* mystify, baffle, bewilder, confound ▷*puzzle* ★**enlighten**

**persecute** *v.* harass, molest, plague, badger ▷*bother* ★**pamper**

**persevere** *v.* persist, hold out, hang on, endure, continue ★**give up**

**persist** *v.* remain, stand fast, abide, carry on ▷*persevere* ★**stop**

**persistent** *adj.* tenacious, relentless, stubborn, obstinate ★**weak**

**person** *n.* individual, human, being, type, somebody, personage, character

**personal** *adj.* individual, intimate, private, special, peculiar

**personality** *n.* individuality, character, disposition, nature

**perspective** *n.* outlook, aspect, proportion

**perspire** *v.* sweat, exude, ooze

**persuade** *v.* convince, wheedle, blandish, entice, cajole *I cajoled my mother into*

*buying me a new swimsuit,* induce ▷*coax* ★**discourage**

**pert** *adj.* saucy, flippant, jaunty, cheeky, brash ★**shy**

**perturb** *v.* upset, disturb, trouble, distress, fluster ▷*bother* ★**reassure**

**peruse** *v.* read, study, pore over, browse, inspect, scrutinize, examine

**pervade** *v.* penetrate, permeate, spread, saturate, suffuse

**perverse** *adj.* contrary, wayward, opposite, disobedient ▷*stubborn* ★**reasonable**

**pessimist** *n.* defeatist, killjoy, wet blanket, cynic *Uncle Bert is a real cynic; he even thinks the lottery is fixed* ★**optimist**

**pessimistic** *adj.* cynical, dismal, fatalistic, defeatist, downhearted ★**optimistic**

**pest** *n.* nuisance, plague, blight, curse, vexation, bug, scourge

**pester** *v.* nag, hector, badger, annoy, disturb, harass ▷*bother*

**pet** ① *v.* fondle, caress, baby, cosset, cuddle ② *n.* favourite, beloved, dear ③ *adj.* endearing, cherished, dearest

**petition** *n.* plea, appeal, entreaty, round robin, request

**petrified** *adj.* spellbound, frightened, scared, terrified

**petty** *adj.* ① paltry, cheap, inferior, trifling ▷*trivial* ★**important** ② mean, measly, stingy

**petulant** *adj.* fretful, displeased, querulous, irritable ▷*peevish*

**phantom** ① *n.* apparition, spectre, spook, ghost ② *adj.* spooky, ghostly, imaginary

**phase** *n.* aspect, appearance, angle, view, period, point FAZE

**phenomenal** *adj.* remarkable, outstanding, marvellous, miraculous, incredible

**phenomenon** *n.* marvel, rarity, curiosity, sensation, spectacle

**philanthropic** *adj.* charitable, kind, generous, humane, benevolent, bountiful, public-spirited ★**selfish**

**philosophical** *adj.* calm, cool, logical, thoughtful, impassive, unruffled

**phobia** *n.* dread, fear, awe, neurosis, hang-

**Pine**

*The flowers in the pot are languishing from lack of water.*

up *My father has a hang-up about bats; he can't stand them,* horror

**phrase** *n.* expression, idiom, saying, utterance, sentence FRAYS

**physical** *adj.* ① material, substantial, solid, concrete ② bodily, personal, sensible

**pick** ① *v.* select, choose, single out, gather ② *n.* pike, pickaxe

**picket** ① *n.* patrol, scout, sentinel, lookout, guard ② *n.* post, rail, panel, fence ③ *v.* strike, demonstrate, blockade

**pickle** ① *n.* preserve ② *n.* difficulty, predicament ③ *v.* cure, salt, preserve, souse

**picture** ① *n.* painting, tableau, portrait, illustration, drawing ② *n.* movie, film ③ *v.* illustrate, imagine, fancy

**picturesque** *adj.* attractive, artistic, pictorial, scenic

**piece** *n.* portion, fragment, lump, morsel, bit ▷*scrap* PEACE

**pier** *n.* wharf, dock, quay, jetty PEER

**pierce** *v.* perforate, drill, bore ▷*penetrate*

**piercing** *adj.* ① loud, deafening, shrill, penetrating ② keen, sharp, cutting

**pigment** *n.* colour, dye, hue, paint, stain

**pile** *n. & v.* heap, mass, stack, load, store

**pilfer** *v.* purloin, rifle, rob, filch ▷*steal*

**pilgrim** *n.* traveller, wanderer, wayfarer

**pilgrimage** *n.* excursion, journey, mission, tour, trip, crusade

**pillage** *v.* plunder, ravage, loot, ransack *Thieves broke into the museum and ransacked all the cases,* rifle

**pillar** *n.* column, shaft, tower, obelisk, monument

**pillow** *n.* cushion, bolster, support

**pilot** *n.* ① guide, steersman, coxswain,

helmsman ② aviator, flyer

**pimple** *n.* zit, blemish, swelling, boil

**pin** ① *n.* fastener, clip, spike, peg ② *v.* fix, fasten, attach, join, tack

**pinch** ① *v.* nip, squeeze, crush, tweak ② *v.* pilfer, steal ③ *n.* dash, drop, splash ④ *n.* crisis, difficulty, jam

**pine** *v.* hanker, yearn, long for, languish *The flowers in the pot are languishing from lack of water,* sicken

**pinnacle** *n.* summit, top, crest, peak, apex

**pioneer** *n.* founder, leader, trail-blazer, explorer, innovator

**pious** *adj.* devout, godly, holy, moral, religious, virtuous, reverent

**pipe** ① *n.* tube, duct, passage, hose, conduit ② whistle, flute

**piquant** *adj.* appetizing, spicy, tangy, savoury, pungent

**pique** *v.* annoy, displease, irritate, affront, vex PEAK

**pirate** ① *n.* corsair *In days of old the ships in the Mediterranean were often raided by corsairs,* buccaneer, privateer, sea-rover ② *v.* copy, plagiarize, steal

**pistol** *n.* gun, revolver, automatic PISTIL

**pit** *n.* ① hole, hollow, crater, trench, mine ② dent, dimple, depression

**pitch** ① *v.* fling, throw, cast, sling, toss ② *v.* fall, drop, descend ③ *v.* raise, set up, erect ④ *n.* angle, slope, degree ⑤ *v.* sales message

**pitcher** *n.* jar, beaker, crock, jug, ewer, vessel

**piteous** *adj.* pitiful, heartbreaking, mournful ▷*pathetic*

**pitiless** *adj.* merciless, unmerciful, cruel, unrelenting ★**merciful**

**pity** ① *n.* mercy, compassion, charity, tenderness ② *v.* spare, forgive, grieve for, sympathize with

**pivot** ① *n.* axle, axis, hinge, turning point, spindle, swivel ② *v.* revolve, rotate, turn, spin

**placate** *v.* appease, pacify, soothe, satisfy ▷*humour* ★**infuriate**

**place** ① *n.* spot, locality, site, situation, position ② *n.* house, apartment, residence

## Planets

*The nine planets of our solar system travel around a star we call the Sun.*

Earth
Jupiter
Mars
Mercury
Neptune
Pluto
Saturn
Uranus
Venus

③ *v.* put, deposit, establish, allocate, arrange

**placid** *adj.* peaceful, quiet, serene, mild ▷ *restful* ★**ruffled**

**plague** ① *n.* epidemic, disease, contagion, pest, blight ② *v.* persecute, pester *We were pestered by flies,* infest, annoy ▷ *badger*

**plain** ① *adj.* unadorned, simple ② *adj.* obvious, clear, apparent ③ *adj.* blunt, direct, candid ④ *adj.* smooth, level, flat ⑤ *n.* prairie, plateau, tableland PLANE

**plan** ① *n.* design, chart, diagram, drawing ② *n.* project, proposal, arrangement, scheme ③ *v.* design, prepare, arrange, invent

**plane** ① *adj.* level, even, flat, smooth ② *n.* aircraft ③ *n.* smoothing tool PLAIN

**planned** *adj.* prepared, ready, arranged

**plant** ① *v.* sow, scatter, implant ② *v.* place, set, establish ③ *n.* herb, shrub, vegetable ④ *n.* equipment, machinery, factory

**plaster** ① *n.* cement, mortar, paste ② *n.* bandage, dressing ③ *v.* spread, smear, daub

**plastic** ① *adj.* mouldable, pliable, malleable, soft, supple ② *n.* thermoplastic

**plate** ① *n.* dish, platter, palette ② *n.* sheet, panel ③ *v.* laminate, cover, gild, anodize

**platform** *n.* rostrum *I was called up to the rostrum to receive my prize,* stage, stand, dais, podium

**plausible** *adj.* believable, credible, convincing, glib, persuasive ★**unlikely**

**play** ① *v.* sport, gambol, frisk, romp, frolic ② *v.* perform, act, represent ③ *n.* drama, performance ④ *n.* sport, amusement, recreation, diversion, pastime, hobby

**player** *n.* actor, sportsman, artist, musician, performer, contestant

**playful** *adj.* frisky, frolicsome, larky, lively, sportive ★**serious**

**plead** *v.* appeal, argue, ask, implore, request, beseech, entreat, beg

**pleasant** *adj.* affable, agreeable, cheerful, nice ▷ *charming* ★**unpleasant**

**please** *v.* ① gratify, enchant, amuse, entertain ▷ *delight* ② like, choose, wish, prefer, desire

**pleased** *adj.* delighted, gratified, satisfied ▷ *contented* ★**annoyed**

**pleasing** *adj.* agreeable, enchanting, entertaining ▷ *satisfying* ★**unpleasant**

**pleasure** *n.* delight, joy, amusement, entertainment, enjoyment ▷ *fun* ★**trouble**

**pledge** ① *n.* promise, vow, undertaking, warrant, oath ② *v.* bind, contract, promise, undertake, vow

**plentiful** *adj.* lavish, ample, profuse, bountiful ▷ *abundant* ★**scanty**

**plenty** *n.* enough, profusion, plethora ▷ *abundance* ★**scarcity**

**pliable** *adj.* supple, flexible, pliant, malleable, mouldable, bendy ★**rigid**

**plight** *n.* predicament, difficulty, condition, dilemma *We made it to the railway station on time, but when we realized we had forgotten our tickets we were in a real dilemma,* jam

**plod** *v.* toil, labour, drudge, slog, grind

**plot** ① *n.* scheme, plan, intrigue ② *n.* story, narrative ③ *v.* hatch, intrigue, scheme

**pluck** ① *v.* gather, pick, pull, yank, catch ② *n.* courage, determination, bravery

**plucky** *adj.* courageous, daring, heroic, hardy ▷*brave* ★**feeble**

**plug** ① *n.* stopper, cork, bung ② *v.* stop, block, choke, cork ③ *v.* publicize, boost, promote, push

**plum** ① *n.* prize, bonus, treasure ② *adj.* best, choice, first-class

**plump** *adj.* buxom, stout, chubby, rotund, pudgy ★**skinny**

**plunder** ① *n.* booty, loot, swag, spoils ② *v.* fleece, rob, ransack, pillage, loot

**plunge** *v.* dive, pitch, submerge, duck, immerse, swoop, hurtle

**poach** *v.* ① pilfer, steal, filch, purloin ② steam, cook

**pocket** ① *n.* compartment, pouch, sack, bag ② *v.* filch, pinch, steal

**poem** *n.* ode, verse, rhyme, ballad, lyric

**poetic** *adj.* artistic, elegant, graceful, flowing, lyrical

**poignant** *adj.* moving, touching, pathetic, biting, penetrating

**point** ① *n.* spike, barb, pike, prong, end, tip ② *n.* locality, place, spot ③ *n.* aspect, object, aim, purpose ④ *n.* headland, cape, ness ⑤ *v.* aim, direct, level, train

**pointless** *adj.* meaningless, senseless, silly, vague, feeble ▷*absurd* ★**significant**

**poise** ① *n.* confidence, assurance, dignity, self-possession, balance ② *v.* stand, hover, brood over

**poison** ① *n.* venom, virus, toxin ② *v.* taint, fester, corrupt, infect

**poisonous** *adj.* deadly, evil, lethal *Don't touch those red berries; they're lethal,* noxious, toxic, venomous

**poke** *v.* jab, push, nudge, jostle, ram, thrust, stab, prod ▷*shove*

**pole** *n.* stick, stave, stake, rod, post, bar, mast, shaft, spar

**policy** *n.* rules, guidelines, course, action, practice, rule, procedure

**polish** ① *v.* burnish, buff, smooth, brighten, clean ② *n.* gloss, glaze, shine ③ *n.* refinement, grace, culture

**polished** *adj.* ① glossy, burnished, shiny ② refined, cultivated, cultured

**polite** *adj.* courteous, attentive, civil, well-bred, elegant, discreet ★**impolite**

**poll** ① *n.* election, vote, count, census, ballot ② *v.* survey, canvas, vote

**pollute** *v.* adulterate, debase, befoul, taint, poison, corrupt ★**purify**

**pomp** *n.* ceremony, show, splendour, pageantry, magnificence ★**simplicity**

**pompous** *adj.* showy, self-important, bombastic ▷*pretentious* ★**modest**

**ponder** *v.* meditate, consider, reflect, deliberate, think about

**pool** ① *n.* lagoon, pond, lake ② *n.* accumulation, funds, reserve, kitty ③ *v.* combine, contribute, share

**poor** *adj.* ① destitute, penniless, miserable ★**rich** ② low quality, faulty, feeble, shoddy *That shirt may be cheap, but it's shoddy and won't last* ★**superior**

**poorly** ① *adj.* ailing, ill, sick, seedy ② *adv.* badly, inexpertly, crudely ★**well**

**pop** *v.* ① bang, burst, crack, explode, go off ② slide, slip, insert

**popular** *adj.* ① well-liked, favourite, in favour, fashionable ② current, common, vulgar, prevailing

**Poisonous Plants**

Aconite
Baneberry
Belladonna
Black nightshade
Deadly nightshade
Foxglove
Hellebore
Hemlock
Henbane
Larkspur
Nux vomica
Poison ivy

**pore** *v.* scan, examine, peruse, scrutinize
POUR

**portable** *adj.* lightweight, convenient, transportable ▷*handy* ★**awkward**

**portion** *n.* piece, fragment, share, fraction, quota, ration, bit, measure ▷*part*

**portly** *adj.* plump, stout, fat, burly, bulky

**portrait** *n.* likeness, painting, picture, profile

**portray** *v.* describe, depict, represent, picture, illustrate, impersonate

**pose** ① *v.* stand, poise, posture, position ② *n.* position, stand, guise, stance *If you want to learn to play golf well, you need a good stance*

**position** *n.* ① spot, situation, location, place, site ② job, post ③ posture, attitude ④ rank, standing, status

**positive** *adj.* ① certain, sure, confident ★**doubtful** ② real, true, absolute ★**negative** ③ precise, definite, irrefutable, unmistakable, conclusive, explicit

**possess** *v.* have, own, hold, occupy ★**lose**

**possessions** *n.* wealth, assets, property, goods, belongings

**possible** *adj.* conceivable, imaginable, likely, feasible, attainable ★**impossible**

**possibly** *adv.* perhaps, maybe, perchance conceivably

**post** *n.* ① rail, pole, beam, banister, stake ② position, employment, job ③ mail

**poster** *n.* placard, bill, advertisement, sign

**posterior** *adj.* hind, behind, after, rear ★**front**

**postpone** *v.* put off, defer, shelve, adjourn ▷*delay* ★**advance**

**posture** *n.* bearing, stance, attitude, pose carriage, deportment

**pot** *n.* basin, bowl, pan, vessel, container, jar

**potential** ① *adj.* possible, probable, latent *The professor discovered that I had a latent talent for languages,* dormant, budding ② *n.* ability, talent, capacity, aptitude, power ▷*flair*

**potion** *n.* beverage, medicine, mixture, tonic, brew, draught

**pouch** *n.* bag, poke, sack, purse, pocket, wallet

**pounce** *v.* strike, lunge, spring, swoop, fall upon ▷*attack*

**pound** ① *v.* beat, batter, crush, hammer ② *n.* enclosure, compound, pen ③ *n.* sterling

**pour** *v.* spout, jet, gush, spill, cascade, rain PORE

**pout** *v.* grimace, glower, sulk, scowl, mope ★**smile**

**poverty** *n.* ① distress, need, bankruptcy, privation ▷*want* ② scarcity, shortage ★**plenty**

**powder** ① *n.* dust, sand, ash, grit, bran ② *v.* pulverize, crunch, grind

**power** *n.* ① authority, command, control, ability ② energy, force, strength

**powerful** *adj.* mighty, vigorous, forceful ▷*strong* ★**weak**

**practical** *adj.* ① useful, effective, workable ② experienced, qualified, trained ▷*skilled* ★**impractical**

**practice** *n.* custom, ① habit, usage ② work, conduct, performance, action ★**theory**

**practise** ① *v.* carry out, apply, do, execute, implement ② rehearse, train ▷*perform*

**praise** ① *v.* acclaim, applaud, glorify, exalt ★**criticize** ② *n.* applause, flattery, compliment, approval ★**criticism** PRAYS, PREYS

**prance** *v.* gambol *I love to watch the lambs gambol in the spring,* frolic, romp, caper, swagger

**prank** *n.* trick, joke, antic, lark, jape, stunt

**prattle** *n.* & *v.* chatter, jabber, gossip, drivel, babble, witter

**pray** *v.* beg, beseech, entreat, implore, crave, solicit, request PREY

**prayer** *n.* petition, entreaty, worship, devotion, supplication

**preach** *v.* lecture, moralize, advocate *The president advocated a programme to feed the poor,* urge, proclaim

**precarious** *adj.* perilous, hazardous, insecure, dangerous ▷*risky* ★**safe**

**precaution** *n.* forethought, provision, anticipation, care, providence ▷*prudence*

**precede** *v.* lead, head, usher, go before, preface ★**follow**

**Prey**

**Pray**

**precious** *adj.* valuable, cherished, treasured, dear, beloved ▷*costly* ★**worthless**

**precise** *adj.* ① definite, exact, pointed, accurate, meticulous ② formal, particular, strict, rigid ★**vague**

**precisely** *adv.* absolutely, just so, exactly, correctly, literally

**precision** *n.* exactness, accuracy, care, detail, correctness

**precocious** *adj.* forward, fast, smart, clever ★**backward**

**predicament** *n.* situation, state, condition, embarrassment, fix ▷*plight*

**predict** *v.* foresee, foretell, prophesy, presage, divine

**predominant** *adj.* leading, main, powerful, superior, ruling, controlling ★**minor**

**preen** *v.* prance, swagger, strut, spruce up, doll up, groom

**preface** *n.* introduction, prelude, prologue, preamble, foreword

**prefer** *v.* choose, select, desire, like better, fancy ▷*favour* ★**reject**

**prejudice** ① *n.* bigotry, intolerance, bias, discrimination ② *v.* influence, warp, twist, distort, undermine ★**benefit**

**prejudiced** *adj.* biased *My opinion of Jessica is biased; she was very cruel to me once*, bigoted, one-sided, unfair, intolerant, narrow-minded, racist, sexist ★**fair**

**preliminary** *adj.* introductory, preparatory, opening, initial ★**final**

**premature** *adj.* untimely, previous, early, immature ★**late**

**premeditated** *adj.* calculated, planned, prearranged, intentional ★**spontaneous**

**premier** ① *n.* prime minister, first minister, head of government ② *adj.* chief, first, head, leading, principal

**premises** *n.* grounds, house, building, lands

**prepare** *v.* arrange, adapt, provide, get ready, concoct, plan ★**demolish**

**preposterous** *adj.* absurd, ridiculous, laughable ▷*unreasonable* ★**reasonable**

**prescribe** *v.* indicate, order, propose, recommend, specify

**presence** *n.* ① existence, appearance, aspect ② nearness, neighbourhood, proximity
PRESENTS

**present** ① *n.* (*pres*-ent) gift, donation, bounty, favour ② (*pres*-ent) *adj.* here, on the spot, ready, current ③ *v.* (pre-*sent*) offer, tender, bestow, award, exhibit

**presently** *adv.* soon, shortly, before long, immediately

**preserve** ① *v.* protect, safeguard, conserve, shield ▷*keep* ② *n.* jam, jelly, pickle

**press** ① *v.* bear down, depress, clamp, jam, compress, flatten ② *n.* printing machine ③ *n.* newspapers, reporters, journalism

**pressure** *n.* ① strain, tension, stress, urgency ② weight, compression, force

**prestige** *n.* repute, authority, weight, power

**presume** *v.* infer *I infer from your smile that you have passed your exam*, suppose, grant, take for granted, assume

**presumptuous** *adj.* arrogant, bold, audacious, insolent ▷*forward* ★**modest**

**pretend** *v.* ① make believe, simulate, sham, feign, masquerade ② aspire, claim, strive for ③ allege, profess

**pretext** *n.* excuse, pretence, guise, device

**pretty** *adj.* attractive, beautiful, comely,

dainty, bonny ▷*lovely* ★**ugly**

**prevail** *v.* obtain, overcome, predominate
▷*triumph* ★**lose**

**prevalent** *adj.* current, common, popular, in
use, accepted ★**uncommon**

**prevent** *v.* avert, forestall, ward off,
discourage, stop ▷*hinder* ★**help**

**previous** *adj.* former, prior, earlier,
premature, untimely ★**later**

**prey** *n.* quarry, chase, booty, victim PRAY

**prey on** *v.* plunder, fleece, oppress, terrorize

**price** *n.* cost, amount, expense, payment,
value, worth

**priceless** *adj.* ① invaluable, precious,
cherished, costly ② amusing, comic,
humorous, hilarious *The clown's antics
were hilarious*

**prick** *v.* jab, jag, puncture, stab, pierce

**pride** *n.* conceit, vanity, egotism, self-
importance, honour, exaltation, pleasure
PRIED

**prim** *adj.* puritanical, demure, starchy,
priggish ★**informal**

**primary** *adj.* first, original, chief, essential,
fundamental

**prime** *adj.* ① principal, chief, basic, original
② best, finest, choice

**primitive** *adj.* ① simple, austere, crude
② uncivilized, savage, barbarous

**principal** ① *adj.* main, chief, head, leading,
foremost ② *n.* head, leader, boss, director,
manager, superintendent PRINCIPLE

**principle** *n.* ① law, regulation, rule, doctrine
② virtue, worth, integrity, rectitude *The
president of the club was honoured by the
mayor as a 'person of high moral
rectitude'* ★**wickedness** PRINCIPAL

**print** ① *v.* impress, stamp, brand, publish
② *n.* impression, printing, imprint

**prior** ① *adj.* previous, former, earlier,
preceding ② *n.* abbot, monk

**prison** *n.* jail, penitentiary, dungeon, lock-up

**private** *adj.* ① particular, personal, special,
own ② solitary, remote *He spent his
holidays on a remote island,* quiet
★**public**

**privilege** *n.* ① advantage, benefit, exemption

**Printing**

Collotype
Computer-setting
Cylinder press
Flatbed press
Intaglio
Letterpress
Linotype
Lithography
Monotype
Photogravure
Rotary press
Silk screen
Type
Web offset

② right, authority, entitlement, prerogative
*It was the emperor's prerogative to pardon
offenders*

**prize** ① *n.* reward, premium, trophy, honour
② *n.* booty, spoils, plunder ③ *adj.* best,
champion, winning ④ *v.* value, appreciate,
cherish ⑤ *v.* force, lever, pry, lift, raise PRIES

**probable** *adj.* likely, presumable,
reasonable, possible ★**improbable**

**probe** *v.* ① poke, prod ② examine,
investigate, scrutinize

**problem** ① *n.* puzzle, question, riddle,
poser, quandary ② difficulty, dilemma,
snag, complication, predicament

**proceed** *v.* ① advance, continue, go on,
progress ★**recede** ② arise, flow, spring,
emanate *A strong sulphurous odour
emanated from the crater of the volcano*

**process** ① *n.* procedure, operation,
movement, system, method ② *v.* convert,
alter, handle, refine

**procession** *n.* parade, pageant, march,
cavalcade, cortege

**proclaim** *v.* declare, announce, advertise,
publish, expound

**procure** *v.* secure, acquire, win, gain, attain,
get ★**lose**

**prod** *v.* goad, poke, nudge, incite, urge,
shove, egg on

**prodigal** *adj.* extravagant, reckless, lavish
▷*spendthrift* ★**thrifty**

**prodigious** *adj.* ① miraculous, abnormal,
amazing, remarkable ▷*extraordinary*

★**ordinary** ② huge, mighty ▷ *enormous* ★**tiny**

**produce** ① *n.* (*pro*-duce) product, output, yield, crop, harvest ② *v.* (pro-*duce*) provide, yield, create, deliver, put forward

**product** *n.* output, crop, harvest, return, merchandise, commodity

**profane** *adj.* impious, blasphemous, unholy, worldly, sinful ★**sacred**

**profess** *v.* declare, avow, acknowledge, own

**profession** *n.* ① occupation, career, job, calling, employment ② avowal, admission

**professional** *adj.* skilled, efficient, experienced ▷ *expert* ★**amateur**

**proffer** *v.* present, offer, tender, submit

**proficient** *adj.* competent, able, skilled, trained ▷ *expert* ★**clumsy**

**profit** ① *n.* benefit, gain, advantage, acquisition ★**loss** ② *v.* improve, gain, reap, acquire ★**lose** PROPHET

**profound** ① *adj.* deep, penetrating, fathomless ② wise, shrewd, learned, sagacious *The leader of the tribe was old, wise and sagacious* ★**shallow**

**profuse** *adj.* bountiful, extravagant, exuberant, prolific, sumptuous ▷ *lavish* ★**sparse**

**progress** ① *n.* (*prog*-ress) advancement, growth, development ★**decline** ② *v.* (pro-*gress*) advance, proceed, go, forge ahead, travel, grow, make headway

**prohibit** *v.* forbid, bar, deny, ban, obstruct, hinder ▷ *prevent* ★**permit**

**project** ① *n.* (*pro*-ject) work, affair, plan, scheme, undertaking ② *v.* (pro-*ject*) propel, hurl, jut, protrude ③ *v.* contrive, scheme, plan ④ *v.* protrude, bulge out

**prolific** *adj.* fruitful, creative, productive, fertile ★**scarce**

**prolong** *v.* lengthen, stretch, draw out, spin out ▷ *extend* ★**shorten**

**prominent** *adj.* ① famous, notable, distinguished ★**minor** ② projecting, standing out, bulging, jutting

**promise** ① *n.* commitment, undertaking, warrant, pledge ② *v.* agree, guarantee, vow

**promote** *adj.* ① cultivate, advance, assist ▷ *encourage* ② dignify, elevate, upgrade, honour ★**degrade**

**prompt** ① *adj.* punctual, timely, quick, smart, ready ★**tardy** ② *v.* hint, remind, urge ▷ *encourage* ★**deter**

**prone** *adj.* ① inclined, apt, liable, disposed ★**unlikely** ② prostrate *The poor fellow lay prostrate on the ship's deck,* face down, recumbent ★**upright**

**pronounce** *v.* ① speak, utter, say, articulate ② declare, decree, proclaim

**pronounced** *adj.* outstanding, striking, noticeable ▷ *distinct* ★**vague**

**proof** *n.* evidence, testimony, confirmation, criterion, scrutiny ★**failure**

**prop** *n.* & *v.* stay, brace, truss, support

**propel** *v.* start, push, force, impel, send ▷ *drive* ★**stop**

**proper** *adj.* ① correct, without error, right, accurate, exact ② respectable, decent, becoming, seemly ★**improper** ③ personal, own, special ★**common**

**property** ① *n.* possessions, wealth, chattels, buildings, belongings ② quality, virtue, characteristic, peculiarity

**prophecy** *n.* forecast, divination, prediction, prognostication

**prophesy** *v.* predict, foretell, foresee, declare

**proportion** ① *n.* ratio, percentage, part, fraction ② adjustment, arrangement

**proposal** *n.* proposition, offer, outline

**propose** *v.* ① put forward, offer, suggest ② ask for the hand of *Sir, I have the honour to ask you for the hand of your daughter in marriage,* pop the question

**proprietor** *n.* owner, possessor, landlady, landlord, leaseholder

**prosaic** *adj.* tedious, uninteresting, boring, dull, mundane, ordinary ★**interesting**

**prosecute** *v.* ① indict, put on trial, summon, sue ② continue, pursue, carry on, conduct ★**abandon**

**prospect** *n.* ① outlook, forecast, promise, expectation ② view, landscape, vista, aspect

**prosper** *v.* succeed, flourish, grow ★**fail**

**prosperous** *adj.* affluent, wealthy, rich, successful, thriving ★**unsuccessful**

**protect** v. defend, preserve, guard, secure, shelter, support ★**endanger**

**protest** ① v. (pro-*test*) complain, object, dispute, challenge ★**accept** ② n. (*pro*-test) objection, complaint, dissent, outcry

**protracted** adj. extended, drawn out, lengthy, prolonged ★**shortened**

**protrude** v. project, bulge, jut ★**recede**

**proud** ① adj. arrogant, haughty, supercilious, boastful ★**humble** ② lofty, majestic, noble, splendid ★**mean**

**prove** v. show, demonstrate, authenticate, confirm, verify ★**disprove**

**provide** v. supply, furnish, equip, contribute, afford ★**withhold**

**province** n. ① realm, sphere, orbit, place, department ② region, state, county

**provoke** v. prompt, incite, excite, enrage, inflame ▷*aggravate* ★**appease**

**prowess** n. ability, strength, might, bravery ▷*valour* ★**clumsiness**

**prowl** v. stalk *Somewhere in the darkness a large grey cat stalked its prey,* roam, slink

**prudent** adj. careful, cautious, discreet, shrewd ▷*thrifty* ★**rash**

**prudish** adj. strait-laced, narrow-minded, demure, priggish ▷*prim*

**prune** ① v. cut, shorten, trim, crop ② n. dried plum

**pry** v. snoop, peep, meddle, intrude

**public** ① adj. communal, civil, popular, social, national ② n. the people, the populace, society, the nation

**publish** v. broadcast, distribute, circulate, communicate, bring out, issue

**pucker** v. fold, crease, cockle, furrow, wrinkle ★**straighten**

**puerile** adj. callow, immature, juvenile

**puff** v. inflate, swell, blow, pant, distend

**pull** v. ① haul, drag, tow, heave ★**push** ② gather, pluck, detach, pick

**pump** v. ① inflate, expand, swell, fill, inject, siphon, draw ② interrogate, question, grill

**punch** v. ① strike, beat, hit, cuff ② puncture, pierce, perforate, bore

**punctual** adj. prompt, on time, precise, in good time, timely ★**tardy**

**puncture** n. perforation, hole, leak, wound

**pungent** adj. sharp, bitter, poignant, biting ▷*acrid* ★**mild**

**punish** v. chastise, correct, discipline, chasten, reprove, scold

**puny** adj. feeble, weak, frail, small, petty, stunted, insignificant ★**large**

**pupil** n. student, scholar, schoolchild, learner

**puppet** n. ① doll, marionette ② cat's-paw *The prisoner was not the true culprit, but only the ringleader's cat's-paw,* figurehead, pawn

**purchase** ① v. buy, procure, secure, obtain, get ▷*buy* ★**sell** ② n. bargain, investment

**pure** adj. ① immaculate, spotless, stainless, clear ▷*clean* ★**impure** ② virtuous, chaste, honest, blameless

**purely** adv. simply, barely, merely, only

**purge** v. ① purify, clean, scour, cleanse ② liquidate, exterminate, kill

**purify** v. clean, clarify, wash, purge

**purloin** v. rob, thieve, take, filch, pilfer ▷*steal*

**purpose** n. intent, design, will, goal, target

**purse** ① n. wallet, pouch, reticule, ② v. pucker, crease, compress, wrinkle

**pursue** v. ① follow, track, trace ▷*chase* ② practise, maintain, work for

**pursuit** n. ① hunt, chase, hue and cry ② occupation, hobby, interest *Stamp collecting has always been one of my main interests*

**push** ① v. shove, thrust, press, drive, propel ② n. advance, assault, drive

**put** v. ① set, place, deposit, repose, lay ② express, propose, state

**put down** v. ① write, jot down, record, note ② crush, humiliate, subdue ③ kill

**put off** v. ① postpone, defer, delay, adjourn ② dishearten, unsettle, perturb

**putrid** adj. decomposed, rotten, rancid, rank, stinking ★**wholesome**

**puzzle** ① v. baffle, confuse, mystify, perplex ▷*bewilder* ② n. conundrum, brainteaser, problem, dilemma

**puzzling** adj. baffling, curious, strange, bewildering ▷*peculiar*

**pyromaniac** n. arsonist, incendiary

# Q q

**quack** *n.* impostor, charlatan *She pretended to tell fortunes by cards, but she was nothing but a charlatan,* humbug, fake

**quaff** *v.* imbibe, swallow ▷*drink*

**quagmire** *n.* bog, mire, marsh ▷*swamp*

**quail** *v.* tremble, flinch, shrink, cower, succumb ★**withstand**

**quaint** *adj.* curious, whimsical, fanciful, singular, old-fashioned, droll

**quake** ① *v.* tremble, quaver, shiver, quiver, shudder ② *n.* shock, convulsion, tremor *The tremors from the earthquake were felt hundreds of miles away*

**qualification** *n.* ① fitness, capacity, ability, accomplishment ② restriction, limitation, modification *The engineer's design was accepted with certain modifications*

**qualify** *v.* ① empower, enable, fit, suit ② moderate, limit, restrict

**quality** *n.* ① characteristic, condition, power ② excellence, worth, goodness

**qualm** *n.* doubt, misgiving, hesitation

**quandary** *n.* difficulty, doubt ▷*dilemma*

**quantity** *n.* amount, number, volume, sum

**quarrel** ① *n.* dispute, squabble, wrangle, disagreement ★**harmony** ② *v.* argue, bicker, brawl, squabble ★**agree**

**quarry** *n.* ① game, prey, object, victim, target ② mine, excavation, pit

**quarter** *n.* ① area, territory, place, district ② one-fourth ③ mercy *The commander of the invading army showed no mercy to the local defenders,* grace, lenience

**quarters** *n.* lodgings, dwelling, billet, rooms

**quash** *v.* abolish, nullify, suppress, overthrow, subdue

**quaver** *v.* shake, tremble, shiver, shudder, vibrate, oscillate, quake

**quay** *n.* pier, dock, wharf, landing, jetty KEY

**queasy** *adj.* bilious, squeamish, sick, faint

**queer** *adj.* strange, odd, whimsical, peculiar

**quell** *v.* crush, stifle, extinguish, defeat

**quench** *v.* ① douse *We carefully doused our campfire before leaving the site,* put out, cool, check ② slake *The cattle rushed to the river and slaked their thirst,* cool, allay

**query** ① *n.* question, doubt, objection ② *v.* ask, inquire, question, doubt ★**accept**

**quest** *n.* chase, hunt, search, pursuit, venture

**question** ① *n.* query, inquiry, interrogation, ② *n.* topic, problem, issue ③ *v.* ask, inquire, interrogate ★**answer**

**questionable** *adj.* doubtful, uncertain, undecided, unbelievable ★**certain**

**queue** *n.* ① row, line, procession, line-up ② pigtail, coil, braid, ponytail CUE

**quibble** *v.* argue, trifle, split hairs, carp *If you like our plan, don't carp about the details*

**quick** *adj.* ① speedy, rapid, express, swift ▷*fast* ② alert, active, agile, lively ★**slow** ③ clever, intelligent, acute ★**dull** ④ hasty, sharp, touchy ★**mild**

**quicken** *v.* accelerate ▷*hasten* ★**delay**

**quiet** ① *adj.* silent, soundless, noiseless, hushed ★**noisy** ② *adj.* placid, smooth, undisturbed ★**busy** ③ *n.* peace, rest, tranquillity, silence ★**tumult**

**quilt** *n.* blanket, cover, duvet, eiderdown

**quip** *n.* joke, gag, gibe, jest, wisecrack, retort

**quirk** *n.* pecularity, curiosity, foible *Despite his age and one or two foibles, old Uncle Fred was very agile,* mannerism ▷*habit*

**quit** *v.* ① cease, desist, stop ② leave, depart, relinquish ③ give up, surrender

**quite** *adv.* absolutely, altogether, wholly

**quits** *adj.* even *If I pay what I owe, it makes us even,* all square, level, equal

**quiver** ① *v.* tremble, quake, shiver, shudder ② *n.* holster, scabbard, sheath

**quiz** ① *v.* question, ask, examine, grill ② *n.* test, examination, contest *Barbara was the winner in the spelling contest*

**quizzical** *adj.* ① incredulous, sceptical, suspicious ② whimsical, teasing, amused

**quota** *n.* allowance, allocation, ration

**quotation** *n.* ① extract, selection, passage ② cost, estimate, price

**quote** *v.* recite, cite, recount, recollect, tell, mention

# R r

**rabble** *n.* crowd, mob, scum, riffraff

**race** ① *n.* competition, contest, chase, dash ② *n.* people, nation, folk, stock, breed, tribe ③ *v.* run, speed, hurry, scamper, gallop, sprint

**rack** ① *n.* shelf, stand, frame, framework ② *v.* distress, strain, torment, pain WRACK

**racket** *n.* ① uproar, noise, hubbub, tumult ▷*din* ② fraud, deception, swindle

**racy** *adj.* ① pungent, piquant, zestful ② spirited, smart, lively

**radiant** *adj.* ① brilliant, bright, luminous, shining ② splendid, glorious, happy ★**dull**

**radiate** *v.* ① gleam, sparkle, beam, shine ② emit, spread, diffuse

**radical** *adj.* ① extreme, fanatical, deep-seated ② original, fundamental *The new teacher made some fundamental changes in our lessons,* natural ★**superficial**

**raffle** *n.* draw, sweepstakes, lottery

**rafter** *n.* joist, girder, beam, support

**ragamuffin** *n.* scarecrow, urchin ▷*waif*

**rage** ① *n.* wrath, fury, ferocity, passion, madness ▷*anger* ② *v.* rave, fret, fume *The mad bull was fuming with rage as we leapt over the fence,* storm, flare up

**ragged** *adj.* shabby, seedy, shaggy, rough, torn ★**smart**

**raid** ① *n.* invasion, attack, strike, sortie ② *v.* attack, invade, ransack, maraud, descend on, plunder *The ship was attacked and plundered by pirates* RAYED

**rail** ① *n.* post, picket, fence, railing ② *v.* scold, rant, blast, reproach

**rain** *n. & v.* deluge, drizzle, flood, shower, torrent REIGN, REIN

**raise** *v.* ① elevate, lift, erect, hoist *The flag was hoisted as the ship came into port* ★**lower**
② excite, awaken, rouse ③ promote, increase, advance ④ cultivate, grow, breed RAZE

**rake** *v.* grope, scrape, collect, gather, assemble

**rally** *v.* ① meet, assemble, convene *The members of the club will convene next month* ★**disperse** ② encourage, restore, reunite

**ram** *v.* ① cram, crowd, push, pack, stuff, poke, wedge ② charge, beat, crash, drive

**ramble** *v.* ① stroll, meander, saunter, roam, rove ② chatter, digress *Joe's speech was very long, as he kept digressing from the point,* dodder

**ramp** *n.* gradient, slope, incline, grade

**rampage** ① *n.* storm, rage, riot, uproar, tumult ② *v.* rave, rush, run wild *Someone left the gate open, and the pigs ran wild in the cabbage patch*

**ramshackle** *adj.* unstable, shaky, unsteady, flimsy, rickety ▷*decrepit* ★**stable**

**rancid** *adj.* sour, curdled, rank, putrid, musty

**rancour** *n.* spite, grudge, animosity, hatred ▷*malice* RANKER

**random** *adj.* haphazard, vague, casual, accidental ▷*chance* ★**deliberate**

**range** ① *n.* extent, length, span, magnitude, area ② *n.* kind, sort, class, order ③ *v.* wander, rove, roam, stray

**rank** ① *n.* grade, class, position, level ② *adj.* foul, musty, offensive, coarse ③ *adj.* luxuriant, fertile, dense ④ utter, total, complete, absolute, out and out

**rankle** *v.* burn, smoulder, fester, be embittered

**ransack** *v.* plunder, pillage, search, scour

**ransom** ① *n.* release, deliverance, payoff, price ② *v.* rescue, redeem *Jill was lazy at school to begin with, but later redeemed herself with hard work,* liberate

**rant** *v.* rave, declaim, bluster, roar, shout

**rap** *v.* tap, pat, strike, knock

**rape** *v.* violate, abuse, assault, attack

**rapid** *adj.* speedy, quick, swift ▷*fast* ★**slow**

**rapt** *adj.* engrossed, intent, captivated, fascinated, delighted RAPPED, WRAPPED

**rapture** *n.* bliss, ecstasy, delight ▷*joy* ★**sorrow**

**rare** *adj.* ① unusual, uncommon, scarce, occasional ② valuable, fine, precious ★**common** ③ underdone, lightly cooked

**rascal** *n.* rogue, knave, villain, scamp, scoundrel, blackguard ★**gentleman**

**rash** ① *adj.* headstrong, audacious, hasty,

foolhardy ▷ *reckless* ★**cautious** ② *n.*
eruption, outbreak, epidemic *There has been an epidemic of chickenpox in our neighbourhood*

**rashness** *n.* audacity, carelessness, hastiness, recklessness ★**carefulness**

**rasp** ① *v.* file, grate, grind ② *v.* irk, irritate, vex ③ *n.* file, tool

**rate** ① *n.* pace, tempo *It took us a while to get used to the tempo of life in the city,* velocity, speed ② *n.* tax, charge, cost ③ *v.* appraise, assess, estimate, merit, value

**rather** *adv.* ① somewhat, to some extent, sort of ② first, preferably, sooner

**ration** ① *n.* portion, share, allotment, helping ② *v.* allocate, allot, restrict, control

**rational** *adj.* ① sensible, sound, wise, intelligent, sane ★**irrational** ② reasonable, fair, proper ★**absurd**

**rattle** *v.* ① jangle, jingle, vibrate ② muddle, confuse, daze ▷*bewilder*

**raucous** *adj.* harsh, hoarse, rough, strident, gutteral, rasping, jarring

**ravage** *v.* devastate, destroy, pillage, ransack, desolate, wreck

**rave** *v.* ① rant, ramble *The old man rambled on for hours about his youth,* roar, rage, storm ② favour, be ecstatic about

**ravenous** *adj.* hungry, starving, famished, voracious ▷*greedy*

**ravishing** *adj.* beautiful, bewitching, delightful, charming ▷*enchanting*

**raw** *adj.* ① uncooked ② unripe, green *I was pretty green during the first six months in the job,* inexperienced ③ sensitive, painful, tender ④ cold, exposed, chilly

**ray** *n.* beam, gleam, glimmer, shaft, stream

**raze** *v.* demolish, destroy, flatten, obliterate, ruin RAISE, RAYS

**reach** ① *v.* arrive at, gain, get to, attain, grasp ② *v.* stretch, extend ③ *n.* extent, length, grasp, distance, scope

**react** *v.* respond, reverberate *The sound of the church bell reverberated through the village,* behave, respond

**read** *v.* ① peruse, pore over, study, browse, understand ② recite ③ record, register REED

**Read**

**Reed**

**readily** *adv.* easily, eagerly, freely, gladly, promptly ★**reluctantly**

**ready** *adj.* ① prepared, alert, prompt, willing ★**reluctant** ② convenient, handy ★**remote** ③ skilful, facile, expert ★**clumsy**

**real** *adj.* ① genuine, authentic, factual ★**false** ② substantial, existent, actual ★**imaginary** REEL

**realistic** *adj.* ① authentic, lifelike ② practical, down-to-earth *Sue is a real romantic type, but her boyfriend is much more down-to-earth,* unromantic, businesslike, matter of fact ★**fanciful**

**realize** *v.* ① understand, comprehend, feel ② earn, gain, obtain, acquire

**really** *adv.* truly, indeed, actually, absolutely

**realm** *n.* domain, province, sphere *My mother has taken up writing and is very involved in the sphere of books,* region, territory, orbit, field

**reap** *v.* harvest, gather, obtain, realize, derive, gain ★**squander**

**rear** ① *n.* back, end, tail, behind, posterior ② *adj.* hind, after, following ③ *v.* foster, breed, educate ④ *v.* lift, raise, elevate

**reason** ① *n.* purpose, motive, basis, cause, explanation ② *n.* wisdom, sense, intellect ③ *v.* consider, think, argue

**reasonable** *adj.* ① sensible, valid, rational ★**absurd** ② moderate, fair, just, modest ③ inexpensive, low-priced *Everything in the new supermarket is low-priced* ★**excessive**

**reassure** *v.* inspire, hearten, convince ▷*encourage* ★**discourage**

**rebate** *n.* refund, repayment, discount, allowance, deduction

**rebel** ① *v.* (re-*bel*) revolt, mutiny, disobey, resist ② *n.* (*reb*-el) revolutionary, mutineer *Fletcher Christian was the leader of the mutineers on the* Bounty, traitor

**rebellious** *adj.* defiant, disobedient, mutinous, resistant ★**obedient**

**rebuke** *v.* reprimand, reproach, scold, tell off ★**praise**

**recall** *v.* ① recollect, remember ② cancel, overrule, countermand *We were just about to pull down the building when our orders were countermanded,* call back

**recede** *v.* ebb, retreat, flow back, decline, shrink, withdraw, return ★**proceed**

**receipt** *n.* acknowledgement, voucher

**recent** *adj.* late, new, fresh, novel, modern, current, up-to-date ★**out-of-date**

**recently** *adv.* lately, currently, latterly

**receptacle** *n.* container, holder, vessel, bowl

**reception** *n.* ① entertainment, function, party ② acceptance, acknowledgement

**recess** *n.* ① alcove, corner, socket, niche, slot, nook ② intermission, interlude, pause

**recession** *n.* slump, stagnation, depression, downturn ★**boom**

**recipe** *n.* formula, method *I'll show you my mother's method of making chocolate sponge cake; it never fails,* prescription

**recite** *v.* recount, chant, speak, declaim, relate, describe

**reckless** *adj.* unwary, incautious, daring, brash, heedless ▷*rash* ★**cautious**

**reckon** ① *v.* calculate, figure, count, tally *I have checked the accounts and my figures tally with yours,* account ② judge, expect, believe, fancy, surmise, guess

**reclaim** *v.* recover, redeem, reform, retrieve, restore, salvage

**recline** *v.* lounge, sprawl, lie, rest, loll, repose

**recognize** *v.* ① recall, recollect, remember, identify, know ② see *I will explain my idea slowly and you will see what I mean,* comprehend, understand

**recoil** *v.* ① rebound, backfire, boomerang ② falter, flinch, shrink, quail *My little brother quailed at the sound of the thunder*

**recollect** *v.* recall, recognize, place ▷*remember* ★**forget**

**recommend** *v.* suggest, advise, propose, commend, approve ★**veto**

**recompense** ① *n.* payment, compensation, remuneration ② *v.* reimburse, repay ▷*reward*

**reconcile** *v.* ① accept, harmonize, pacify, placate ★**estrange** ② adjust, settle, square

**record** ① *v.* (re-*cord*) note, register, enter, inscribe, list ② *n.* (*rec*-ord) album, disc, platter, CD, LP ③ chronicle, archive, almanac *We'll get hold of the almanac and check the time of high tide,* register ④ performance, championship

**recount** *v.* ① (re-*count*) relate, tell, recite, describe ② (*re*-count) count again

**recover** *v.* ① reclaim, retrieve, redeem, regain ② get better, recuperate, revive ★**worsen**

**recreation** *n.* pastime, sports, amusement, fun

**recruit** ① *n.* trainee, beginner, apprentice ② *v.* enlist, enrol, draft, mobilize

**rectify** *v.* correct, put right, repair, remedy, restore, mend, adjust

**recuperate** *v.* get better, rally, improve, mend ▷*recover* ★**worsen**

**recur** *v.* return, reappear, come back, repeat, revert, persist

**redden** *v.* crimson, colour, flush ▷*blush*

**redeem** *v.* ① buy back, compensate for, exchange ② save, liberate, free

**reduce** *v.* ① lessen, diminish, curtail, contract ② overcome, defeat, humiliate

**reek** *v.* smell, stink, fume, exhale, smoke

**reel** ① *v.* roll, rock, shake, stagger, falter, totter ② *n.* spool, bobbin, spindle REAL

**refer** *v.* relate, connect, associate, assign, belong, pertain

**referee** *n.* umpire, arbitrator, judge

**reference** *n.* ① allusion, insinuation, innuendo *From your innuendo, it seems that you think I'm joking!* ▷*hint* ② testimonial, recommendation, credentials

**refine** *v.* clarify, purify, filter, process, cultivate

**refined** *adj.* ① civilized, cultivated, cultured ▷*polite* ② purified, pure, clarified ★**coarse**

**reflect** *v.* ① think, contemplate, deliberate, consider ② mirror, copy, imitate, image

**reform** *v.* ① improve, correct ▷*rectify* ② remodel, reorganize, revamp

**refrain** ① *v.* avoid, abstain, forbear, resist, keep from ② *n.* chorus, melody, tune

**refresh** *v.* rejuvenate, renew, restore, cheer, enliven ★**exhaust**

**refrigerate** *v.* chill, cool, freeze

**refuge** *n.* haven, harbour, asylum, sanctuary ▷*shelter*

**refugee** *n.* exile, fugitive, emigrant

**refund** *v.* repay, rebate, reimburse *I must reimburse you for everything you spent on my behalf,* pay back, return

**refuse** ① *v.* (re-*fuze*) decline, say no, demur, repudiate ② *n.* (*ref*-use) trash, garbage, rubbish, waste

**refute** *v.* deny, dispute, disprove, discredit ★**prove**

**regain** *v.* recover, get back, retrieve, redeem

**regal** *adj.* royal, princely, majestic, noble, stately

**regard** ① *v.* esteem, revere, honour, respect ★**dislike** ② *v.* notice, observe, see, gaze ③ *n.* affection, esteem, fondness, repute ★**contempt**

**regardless** ① *adj.* heedless, neglectful, indifferent ★**careful** ② *adv.* anyhow, anyway, in any case

**region** *n.* area, zone, territory, locality, province, country

**register** ① *n.* roll, roster, record, archives *We can trace the town's history from the ancient archives* ② *v.* enter, record, inscribe, enrol, sign on

**regret** ① *v.* repent, rue, deplore, lament, mourn, apologize ★**welcome** ② *n.* remorse, sorrow, apology, grief

**regular** *adj.* ① normal, customary, periodical, formal ★**unusual** ② orderly, steady, unchanging ★**variable**

**regulate** *v.* ① control, manage, govern, determine ② adjust, measure, time, correct

**regulation** *n.* ① rule, law, command, bylaw

*The club bylaws require us to elect a new secretary* ② order, control, government

**rehearse** *v.* repeat, practise, drill, prepare, run through

**reign** ① *n.* rule, sway, power, control ② *v.* govern, rule, dominate, command RAIN, REIN

**rein** *v. & n.* bridle, hold, check, harness RAIN, REIGN

**reinforce** *v.* support, strengthen, toughen, harden, stiffen ★**weaken**

**reject** ① *v.* (re-*ject*) discard, get rid of, throw out, refuse, repel, deny ② *n.* (*re*-ject) cast-off, scrap

**rejoice** *v.* glory, exult, cheer, please, triumph ▷*delight* ★**lament**

**relapse** ① *v.* revert, backslide, turn back, recede ② *n.* repetition, recurrence, setback

**relate** *v.* describe, recount, tell, mention, detail

**related** *adj.* associated, allied, connected, linked, akin ★**different**

**relative** ① *n.* kinsman, kinswoman, cousin, relation, sibling *I have four siblings – three sisters and one brother* ② *adj.* comparative, approximate, relevant

**relax** *v.* diminish, loosen, ease, reduce, relieve, unwind ★**tighten**

**relaxed** *adj.* composed, cool, easy-going, mellow ▷*casual* ★**tense**

**release** *v.* let go, loose, liberate, acquit, discharge ▷*free* ★**detain**

**relent** *v.* relax, soften, yield, ease, give in, unbend ★**harden**

**relentless** *adj.* unmerciful, remorseless, grim, pitiless ▷*cruel* ★**humane**

**relevant** *adj.* applicable, pertinent, appropriate, apt ▷*suitable* ★**irrelevant**

**reliable** *adj.* dependable, trustworthy, responsible, honest ▷*sound* ★**unreliable**

**relic** *n.* fragment, vestige, antique, keepsake, memento *This brooch is a memento of my great-grandmother; she wore it often*

**relief** *n.* aid, assistance, respite, support, succour ▷*help* ★**aggravation**

**relieve** *v.* release, support, comfort, lighten, relax, console ★**aggravate**

**religious** *adj.* pious, devout, orthodox, devoted, God-fearing, faithful

**relinquish** *v.* renounce, let go, waive, disclaim, give up ▷*abandon* ★**retain**

**relish** ① *v.* enjoy, like, approve ▷*appreciate* ★**loathe** ② *n.* savour, flavour, tang, gusto *The fried chicken was a great success; everyone ate with gusto,* zest, sauce

**reluctant** *adj.* hesitant, averse, loth, disinclined, squeamish ★**willing**

**rely on** *v.* depend on, count on, believe in

**remain** *v.* ① stay, tarry, dwell, wait, rest ★**depart** ② persist, last, endure

**remainder** *n.* remnant, residue, leavings

**remark** *v.* ① utter, observe, state, mention ▷*say* ② notice, perceive, note ▷*see*

**remarkable** *adj.* unusual, surprising, curious, prominent ▷*outstanding* ★**ordinary**

**remedy** ① *n.* cure, restorative, medicine ② *n.* relief, solution, treatment, corrective ③ *v.* relieve, heal, cure, put right

**remember** *v.* recollect, recognize, think back ▷*recall* ★**forget**

**remind** *v.* suggest, hint, cue, prompt

**remit** *v.* ① relax, desist, slacken, modify, excuse, forgive ② pay, square, settle up

**remnant** *n.* residue, remains, rest, scrap, leftover ▷*remainder*

**remorse** *n.* regrets, contrition, pity

**remote** *adj.* ① distant, far, isolated ★**near** ② unrelated, alien, foreign ★**significant**

**remove** *v.* take away, transfer, withdraw, carry off

**rend** *v.* split, fracture, tear apart, sever, break

**render** *v.* ① give, present, surrender, deliver ② play, execute, perform

**renew** *v.* ① modernize, mend, prolong, renovate ② reissue *Next week we start to reissue some of the old silent films,* revive

**renounce** *v.* disown, disclaim, give up, repudiate, forsake ★**retain**

**renowned** *adj.* eminent, noted, famed, notable ▷*celebrated* ★**obscure**

**rent** ① *v.* hire, lease, let, charter ② *n.* tear, rip, break, crack, fissure ③ *n.* fee, payment

**repair** ① *v.* fix, mend, correct, remedy, rectify *We are sorry there was an error in your account; we will rectify it right away* ② *n.* restoration, adjustment

**repast** *n.* meal, food, snack, spread

**repay** *v.* ① refund, reimburse, pay ② avenge, retaliate, revenge, punish

**repeal** *v.* revoke, annul, abolish, quash *The man's innocence was proved and his sentence was quashed* ▷*cancel* ★**establish**

**repeat** *v.* duplicate, renew, reiterate, do again

**repel** *v.* ① repulse, deter, reject, push back ② revolt, disgust, nauseate ★**attract**

**repellent** *adj.* distasteful, hateful, discouraging ▷*repulsive* ★**attractive**

**repent** *v.* sorrow, deplore, grieve ▷*regret*

**replace** *v.* ① supersede, succeed, follow, substitute ② put back, reinstate, restore

**replenish** *v.* fill, refill, restock, furnish, provide, top up ★**empty**

**replica** *n.* facsimile, copy, likeness, duplicate

**reply** ① *v.* answer, respond, rejoin, retort, acknowledge ② *n.* answer, response, acknowledgement, riposte

**report** ① *n.* statement, account, message, communication, tidings ② *n.* noise, explosion, bang ③ *v.* tell, disclose, reveal, expose

**repose** ① *v.* rest, settle, lie down, sleep, recline ② *n.* ease, peace, quiet, tranquillity ★**tumult**

**represent** *v.* ① depict, picture, portray, illustrate ② stand for, mean, denote

**representative** ① *n.* agent, delegate, envoy, deputy ② *adj.* typical, figurative

**repress** *v.* restrain, suppress, bottle up, smother, stifle

**reprimand** ① *v.* admonish, blame, rebuke ▷*chide* ② *n.* reproach, talking-to, scolding, telling off, dressing down ★**praise**

**reproach** *v.* scold, reprove, reprimand, blame ▷*rebuke* ★**approve**

**reproduce** *v.* ① copy, duplicate, imitate, simulate ② breed, multiply, generate

**reprove** *v.* reproach, reprimand ▷*rebuke* ★**approve**

**repudiate** *v.* renounce, disown, disavow, disclaim ★**acknowledge**

**repugnant** *adj.* unattractive, disagreeable, offensive ▷*repulsive* ★**pleasant**

**repulse** *v.* repel, rebuff, drive back, reject ▷*spurn* ★**attract**

**repulsive** *adj.* obnoxious, disgusting, loathsome ▷*repugnant* ★**attractive**

**reputation** *n.* standing, position, esteem, honour, good name

**request** ① *v.* demand, beg, entreat, beseech ▷*ask* ② *n.* petition, entreaty, invitation

**require** *v.* ① need, want, demand, crave ② expect, cause, instruct

**rescue** ① *v.* save, set free, liberate, recover, release ② *n.* liberation, deliverance, salvation *Salvation for the shipwrecked crew came when the coastguard lifted them to safety* ★**capture**

**research** *v.* examine, explore, investigate, inquire ▷*study*

**resemble** *v.* look like, mirror, take after, be like ★**differ**

**resent** *v.* resist, begrudge, dislike, take exception to ★**like**

**resentful** *adj.* offended, bitter, piqued, huffy ▷*indignant* ★**contented**

**reserve** ① *v.* hoard, retain, withhold ▷*keep* ② *n.* modesty, shyness, restraint ③ *n.* supply, backlog, stock

**reservoir** *n.* lake, spring, pool, container

**reside** *v.* live, occupy, inhabit, lodge ▷*dwell*

**residence** *n.* house, home, habitation, dwelling, mansion RESIDENTS

**resign** *v.* retire, abdicate, step down, give notice, abandon ▷*quit* ★**join**

**resign oneself to** *v.* accept, comply, reconcile *Robinson Crusoe became reconciled to loneliness on his island*, yield, give in ▷*submit* ★**resist**

**resist** *v.* withstand, oppose, defy, refrain, hinder ▷*thwart* ★**submit**

**Rescue**

*Salvation for the shipwrecked crew came when the coastguard lifted them to safety.*

**resistance** *n.* defiance, obstruction, opposition, hindrance ★**acceptance**

**resolute** *adj.* determined, resolved, obstinate, stubborn, dogged *Despite the bad weather, the climbers were dogged in their will to reach the peak* ★**weak**

**resolve** ① *v.* determine, intend, decide ② *v.* decipher, unravel, disentangle ③ *n.* resolution, purpose, will

**resort** ① *v.* frequent, haunt, visit ② *n.* alternative, chance, course ③ *n.* spa, watering place, hotel, holiday centre

**resourceful** *adj.* clever, ingenious, bright

**respect** ① *n.* esteem, honour, regard, repute, dignity ② *v.* esteem, honour, revere, venerate *The names of the pioneers and explorers will always be venerated*

**respectable** *adj.* decent, admirable, honest, honourable, proper ★**disreputable**

**respectful** *adj.* deferential, courteous, polite, dutiful ★**disrespectful**

**respite** *n.* break, halt, interval, lull, recess, let-up

**respond** *v.* answer, reply, retort, tally, accord, agree ★**differ**

**responsible** *adj.* ① accountable, dependable, sensible ▷*reliable* ★**unreliable** ② liable, guilty

**rest** ① *n.* repose, relaxation, peace, tranquillity ② *n.* break, pause, respite, spell ③ *n.* remainder, residue, balance ④ *v.* repose, settle, sleep, relax wrest

**restful** *adj.* peaceful, quiet, calm, placid ★**disturbing**

**restless** *adj.* uneasy, fitful, agitated, nervous, fretful ★**calm**

**restore** *v.* ① replace, reinstate, return ② refurbish, recondition, renovate *We renovated this old sofa which we found in a junk shop*

**restrain** *v.* stop, prevent, hold back, subdue ▷*check* ★**encourage**

**restrict** *v.* confine, limit, cramp, handicap ▷*regulate* ★**free**

**result** ① *n.* effect, consequence, outcome, end ★**cause** ② *v.* ensue, happen, turn out, follow, emerge, occur

**resume** *v.* renew, recommence, start again, go back to ▷*continue* ★**interrupt**

**retain** *v.* hold, restrain, withhold, detain ▷*keep* ★**relinquish**

**retaliate** *v.* avenge, reciprocate, fight back, repay, retort ★**submit**

**retire** *v.* ① retreat, go back ▷*withdraw* ★**advance** ② abdicate, resign, relinquish

**retort** ① *n.* riposte, reply, rejoinder ② *v.* return, answer, reply

**retract** *v.* recant, deny, disavow, take back, repudiate, revoke ★**maintain**

**retreat** ① *v.* retire, depart, shrink ▷*withdraw* ★**advance** ② *n.* sanctuary *This section of the park is being made into a bird sanctuary,* shelter, den, haven

**retrieve** *v.* redeem, recover, regain, rescue ▷*salvage* ★**lose**

**return** ① *v.* rejoin, come back, reappear ② *v.* restore, give back, repay, refund ③ *n.* form, tax form, document, list

**reveal** *v.* disclose, expose, show, display, uncover, divulge ★**hide**

**revel** ① *v.* make merry, celebrate, have fun ② *n.* celebration, gala, party, spree

**revenge** ① *n.* vengeance, reprisal, retaliation ② *v.* avenge, get one's own back

**revenue** *n.* income, receipts, earnings

**revere** *v.* honour, esteem, regard, adore, venerate, respect ★**despise**

**reverse** ① *v.* cancel, change, overrule, repeal, revoke ② *n.* adversity, disaster, bad luck, misfortune ③ *adj.* backward, contrary, opposite *We turned the car around and drove back in the opposite direction*

**review** ① *v.* reconsider, examine, survey ② *n.* inspection, examination ③ *n.* synopsis, journal, magazine REVUE

**revise** *v.* edit, amend, improve, rewrite, alter

**revive** *v.* awaken, rally, recover, refresh, restore, invigorate ▷*rouse*

**revoke** *v.* repeal, abolish *The principal refuses to abolish the school dress code,* cancel, quash, reverse, withdraw

**revolt** ① *v.* rebel, mutiny, riot ② *v.* nauseate, sicken, disgust ③ *n.* rebellion, uprising, revolution

**revolting** *adj.* obnoxious *The chemical factory's chimney was giving off obnoxious fumes,* repulsive, offensive ▷*repugnant* ★**pleasant**

**revolve** *v.* rotate, spin, gyrate, turn

**reward** ① *n.* award, payment, benefit, bonus, profit ★**punishment** ② *v.* compensate, repay, remunerate ★**punish**

**rhyme** *n.* verse, poem, ditty, ode RIME

**rhythm** *n.* beat, pulse, throb, stroke, timing

**ribald** *adj.* smutty, vulgar, coarse, gross

**rich** *adj.* ① wealthy, prosperous, affluent, opulent ★**poor** ② fertile, loamy, fruitful, abundant ★**barren** ③ delicious, sweet, luscious, delicate

**rid** *v.* get rid of, unburden, expel, free

**riddle** ① *n.* puzzle, cryptogram, enigma ② *v.* puncture, bore, perforate, pierce

**ride** ① *v.* sit, travel, drive, journey ② *n.* journey, jaunt, lift, trip

**ridge** *n.* ① groove, furrow, fold ② highland, chain, range *A range of hills could be seen in the distance*

**ridicule** ① *n.* scorn, derision, travesty, sarcasm, mockery ② *v.* deride, mock, jeer,

### Rivers and Waterways

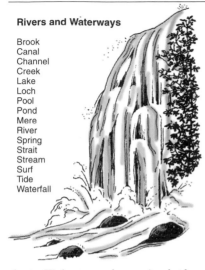

Brook
Canal
Channel
Creek
Lake
Loch
Pool
Pond
Mere
River
Spring
Strait
Stream
Surf
Tide
Waterfall

banter *His banter can be amusing, but he doesn't know when to stop and sometimes offends people*

**ridiculous** *adj.* laughable, absurd, foolish, preposterous ▷*silly* ★**sensible**

**rife** *adj.* common, current, frequent, prevalent ▷*widespread* ★**scarce**

**rifle** ① *v.* loot, rob, plunder ▷*ransack* ② *n.* gun, musket, firearm

**rift** *n.* ① fissure, breach, crack, spilit, cleft ② disagreement, clash, break

**right** ① *adj.* correct, proper, true ★**incorrect** ② *adj.* honest, upright, fair ③ *adj.* seemly, fit, suitable, becoming ★**improper** ④ *n.* truth, justice, honesty ★**wrong** RITE, WRITE

**righteous** *adj.* honourable, upright, moral

**rigid** *adj.* ① stiff, firm, inflexible ② stern, austere, harsh ★**flexible**

**rigorous** *adj.* stern, severe, strict, rigid

**rim** *n.* border, margin, edge, verge *We knew we were on the verge of disaster,* brink

**ring** ① *n.* circle, band, collar ② *n.* bell, chime, tinkle ③ *v.* chime, strike, jingle, sound WRING

**riot** ① *n.* uproar, tumult, brawl, broil ★**calm** ② *v.* revolt, rampage, rebel

**ripe** *adj.* ① mellow, mature, seasoned ② developed, adult, full-grown

**rise** ① *v.* ascend, mount, soar, arise, grow ★**fall** ② *v.* appear, occur, happen ★**vanish** ③ *n.* ascent, advance, increase ★**fall**

**risk** ① *v.* chance, dare, hazard, gamble ② *n.* adventure, peril, danger, jeopardy ★**safety**

**risky** *adj.* perilous, chancy, dangerous, tricky, uncertain ★**safe**

**rite** *n.* custom, ritual, practice RIGHT

**rival** ① *adj.* opposing, competing, conflicting ② *n.* opponent, adversary ★**associate**

**river** *n.* stream, waterway, brook, torrent *Before the rains came, this torrent was only a trickle*

**road** *n.* street, avenue, drive, lane, highway, motorway, route, way RODE, ROWED

**roam** *v.* rove, ramble, range, stroll, wander

**roar** *v.* bellow, bawl, yell, blare, cry

**rob** *v.* cheat, defraud, loot, plunder ▷*steal*

**robber** *n.* bandit, brigand, thief, crook

**robe** *n.* costume, dress, gown, habit

**robust** *adj.* strong, healthy, lusty, sturdy ▷*vigorous* ★**delicate**

**rock** ① *n.* stone, boulder, cobble, pebble, crag, reef ② *v.* totter, reel, sway, falter ③ *v.* quiet, still, tranquillize, soothe

**rod** *n.* baton, stick, stave, pole, perch, cane

**rogue** *n.* rascal, blackguard, scamp, knave ▷*scoundrel* ★**gentleman**

**role** *n.* character, post, duty, function *At the end of the party, my function will be to clear up*

**roll** ① *n.* record, register, list ② *n.* spool, scroll, reel ③ *v.* revolve, rotate, turn ④ *v.* smooth, level, press ⑤ *v.* lurch, reel, pitch, ROLE

**romance** *n.* ① love story, novel, love affair ② adventure, excitement, fantasy, glamour

**romantic** *adj.:* ① amorous, passionate, loving ② visionary, fanciful *Many people have a fanciful idea of how things were in the old days,* fantastic, extravagant ★**ordinary**

**romp** *v.* gambol, caper, frolic, prance, play

**roof** *n.* ceiling, covering, cover, canopy

**room** *n.* ① apartment, chamber, area, compartment, salon ② space, capacity

**root** *n.* ① seed, source, radicle ② basis, element, stem, origin

**rope** *n.* cable, cord, hawser, line, lasso

**rosy** *adj.* ① cheerful, encouraging, hopeful, optimistic ② pink, flesh-coloured

**rot** ① *v.* corrupt, crumble, decay, perish ② *n.* bunkum *The last speaker at the meeting was talking a lot of bunkum,* balderdash, bosh, poppycock, claptrap

**rotate** *v.* revolve, turn, spin, pivot, gyrate

**rotten** *adj.* ① decayed, putrid, decomposed, fetid ② deplorable, despicable, nasty, vicious ③ ill, poorly, grotty

**rough** *adj.* ① wrinkled, craggy, coarse, shaggy, broken ② rude, crude, imperfect ③ blunt, gruff, brusque, discourteous RUFF

**round** ① *adj.* circular, rotund, spherical ② *n.* ring, circle, loop

**rouse** *v.* ① waken, arouse, excite, disturb ② anger, inflame, incite ★calm

**rout** *v.* crush, defeat, conquer, overthrow

**route** *n.* road, track, way, journey, direction

**routine** *n.* usage, practice, formula, technique, method, habit *After being alone for so long, I have got into the habit of talking to myself*

**rove** *v.* tramp, roam, wander, stroll, drift

**row** ① *n.* (*ro*) string, line, queue, rank, column ② *v.* paddle, scull ROE ③ *n.* (rhymes with *now*) fight, squabble, noise, quarrel, dispute, tiff ★calm

**rowdy** *adj.* rough, unruly, boisterous, noisy, wild, riotous ★quiet

**royal** *adj.* sovereign, princely, stately, majestic ▷*regal*

**rub** *v.* stroke, brush, scrub, wipe, polish

**rubbish** *n.* debris, trash, junk, garbage, refuse, waste

**rude** *adj.* ① coarse, primitive, ill-bred, impolite, boorish, bad-mannered ② crude, formless ★polished ROOD, RUED

**rue** *v.* be sorry for, deplore, grieve ▷*regret*

**ruffian** *n.* hoodlum, hooligan, lout, scoundrel, rogue, ▷*rascal*

**ruffle** *v.* ① fluster, worry, excite, agitate ② crumple, rumple, crease

**ruffled** *adj.* upset, worried, flustered

### Rulers, Monarchs, and Leaders

| | |
|---|---|
| Caesar | Prime |
| Czar | Minister |
| Czarina | Prince |
| Emperor | Princess |
| Empress | Queen |
| King | Rajah |
| Mikado | Sultan |
| Mogul | |
| Pharaoh | |
| President | |

**rugged** *adj.* ① rough, craggy, shaggy, ragged ② rigorous, robust, strong, strenuous

**ruin** *v.* ① demolish, wreck, damage, smash ② bankrupt, impoverish, overwhelm

**rule** ① *v.* control, govern, command, manage, direct ② *v.* decide, determine, judge ③ *n.* law, regulation ④ *n.* straight-edge

**ruler** ① *n.* leader, director, king, queen, monarch, governor ② rule, straight-edge

**rumble** *v.* roar, thunder, boom, roll

**rumour** *n.* hearsay, report, gossip, scandal *The bribery scandal, added to high taxes, brought down the government*

**rumpus** *n.* uproar, racket, riot, commotion, hurly-burly ★calm

**run** ① *v.* hurry, hasten, speed, sprint ★saunter ② *v.* leak, flow, ooze ③ *v.* operate, propel, drive ④ *n.* race, sprint, spurt, dash, rush

**run away** *v.* escape, flee, bolt, abscond ★stay

**rupture** *v. & n.* break, burst, puncture, split

**rural** *adj.* rustic, countrified, pastoral, agrarian ★urban

**ruse** *n.* dodge, hoax, scheme, trick, ploy RUES

**rush** *v. & n.* dash, speed, hurry, scramble, stampede, rampage ★saunter

**rust** *n.* corrosion, mould, blight, mildew, stain, deterioration

**rustic** *adj.* rural, pastoral, country, homely, simple, sylvan

**rustle** *n. & v.* crackle, swish, murmur, whisper

**rut** *n.* furrow, channel, groove, score, track

**ruthless** *adj.* cruel, savage, harsh, ferocious, pitiless ★merciful

# S s

**sack** ① *n.* bag, pouch, pack ② *v.* rob, plunder, pillage ③ discharge, dismiss, lay off SAC

**sacred** *adj.* holy, blessed, hallowed, spiritual, consecrated, review ★**profane**

**sacrifice** ① *n.* offering ② *v.* forfeit, give up, relinquish ▷*abandon*

**sad** *adj.* sorrowful, melancholy, unhappy, mournful, woeful ▷*sorry* ★**happy**

**sadden** *v.* mourn, grieve, distress, lament, dismay, dishearten ★**please**

**safe** ① *adj.* secure, protected, sure ★**unsafe** ② *n.* vault, coffer, cash-box, strongbox

**safety** *n.* shelter, security, sanctuary, protection, refuge ★**danger**

**sag** *v.* bend, curve, bow, decline, flag, slump ▷*droop* ★**bulge**

**sage** ① *adj.* wise, sensible, shrewd, sagacious ★**foolish** ② *n.* wise person, savant *We were taught by an old savant of the university, Professor Hankins,* philosopher ★**fool**

**said** *adj.* expressed, stated

**sail** *v.* cruise, voyage, navigate, float, skim, weigh anchor SALE

**sailor** *n.* seaman, seafarer, mariner, jack tar, seadog, yachtsman, yachtswoman

**sake** *n.* motive, reason, purpose, object, principle

**salary** *n.* pay, earnings, reward, wages, income, emolument

**sale** *n.* auction, transaction, selling, trade, disposal SAIL

**sally** *n.* jest, joke, crack, riposte ▷*quip*

**salute** ① *v.* greet, accost, welcome, hail, honour ② *n.* greetings, welcome, acknowledgement

**salvage** *v.* save, conserve, rescue, restore, reclaim ▷*preserve* ★**abandon**

**same** *adj.* ① identical, duplicate, alike, similar ② aforesaid, aforementioned *I leave all my possessions to my wife, the aforementioned Angela Gomez*

**sample** ① *n.* specimen, example, model, pattern, illustration ② *v.* inspect, try, taste

**sanction** *v.* permit, allow, authorize, approve

**sanctuary** *n.* retreat, shelter, shrine, asylum, haven ▷*refuge*

**sane** *adj.* normal, rational, reasonable, lucid ▷*sensible* ★**insane**

**sap** *v.* bleed, drain, exhaust, reduce, weaken ★**strengthen**

**sarcastic** *adj.* biting, cutting, sardonic, cynical, ironic, caustic *My cousins made some caustic remarks after I played the violin*

**satire** *n.* invective, sarcasm, burlesque, ridicule, parody

**satisfaction** *n.* contentment, delight, gratification, compensation ★**grievance**

**satisfy** *v.* gratify, fulfil, appease, suit, please ▷*delight* ★**disappoint**

**saturate** *v.* soak, steep, drench, souse, waterlog *I am afraid that old canoe is too waterlogged ever to be used again*

**saucy** *adj.* forward, pert, impudent, cheeky, disrespectful ★**civil**

**saunter** *v.* roam, loiter, wander, linger, dawdle, amble ▷*stroll* ★**hasten**

**savage** ① *adj.* barbaric, wild, uncivilized, ferocious, brutal ★**civilized** ② *n.* brute, oaf, barbarian

**save** *v.* ① liberate, set free, rescue, protect,

### Sacred Books

| | |
|---|---|
| Apocrypha | Koran |
| Bhagavad-Gita | Talmud |
| Bible | Torah |
| Book of Mormon | Tripitaka |
| Book of Common Prayer | Upanishad |
| Granth | Veda |

guard ② keep, preserve, salvage, hoard, put aside ★**squander**

**savoury** *adj.* appetizing, flavourful, luscious, agreeable ★**tasteless**

**say** *v.* speak, utter, state, pronounce, talk, tell, assert

**saying** *n.* proverb, statement, adage, idiom, maxim, aphorism

**scale** ① *n.* measure, balance, calibration ② *n.* crust, plate, flake ③ *n.* clef, key *I will play this next piece in the key of C,* mode ④ *v.* climb, ascend, clamber

Scales

Scale

**scamp** *n.* knave, rogue, rascal, scoundrel, scallywag *Someone rang our doorbell, but when I opened the door, the scallywag had gone*

**scamper** *v.* hurry, run, scurry, hasten, sprint, scoot, fly ▷*rush*

**scan** *v.* examine, glance at, scrutinize, pore over ▷*check*

**scandal** *n.* disgrace, libel, slander, offence, infamy, rumour, discredit ★**honour**

**scanty** *adj.* meagre, insufficient, sparse, inadequate, poor, scant ★**plenty**

**scar** ① *n.* blemish, mark, stigma, wound ② *v.* brand, damage, disfigure

**scarce** *adj.* rare, infrequent, sparse, scanty, uncommon ★**common**

**scarcity** *n.* lack, deficiency, dearth, rarity, infrequency ★**abundance**

**scare** *v.* frighten, startle, shock, alarm, dismay ★**reassure**

**scatter** *v.* spread, disperse, strew, broadcast, sow, shower, disseminate ▷*sprinkle* ★**collect**

**scene** *n.* sight, spectacle, vision, view, exhibition, landscape SEEN

**scent** ① *n.* aroma, tang, fragrance, smell, odour ② *v.* detect, sniff, smell CENT, SENT

**sceptical** *adj.* doubtful, unbelieving, incredulous ▷*dubious* ★**convinced**

**schedule** *n.* timetable *We checked the timetable before buying our train tickets,* programme, catalogue, diary

**scheme** *n.* plot, plan, project, design, proposal, idea

**scholar** *n.* ① pupil, student, schoolchild, learner ② intellectual *That café is a favourite gathering place for intellectuals,* savant, academic

**scholarly** *adj.* learned, educated, literate, cultured ★**illiterate**

**scoff** *v.* sneer, mock, deride, jeer, ridicule

**scold** *v.* rebuke, admonish, reprove, find fault with ▷*chide* ★**praise**

**scoop** ① *v.* bail, ladle, spoon, excavate, gouge, hollow ② exclusive, coup, inside story

**scope** *n.* extent, margin, compass, range, latitude, field

**scorch** *v.* sear, burn, singe, blister, shrivel

**score** *v.* ① cut, mark, scratch ② register, record, win

**scorn** ① *n.* mockery, disdain, ridicule, disregard ② *v.* despise, mock, spurn, slight

**scoundrel** *n.* rascal, knave, thief, rogue, villain ▷*vagabond* ★**gentleman**

**scour** *v.* ① cleanse, rinse, scrub, purge ② search, seek, ransack, rake

**scourge** ① *v.* beat, whip, thrash, cane ② *n.* curse, evil, misfortune, plague ★**blessing**

**scowl** *v. & n.* frown, glower, grimace, glare ★**smile**

**scramble** ① *v.* clamber, climb ② *v.* jostle, struggle, swarm, push ③ *n.* turmoil, bustle, confusion ★**order**

**scrap** ① *n.* piece, morsel, bit, portion, fragment, grain ② *v.* abandon, discard, junk

**scrape** ① *v.* scratch, groove, abrade, file, grate, scour ② *n.* predicament, fix, difficulty

**scratch** *v. & n.* wound, cut, mark, score

**scream** *v. & n.* screech, cry, shriek, howl, yell

**screen** ① *n.* awning *Before the ceremony, an awning was erected over the entrance to the hotel,* canopy, shade, protection ② *v.* protect, hide, conceal, veil

**screw** *v.* twist, turn, wrench, tighten, compress

**scribble** *v.* write, scrawl, scratch, doodle

**scribe** *n.* writer, penman, clerk, historian

**script** *n.* handwriting, manuscript, text, words, libretto *Sir Arthur Sullivan wrote the music for* The Mikado, *and W. S. Gilbert wrote the lyrics and libretto*

**scrub** ① *v.* scour, brush, mop, cleanse ② *n.* brushwood, undergrowth

**scruffy** *adj.* messy, dirty, frowzy, seedy, shabby, sloppy ▷*slovenly* ★**neat**

**scrumptious** *adj.* delightful, delicious, appetizing, exquisite

**scrupulous** *adj.* painstaking, particular, rigorous, strict, conscientious ★**careless**

**scrutinize** *v.* examine, inspect, peruse, study

**scuffle** *v. & n.* tussle, skirmish, fight, struggle, squabble

**scum** *n.* dross, foam, froth, dregs, crust

**scuttle** *v.* ① scramble, scamper, scoot, hurry ② destroy, smash, wreck

**seal** ① *n.* signet, stamp ② *n.* cork, bung, closure ③ *n.* sea mammal ④ *v.* fasten, close, shut, stop

**seam** ① *n.* ridge, scar, lode, furrow ② hem, pleat, tuck SEEM

**search** ① *v.* seek, quest, hunt, trail, track, scour, explore ② *n.* exploration, probe investigation, quest, pursuit

**season** ① *n.* period, time, occasion, term ② *v.* accustom, acclimatize, mature ③ *v.* flavour, spice, salt

**seat** ① *n.* bench, chair, stool, sofa, couch, throne ② *n.* headquarters, place, site ③ *v.* accommodate, locate, place

**secret** *adj.* mysterious, hidden, concealed, obscure, private ★**public**

**section** *n.* division, group, department, segment, portion

**secure** ① *adj.* safe, protected ② *adj.* confident, certain, sure, stable ★**uncertain** ③ *v.* fasten, protect, close, lock ★**unfasten** ④ *v.* acquire, procure, obtain ★**lost**

**sedate** *adj.* staid, sober, demure, earnest ▷*steady* ★**flippant**

**see** *v.* ① behold, witness, sight, observe ② heed, examine, watch, note ③ understand, comprehend, know SEA

**seedy** *adj.* shabby, squalid, poor, grubby, unkempt ▷*slovenly* ★**spruce**

**seek** *v.* look for, search, inquire, endeavour, hunt, strive

**seem** *v.* appear, look like, sound like, look as if SEAM

**seemly** *adj.* fit, suitable, proper, decent, decorous ★**unseemly**

**seethe** *v.* simmer, fizz, bubble, boil, foam

**seize** *v.* grasp, snatch, take, clutch, arrest ▷*grab* ★**abandon** SEAS, SEES

**seldom** *adv.* rarely, infrequently, hardly, scarcely ★**often**

**select** ① *adj.* choice, preferred, fine, prime *All the fruit on the trees in the orchard is in its prime,* first-class ★**common** ② *v.* choose, pick out, single out, prefer

**selfish** *adj.* greedy, self-centred, narrow, illiberal ▷*stingy* ★**generous**

**sell** *v.* vend, market, retail, trade, peddle, barter, deal in ★**buy**

**send** *v.* transmit, dispatch, forward, mail, direct ★**detain**

**send for** *v.* command, order, summon, request ★**dismiss**

**sensation** *n.* ① feeling, perception, impression, awareness ② excitement, commotion, scandal

**sensational** *adj.* exceptional, scandalous, lurid ▷*exciting* ★**ordinary**

**sense** *n.* ① sensation, impression, feeling ② understanding, mind, tact, intellect ③ wisdom, significance, meaning CENTS

**senseless** *adj.* silly, stupid, absurd, unwise ▷*foolish* ★**sensible**

**sensible** *adj.* ① wise, intelligent, astute, shrewd ② reasonable, rational ③ conscious, aware, mindful ★**senseless**

**sensitive** *adj.* ① susceptible, responsive, acute, impressionable *Because Rachel is at such an impressionable age, her mother does not want her to see the film* ② thin-skinned, touchy, irritable, tender

**sentence** *n.* ① phrase, clause ② judgement, decision, condemnation, doom, irritable

**sentimental** *adj.* romantic, tender, emotional

**separate** ① *adj.* disconnected, apart, detached ★**united** ② *v.* detach, part, divide, break, disconnect ★**unite**

**sequel** *n.* continuation, consequence, result, outcome, follow-up

**serene** *adj.* tranquil, calm, peaceful, undisturbed, clear ★**tempestuous**

**series** *n.* sequence, progression, succession, run, string

**serious** *adj.* grave, earnest, solemn, thoughtful, severe, grim ★**trivial**

**serve** *v.* attend, assist, aid, oblige, help, officiate, act

**service** *n.* ① aid, help, assistance, attendance, employment ② ceremony, rite *Stuart is at college studying the marriage rites of the Incas*

**set** ① *n.* group, pack, outfit, series ② *v.* settle, put, place, seat, locate ③ *v.* stiffen, congeal, harden ④ *adj.* decided, resolved, determined, fixed

**setback** *n.* defeat, delay, problem, snag, hold-up ★**advantage**

**settle** *v.* ① establish, regulate, fix ② pay, liquidate, finish ③ populate, colonize ④ live, dwell, reside

**several** *adj.* various, numerous, sundry, separate, assorted

**severe** *adj.* strict, rigid, unkind, hard, austere ▷*stern* ★**lenient**

**sew** *v.* stitch, tack, baste, fasten sow

**shabby** *adj.* torn, ragged, mean, shoddy, tacky ▷*squalid* ★**neat**

**shack** *n.* hut, cabin, shanty, shed, hovel

**shackle** *v. & n.* manacle, handcuff, chain, rope, fetter

**shade** *n.* ① shadow, gloom, darkness, dusk ② blind, awning, screen ③ colour, tint, hue, tone ④ ghost, spirit, wraith *Out of the darkness, a wraithlike figure loomed up before us*

**shadow** ① *n.* shade ② *v.* follow, stalk, tail

**shady** *adj.* ① shadowy, shaded ★**sunny**

② crooked, infamous, disreputable ★**honest**

**shaft** *n.* ① pillar, column, support ② hilt, handle, rod ③ mine, pit, well, tunnel

**shaggy** *adj.* hairy, tousled, unkempt, rough, dishevelled ★**smooth**

**shake** *v.* flutter, tremble, throb, shudder ▷*quiver*

**shallow** *adj.* ① not deep ② trivial, empty, silly, empty-headed ★**profound**

**sham** *adj.* false, imitation, counterfeit, forged, fake ▷*bogus* ★**genuine**

**shame** *n. & v.* dishonour, discredit ▷*disgrace*

### Ships and Boats

Gondola

Catamaran

Kayak

**shameful** *adj.* disgraceful, scandalous, outrageous ▷*disreputable* ★**honourable**

**shape** ① *n.* form, structure, outline, pattern ② *v.* form, fashion, make, create

**share** ① *v.* allot, divide, participate, co-operate ② *n.* portion, allotment, allowance

**sharp** *adj.* ① acute, keen, pointed ② clear, distinct, clean-cut ③ painful, severe, intense ④ pungent, acrid, acid ⑤ alert, shrewd, acute ▷*clever* ★**dull**

**shatter** *v.* smash, wreck, break, fracture, ruin ▷*destroy*

**shave** *v.* shear, crop, slice, shred, graze, trim

**shear** *v.* fleece, strip, cut ▷*shave* SHEER

**sheath** *n.* scabbard, quiver, holster, holder, case, casing

**shed** ① *n.* hut, barn, lean-to, shanty ② *v.* cast off, moult *Our parrot is moulting and is leaving feathers all over the carpet,* spill ③ *v.* beam, radiate

**sheepish** *adj.* timid, diffident, foolish, embarrassed, shamefaced ★**unabashed**

**sheer** *adj.* ① absolute, simple, pure, unmixed ② transparent, filmy, thin ③ steep,

Ferry

Motorboat

Liner

abrupt, perpendicular *The trail ended at the foot of a huge, perpendicular cliff* SHEAR

**shell** *n.* pod, case, husk, hull, shuck, crust

**shelter** ① *n.* roof, sanctuary, safety, home, retreat, cover ② *v.* shield, cover, protect, screen ★**expose**

**shield** *n. & v.* guard, screen, safeguard ▷*shelter*

**shift** ① *v.* alter, move, change, displace, remove ② *n.* turn, spell, stint

**shifty** *adj.* untrustworthy, devious, treacherous ▷*wily* ★**honest**

**shine** *v. & n.* glow, gleam, glitter, sparkle, flash

**ship** ① *n.* boat, barge, craft, vessel ② *v.* export, send, transport *(see page 114)*

**shirk** *v.* dodge, avoid, shun, evade, slack

**shiver** *v.* quaver, quiver, shake, shudder ▷*tremble*

**shock** ① *n.* blow, jolt, clash, collision ② *n.* scare, start, turn ③ *v.* stupefy, daze, stun

**shocking** *adj.* scandalous, awful, frightful ▷*horrible* ★**agreeable**

**shoot** *v.* ① fire, discharge, bombard, propel ② *v.* germinate *We grew some beans in a glass jar and watched them germinate,* grow, bud, sprout ③ *n.* bud, twig, sprout CHUTE

**shop** ① *n.* store, market, emporium ② *v.* buy, market, purchase

**shore** ① *n.* beach, coast, strand, seashore, seaside ② *v.* prop, support, bolster up

**short** *adj.* ① brief, concise, condensed ★**long** ② deficient, incomplete, scanty ★**full** ③ sharp, severe, bad-tempered ④ small, puny, squat, diminutive, tiny ★**tall**

**shortcoming** *n.* defect, fault, flaw, inadequacy, ▷*weakness*

**shorten** *v.* cut, crop, abbreviate, lessen ▷*diminish* ★**lengthen**

**shortened** *adj.* abbreviated, abridged, condensed ★**enlarged**

**shortly** *adj.* presently, soon, before long, directly

**shout** *n. & v.* cry, scream, roar, shriek, cheer, whoop, bellow

**shove** *v.* push, jostle, prod, nudge, move, propel ★**pull**

**show** ① *v.* display, parade, exhibit, flaunt, reveal ★**hide** ② *v.* prove, testify to, demonstrate ③ *v.* explain, teach, instruct ④ *n.* exhibition, display, ceremony, play

**shower** ① *v.* scatter, spray, sprinkle, rain ② *n.* downpour, cloudburst ③ *n.* barrage, volley, discharge

**shred** ① *n.* particle, piece, scrap, tatter, fragment ② *v.* tear, rip, strip

**shrewd** *adj.* profound, deep, discerning ▷*wise* ★**obtuse**

**shriek** *n. & v.* screech ▷*shout*

**shrill** *adj.* treble, high-pitched, screeching, ear-piercing

**shrink** *v.* ① contract, dwindle, shrivel, become smaller ② flinch, cringe, recoil, withdraw

**shrivel** *v.* wither, contract, wrinkle, decrease, pucker, parch ▷*wilt*

**shudder** *v.* shake, quake, tremble ▷*quiver*

**shuffle** *v.* ① mix, jumble, rearrange ② hobble, limp

**shun** *v.* avoid, elude, ignore, spurn, steer clear of ★**accept**

**shut** *v.* fasten, close, secure, slam, bar, latch, lock ★**open**

**shut up** *v.* ① imprison, cage, intern ② be silent, hold one's tongue, be quiet

**shy** ① *adj.* bashful, diffident, timid, wary, shrinking ★**bold** ② *v.* flinch, quail, recoil

**sick** *adj.* ① ill, poorly, ailing, unwell, feeble ② weary, fed up, displeased ③ nauseated

**side** *n.* ① border, edge, flank, margin, half ② party, sect, group, team SIGHED

**sift** *v.* strain, drain, separate, screen, sieve, riddle

**sigh** *v.* ① grieve, lament, moan, complain ② wheeze, breathe

**sight** ① *n.* appearance, spectacle, scene, mirage ② *n.* seeing, perception, visibiity ③ *v.* behold, glimpse, observe CITE, SITE

**sign** ① *n.* symbol, emblem, mark ② *n.* omen, token ③ *n.* signboard, signpost, placard ④ *v.* endorse, autograph, inscribe

**signal** ① *n.* beacon *As soon as the ships*

*were sighted, beacons were lit all along the coast,* sign, flag, indicator ② *adj.* distinguished, impressive, outstanding

**significant** *adj.* symbolical, meaningful, weighty ▷*important* ★**unimportant**

**signify** *v.* denote, indicate, suggest, imply ▷*mean*

**silence** *n.* quiet, hush, peace, tranquillity ★**noise**

**silent** *adj.* hushed, noiseless, soundless, still, mute ▷*quiet* ★**noisy**

**silly** *adj.* absurd, senseless, stupid, fatuous, childish, puerile ▷*foolish* ★**wise**

**similar** *adj.* resembling, alike, harmonious, common ▷*like* ★**different**

**simple** *adj.* ① elementary, plain, uncomplicated ▷*easy* ② trusting, open, naive ★**intricate**

**simply** *adv.* ① merely, purely, barely, solely, only ② easily, directly

**sin** ① *n.* misdeed, wrong, vice, evil, wickedness ② *v.* err, offend, trespass, stray, do wrong

**since** ① *conj.* because, as, for, considering ② *prep.* subsequently, after

**sincere** *adj.* true, unaffected, frank, open, truthful ▷*genuine* ★**insincere**

**sing** *v.* vocalize, warble, yodel, trill, croon, chant, carol, hum, chirp

**singe** *v.* scorch, burn, scald, sear, char

**singer** *n.* vocalist, minstrel, songster, chorister, crooner

**single** *adj.* ① one, only, sole ② solitary, alone, separate ③ unmarried, celibate *The priests of the Roman Catholic Church are celibate*

**singular** *adj.* odd, peculiar, curious, surprising ▷*unusual* ★**ordinary**

**sinister** *adj.* menacing, threatening, unlucky, disastrous ▷*evil* ★**harmless**

**sink** ① *v.* drop, dip, descend, decline ▷*fall* ★**rise** ② *n.* basin, drain

**sit** *v.* perch, seat, squat, roost, rest, settle

**site** *n.* spot, plot, locality, place, station, post ▷*situation* CITE, SIGHT

**situation** *n.* ① position, location, place, site, whereabouts, standpoint ② predicament,

**Singers**

Alto
Baritone
Bass
Basso profundo
Cantor
Chorister
Contrabass
Contralto
Countertenor
Mezzo-soprano
Prima donna
Soprano
Tenor
Treble
Vocalist

plight, state of affairs, condition

**size** *n.* ① dimensions, proportions, measurement ② magnitude, bulk, volume, weight SIGHS

**sketch** ① *n.* drawing, picture, cartoon ② *n.* draft, blueprint, outline ③ *v.* draw, portray, depict, outline, delineate

**skilful** *adj.* adroit, able, adept, dexterous, expert, competent ▷*clever* ★**clumsy**

**skill** *n.* ability, expertness, knack, facility ▷*talent*

**skim** *v.* brush, touch, graze, float, glide

**skimp** *v.* stint, scrimp, economize, scrape

**skin** *n.* peel, rind, hide, husk, pelt

**skinny** *adj.* thin, lean, scraggy, weedy ★**fat**

**skip** *v.* ① jump, hop, dance, caper ② pass over, miss, disregard, omit

**skirmish** *n. & v.* scuffle, fight, affray, scrap, combat, clash, set-to

**skirt** ① *n.* petticoat, kilt ② *n.* border, hem, edge, margin ③ *v.* border, flank, evade, avoid

**skulk** *v.* lurk, hide, cower, slink, sneak

**slab** *n.* board, stone, boulder, piece, chunk

**slack** *adj.* ① limp, flabby, loose, relaxed ★**tight** ② lazy, sluggish ▷*idle* ★**busy**

**slander** *v.* libel, malign, accuse, abuse ▷*defame* ★**praise**

**slaughter** ① *v. & n.* incline, angle, list ▷*slope*

**slap** *v.* smack, whack, strike, hit, spank

**slash** *v. & n.* cut, slit, gash, hack, rip

**slaughter** *v.* slay, butcher, massacre ▷*kill*

**slave** ① *n.* bondsman, bondswoman, serf, vassal, drudge, captive ② *v.* drudge, toil, labour, grind

**slavery** *n.* bondage, enslavement, serfdom, servility, drudgery, captivity ★**freedom**

**slay** *v.* murder, massacre ▷*kill* SLEIGH

**sleek** *adj.* shiny, smooth, glossy, slick

**sleep** *v. & n.* snooze, nap, doze, drowse, repose, slumber

**slender** *adj.* ① narrow, thin, fine, slight ▷*slim* ★**thick** ② trivial, inadequate, meagre, scanty

**slice** ① *v.* shred, shave, cut, strip, segment ② *n.* segment, piece, cut, slab

**slick** *adj.* ① shiny, smooth ▷*sleek* ② glib, suave, plausible

**slide** *v.* slip, slither, glide, skim, skate

**slight** ① *adj.* delicate, tender ▷*slender* ② *adj.* small, little, meagre, trifling, trivial ★**significant** ③ *n. & v.* snub, insult, disdain

**slim** *adj.* fine, slight, thin ▷*slender* ★**fat**

**slime** *n.* mire, ooze, mud, filth

**sling** ① *v.* hurl, toss, throw ② *n.* loop, bandage, strap, support

**slink** *v.* prowl, creep, sidle, sneak ▷*skulk*

**slip** ① *v.* slide, slither, glide ② *v.* fall, lurch, drop, slip over ③ *v. & n.* blunder, slip up

**slippery** *adj.* ① smooth, glassy ② cunning, untrustworthy, tricky ▷*shifty* ★**trustworthy**

**slit** *v.* gash, cut, rip ▷*slash*

**slogan** *n.* motto, catchword, war cry, saying

**slope** ① *n.* slant, grade, gradient, incline, ascent, descent, rise ② *v.* lean, incline, descend, ascend

**sloppy** *adj.* ① careless, slipshod, inattentive ▷*slovenly* ② dowdy, messy, tacky ③ dingy, dirty ④ schmaltz, sentimental, slushy

**slot** *n.* recess, opening, hole, groove

**slovenly** *adj.* slipshod, careless, negligent, disorderly, sloppy, untidy, dowdy

**slow** ① *adj.* inactive, tardy, late, slack, leisurely ▷*sluggish* ★**fast** ② *v.* slow down, slacken, lose speed, relax ★**accelerate** SLOE

**sluggish** *adj.* slothful, lazy, inactive, languid, indolent, lifeless ▷*idle* ★**brisk**

**slumber** *v.* snooze, doze ▷*sleep* ★**awaken**

**sly** *adj.* cunning, tricky, furtive, sneaky, artful ▷*wily* ★**frank**

**smack** *v.* slap, strike, spank ▷*hit*

**small** *adj.* ① minute, tiny, slight, diminutive ▷*little* ★**large** ② trivial, petty, feeble, paltry, inferior

**smart** ① *adj.* alert, bright ▷*intelligent* ② *adj.* elegant, neat, spruce, dressy ★**dull** ③ *v.* sting, burn, throb ▷*ache*

**smash** *v.* break, hit, destroy, wreck, demolish, destroy, defeat, crush

**smear** *v.* plaster, daub, coat, varnish, cover, spread, smudge

**smell** *n.* aroma, fragrance, scent, perfume, stink, stench, odour, tang

**smile** *v.* grin, simper, smirk, beam ▷*laugh*

**smoke** ① *n.* vapour, mist, gas ② *v.* fume, reek, whiff, smoulder, vent

**smooth** ① *adj.* level, even, flat, plain, sleek ★**rough** ② *v.* flatten, level, press

**smother** *v.* choke, throttle, stifle, restrain

**smudge** *n. & v.* mark, smear, blur, stain, blight, daub

**smug** *adj.* self-satisfied, content, holier-than-thou, complacent, conceited

**smut** *n.* dirt, smudge, blot, spot, smear

**snack** *n.* lunch, repast, morsel, bite

**snag** *n.* catch, complication, drawback, hitch

**snap** *v.* ① break, crack, snip ② snarl, growl

**snare** ① *v.* trap, catch, seize, net ② *n.* trap, noose, pitfall

**snatch** *v.* seize, grab, clutch, grip, take, pluck, grasp

**sneak** ① *v.* slink, prowl, crouch ▷*skulk* ② *n.* wretch, coward, informer

**sneer** *v.* jeer, scoff, gibe, scorn, ridicule, taunt, deride

**sniff** *v.* smell, breathe in, inhale, scent

**snivel** *v.* weep, cry, blub, sniffle

**snobbish** *adj.* condescending, snooty, lofty, patronizing, stuck-up

**snoop** *v.* pry, eavesdrop, peep, peek, sneak

**snooze** *v.* doze, nap, slumber ▷*sleep*

**snub** *v.* slight, slur, spurn, cut ▷*humiliate*

**snug** *adj.* cosy, sheltered, secure, safe,

restful, close-fitting ▷ *comfortable*

**so** *adv.* accordingly, thus, therefore, likewise
SEW, SOW

**soak** *v.* moisten, wet, douse, saturate, steep

**soar** *v.* glide, fly, rise, hover, tower SORE

**sob** *v.* lament, cry, sigh ▷ *weep*

**sober** *adj.* temperate, abstemious *Uncle
Arthur was very abstemious and never
drank anything alcoholic,* calm, composed,
serious, sombre ★**excited**

**sociable** *adj.* companionable, affable,
friendly, genial ★**withdrawn**

**social** *adj.* neighbourly, civic, public
② convivial ▷ *sociable*

**soft** *adj.* ① pliable, plastic, flexible, supple
★**hard** ② kind, gentle, mild ▷ *tender*
★**harsh** ③ low, faint, quiet ★**loud**

**soften** *v.* ① melt, dissolve, mellow
★**solidify** ② moderate, diminish, quell

**soil** ① *n.* earth, dirt, mould, clay, loam ② *v.*
foul, dirty, sully, taint

**sole** *adj.* only, single, lone, one SOUL

**solemn** *adj.* ① grim, serious ▷ *sombre*
② impressive, stately, sedate ★**frivolous**

**solid** *adj.* ① steady, firm, stable, sturdy
② dense, compact, hard ★**soft**

**solidify** *v.* congeal, harden, clot, cake, set
★**soften**

**solitary** *adj.* alone, lonely, remote, separate,
only

**solution** *n.* ① blend, mixture, brew, fluid
② answer, explanation, key

**solve** *v.* unravel, untangle, elucidate
▷ *explain* ★**complicate**

**sombre** *adj.* dark, serious, solemn, grim,
gloomy, funereal ★**bright**

**some** *adj.* any, more or less, about, several
SUM

**sometimes** *adv.* at times, from time to time,
occasionally

**somewhat** *adv.* in part, a little, not much

**song** *n.* air, tune, carol, ballad, ode, ditty
*The new pop song was based on an old
sailors' ditty*

**soon** *adv.* presently, shortly, before long

**soothe** *v.* pacify, appease, mollify, ease, lull,
comfort ★**irritate**

Soar

Sore

**sordid** *adj.* shabby, miserable, dirty, base,
sleazy, tawdry ▷ *squalid*

**sore** ① *adj.* tender, aching, painful, inflamed
② *adj.* annoyed, upset, grieved
③ *n.* ulcer, boil, carbuncle SOAR

**sorrow** ① *n.* grief, woe, remorse, anguish
★**joy** ② *v.* mourn, grieve, lament ★**rejoice**

**sorrowful** *adj.* sad, disconsolate, mournful,
dejected ★**joyful**

**sorry** *adj.* ① pained, grieved, hurt, dejected,
doleful ★**glad** ② wretched, mean, poor,
shabby ★**delighted**

**sort** ① *n.* kind, type, variety, group, class
② *v.* sift, arrange, catalogue, classify

**soul** *n.* spirit, substance, mind, vitality, fire,
essence SOLE

**sound** ① *n.* noise, din, tone ★**silence** ② *v.*
blare, blast *We were startled by a blast
from the trumpets,* blow ③ *adj.* hearty,
virile, whole, perfect ▷ *healthy* ★**unfit**

**sour** *adj.* ① tart, rancid, bitter, acid ★**sweet**
② morose, peevish ▷ *harsh* ★**genial**

**source** *n.* origin, spring, fount, cause,
beginning, wellhead

**souvenir** *n.* token, memento, keepsake,
reminder, relic

**sow** ① *n.* (rhymes with *how*) female pig ② *v.*
(rhymes with *mow*) *v.* plant, scatter, strew
SEW, SO

**space** *n.* ① extent, expanse, capacity, room,
accommodation ② the universe, the
heavens, firmament

**spacious** *adj.* roomy, extensive,
commodious, broad, wide ★**restricted**

**span** ① *n.* stretch, reach, extent, length ② *v.*

cross, bridge, link, connect, traverse

**spare** ① *adj.* extra, reserve, surplus ② *adj.* bare, meagre poor, scanty ▷*sparse* ③ *v.* afford, preserve, give, allow

**sparkle** *v.* glitter, glow, gleam, glint, twinkle

**sparse** *adj.* scanty, thin ▷*meagre* ★**dense**

**spate** *n.* flood, flow, deluge, rush, torrent

**speak** *v.* say, utter, talk, pronounce, lecture, express, articulate, enunciate

**spear** *n.* pike, javelin, lance

**special** *adj.* distinct, different, unique, individual ▷*particular* ★**common**

**species** *n.* breed, kind, sort, class, family

**specific** *adj.* definite, exact, precise ▷*special*

**specimen** *n.* sample, example, type, model, pattern

**speck** *n.* dot, speckle, spot, particle

**spectacle** *n.* sight, scene, exhibition, pageant, presentation ▷*display*

**spectacles** *n.* glasses, eyeglasses

**spectacular** *adj.* wonderful, fabulous, surprising ▷*marvellous*

**spectator** *n.* onlooker, witness, observer

**speech** *n.* ① talk, tongue *The people spoke a strange tongue we had never heard,* language ② address, lecture

**speed** *n.* velocity, rapidity, dispatch, pace, tempo *The tempo of life in the quiet seaside town was much too slow for us*

**speedy** *adj.* swift, rapid, fleet, quick, lively ▷*fast* ★**slow**

**spell** ① *n.* charm, magic, witchcraft ② *n.* period, term, space, time ③ *v.* form words, write out

**spend** *v.* ① expend, lay out, lavish, pay, disburse ② exhaust, use up

**spendthrift** *n.* wastrel, squanderer, prodigal ★**miser**

**sphere** *n.* ① globe, ball, orb, planet ② realm, orbit, domain, field, province

**spice** *n.* seasoning, flavouring, zest, relish, savour

**spill** *v.* pour, stream, run, overflow, spurt, upset, overturn, shed

**spin** *v.* revolve, rotate, turn, whirl, make thread, pirouette

**spine** *n.* backbone, needle, quill *The porcupine is covered in sharp quills,* ridge

**spirit** *n.* ① essence, substance, nature, character ② soul, air, breath ③ vigour, energy, courage ④ phantom, spectre, ghost

**spiritual** *adj.* ① religious, divine, unworldly, holy ② pure, immaterial

**spite** ① *n.* malice, rancour, hostility, hatred ② *v.* grudge, annoy, offend, injure

**spiteful** *adj.* vicious, malicious, vindictive ▷*hateful* ★**kind**

**splash** *v.* wet, spatter, shower, sprinkle

**splendid** *adj.* grand, brilliant, magnificent, showy, glorious ▷*sumptuous* ★**ordinary**

**splendour** *n.* glory, pageantry, brilliance, show, magnificence ▷*pomp*

**split** *v.* cleave, sever *Our family quarrelled with our cousins and severed relationships for years,* crack, snap, splinter

**spoil** *v.* ① hurt, injure, harm ② deface, disfigure, destroy ③ rot, decompose, decay

**spoiled** *adj.* decayed, rotten, broken up, corroded

**spontaneous** *adj.* natural, impulsive, self-generated, voluntary

**spoof** *n.* ① hoax, joke, bluff, prank, satire ② quip, jest, wisecrack

**sport** ① *n.* game, amusement, fun, athletics, recreation ② *v.* play, frolic, gambol, romp

**Spices**

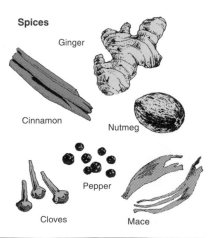

Ginger

Cinnamon

Nutmeg

Pepper

Cloves

Mace

**spot** ① *n.* dot, speck, mark, stain, blemish ② *v.* espy, notice, recognize, distinguish

**spotless** *adj.* pure, clean, unstained, faultless, perfect, immaculate

**sprawl** *v.* recline, stretch, extend, lie ▷*lounge*

**spray** *v.* sprinkle, squirt, splash, shower

**spread** *v.* ① scatter, strew, sow, circulate ② extend, stretch, expand, open

**sprightly** *adj.* lively, vivacious, cheerful, agile ▷*brisk* ★**sluggish**

**spur** *v.* arouse, drive, urge, incite, encourage

**spurious** *adj.* fake, counterfeit, false ▷*bogus* ★**genuine**

**spurn** *v.* reject, scorn, disdain, disregard ▷*snub* ★**respect**

**spurt** *v.* ① stream, squirt, emerge, gush ② hurry, hasten, rush

**spy** ① *n.* agent, detective, observer, snooper, scout ② *v.* see, glimpse, pry, peek, spot

**squabble** ① *n. & v.* quarrel, clash, fight, row ▷*dispute*

**squad** *n.* group, company, troop, force, band, team

**squalid** *adj.* foul, dirty, untended, poverty-stricken ▷*sordid* ★**clean**

**squall** ① *n.* blast, gust, blow, tempest ② *v.* blubber, cry, bawl, howl

**squander** *v.* misspend, waste, fritter, lavish

**squash** *v.* ① mash, crush, squelch, pound ② quell, suppress, humiliate

**squat** ① *adj.* dumpy, stocky, tubby, plump ② *v.* crouch, sit, roost, perch

**squeal** *v.* squawk, squeak, cheep, grunt, cry

**squeamish** *adj.* fastidious, delicate, finicky, nauseous

**squeeze** *v.* compress, press, constrict, force, pinch, clasp, cuddle

**squirm** *v.* wriggle, fidget, twist, flounder ▷*writhe*

**squirt** *v.* spray, splash ▷*spurt*

**stab** *v. & n.* cut, jab, puncture, wound, thrust

**stable** ① *adj.* firm, steady, solid, constant, durable, lasting ★**unstable** ② *n.* barn, cowshed, shed, stall

**stack** ① *n.* pile, pack, bundle, sheaf, heap ② *v.* assemble, pile up, amass, hoard

**staff** *n.* ① stick, cane, pole, rod ② team, workers, force, personnel, crew

**stage** ① *n.* platform, dais, scaffold, podium *The famous conductor stood on the podium and raised his baton,* arena ② *n.* step, degree, position ③ *v.* perform, produce, present, put on

**stagger** *v.* reel, totter, waver, lurch

**stagnant** *adj.* motionless, inactive, still, quiet, sluggish

**staid** *adj.* serious, steady, earnest, sober, demure ▷*sedate* ★**frivolous** STAYED

**stain** ① *n.* blemish, blur, spot, blot ② *n.* disgrace, shame ③ *v.* tarnish, sully, defile, blemish

**stair** *n.* step, rung, spoke, footrest STARE

**stake** ① *n.* stick, stave, paling, spike, pole ▷*staff* ② *n.* bet, claim, wager, involvement ③ *v.* prop, secure, support STEAK

**stale** *adj.* ① musty, old, tasteless, faded ② common, trite, banal, flat ★**fresh**

**stalk** *v.* hunt, chase, follow, pursue, shadow, tail, haunt, track

**stall** ① *v.* tarry, delay, hedge, obstruct, hamper ★**advance** ② *n.* compartment, booth, stand, bay

**stalwart** *adj.* rugged, sturdy, stout, lusty ▷*valiant* ★**timid**

**stamina** *n.* endurance, vitality, strength, power, energy ★**weakness**

**stammer** *v.* stutter, falter, hesitate, stumble

**stamp** ① *v.* print, imprint, mark, impress ② *n.* impression, mark, print, brand ③ *n.* kind, make, genus, cast ④ *n.* seal, sticker

**stand** ① *n.* board, counter, table, platform ▷*stall* ② *v.* rest, put, locate, place ③ *v.* tolerate, put up with, abide, endure ★**oppose** ④ *v.* arise, get up, be erect ★**sit**

**standard** ① *adj.* normal, regular, uniform ② *n.* pattern, criterion, norm ③ *n.* flag, banner, ensign

**staple** *adj.* main, principal, important, leading, key, chief

**stare** *v.* gaze, gape, look, peer STAIR

**stark** *adj.* severe, plain, downright, bare, absolute

**start** ① *v.* commence, begin, found, initiate

② *v.* depart, set out, leave ③ *v.* startle, jump, wince ④ *n.* beginning, commencement ⑤ *n.* shock, scare, fit

**startle** *v.* frighten, alarm, scare, surprise ▷*start*

**starve** *v.* be hungry, famish, want

**state** ① *n.* condition, situation, position ② *n.* country, nation, commonwealth ③ *v.* declare, say, express, utter ▷*speak*

**stately** *adj.* imposing, grand, dignified ▷*magnificent* ★**commonplace**

**statement** *n.* ① declaration, utterance, remark, motto ② bill, account, invoice

**station** ① *n.* post, spot, site, position, terminal ② *v.* park, place, put, establish *We got there early to establish our place in the queue* post, garrison

**stationary** *adj.* still, unmoving, standing, fixed, motionless ★**mobile** STATIONERY

**stationery** *n.* paper, envelopes, ink, pens, pencils STATIONARY

**statue** *n.* carving, bust, figure, effigy

**staunch** *adj.* constant, faithful, true, firm, reliable, dependable ▷*loyal* ★**unfaithful**

**stay** ① *v.* endure, last, remain, stand, linger ② *v.* check, curb, prevent ③ *n.* halt, wait, pause ▷*stop*

**steady** ① *adj.* firm, fixed, established, constant ▷*staunch* ★**uncertain** ② *v.* brace, stabilize, stiffen

**steal** *v.* ① thieve, pilfer, filch, swipe ▷*rob* ② slink, flit, creep ▷*prowl* STEEL

**stealthy** *adj.* furtive, sneaky, sly, secret ▷*underhanded* ★**open**

**steep** ① *adj.* sheer, sharp, hilly, precipitous ② *v.* bathe, soak, souse, submerge

**steer** *v.* guide, direct, pilot, control

**stem** ① *n.* stalk, shoot, stock, trunk ② *v.* arise from, flow from ③ *v.* check, restrain

**step** ① *n.* pace, tread, stride, gait ② *n.* action, method, deed ③ *v.* walk, skip, trip, pace STEPPE

**sterile** *adj.* ① barren, unfertile, arid ② sanitary, disinfected, antiseptic

**stern** ① *adj.* strict, severe, harsh, grim ▷*austere* ★**mild** ② *n.* aft end, rear, poop *The name of the ship was displayed in large letters on the poop*

**stew** *v.* ① cook, simmer, boil ② worry, fuss

**stick** ① *n.* stave, pole, rod, cane, staff ② *v.* adhere, cling, cleave, glue, paste, seal

**sticky** *adj.* gluey, gummy, adhesive

**stick out** *v.* project, bulge, protrude, extrude ▷*jut* ★**recede**

**stiff** *adj.* ① inflexible, firm, stable, unyielding ▷*rigid* ★**flexible** ② formal, stilted, prim, precise ★**yielding**

**stifle** *v.* suffocate, throttle, gag, muzzle ▷*smother*

**stigma** *n.* ① blot, blur, scar ▷*blemish* ② disgrace, dishonour ▷*shame* ★**credit**

**still** ① *adj.* fixed, stable, static ② *adj.* calm, quiet, serene, tranquil, noiseless, hushed ▷*peaceful* ★**agitated** ③ *v.* quiet, hush, muffle ▷*calm* ★**agitate**

**stimulate** *v.* inspire, provoke, arouse, motivate ▷*excite* ★**discourage**

**sting** *v.* prick, wound, pain, hurt, injure

**stingy** *adj.* miserly, tight-fisted, selfish,

**Stationery**

**Stationary**

niggardly, mean ▷*tight* ★**generous**

**stink** *v.* smell, whiff, reek

**stint** ① *n.* job, task, chore ② *n.* turn, spell, share, quota ③ *v.* limit, stop, scrimp, restrict ★**squander**

**stir** ① *v.* move, excite, spur, agitate ▷*stimulate* ② *v.* whisk, mix, blend ③ *v.* waken, arouse ★**calm** ④ *n.* flurry, fuss, uproar

**stock** ① *adj.* standard, regular, established, normal ② *n.* reserve, hoard, supply ③ *v.* provide, supply, equip, hoard

**stocky** *adj.* thickset, chunky, sturdy, pudgy ▷*squat* ★**willowy**

**stodgy** *adj.* dull, heavy, tedious, boring

**stolid** *adj.* stupid, dull, mindless, unintelligent ▷*stodgy* ★**quick**

**stoop** *v.* bend, crouch, kneel, bow

**stop** ① *v.* cease, desist, end, terminate, halt ★**start** ② *v.* prevent, forestall, avoid ③ *v.* arrest, hold, fix ④ *n.* pause, end, cessation *A cessation of hostilities came into force after the peace agreement*

**store** ① *v.* put by, reserve, hoard, save ★**use** ② *n.* stock, supply, reserve ③ *n.* market, shop, emporium

**story** *n.* ① yarn, tale, narrative, account, anecdote ② untruth, lie, fib ③ floor,

**storey** *n.* floor, landing, level, flight deck

**storm** ① *n.* tempest, gale, cyclone, hurricane, tornado ★**calm** ② *n.* turmoil, upheaval, attack ③ *v.* rage, rant, fume, attack

**stout** *adj.* ① sturdy, tough, robust ▷*strong* ★**weak** ② fat, corpulent ▷*plump* ★**thin**

**stow** *v.* deposit, store ▷*pack*

**straight** *adj.* ① right, undeviating, unswerving ▷*direct* ② frank, candid, truthful ▷*honest* ★**crooked** STRAIT

**straightforward** *adj.* open, outspoken, reliable, trustworthy ★**devious**

**strain** ① *n.* tension, fatigue, exertion ▷*stress* ★**relaxation** ② *n.* melody, tune, air ③ *v.* struggle, labour ▷*toil* ★**relax** ④ *v.* wrench, injure ⑤ *v.* filter, sift, separate

**strait** *n.* channel, sound, narrows STRAIGHT

**strait-laced** *adj.* prim, prudish, strict, puritanical *My family was rather puritanical and we were not allowed to play any games on Sundays*

**strand** ① *n.* coast, beach, shore ② *n.* hair, fibre, tress, lock ③ *v.* desert, maroon, abandon

**strange** *adj.* ① unusual, incredible, extraordinary, curious ▷*odd* ★**commonplace** ② foreign, alien, remote

**stranger** *n.* outsider, foreigner, visitor, newcomer ▷*alien* ★**acquaintance**

**strangle** *v.* constrict, choke, garrote, throttle

**strap** *n.* belt, harness, thong, leash

**stray** *v.* ① wander, deviate, depart, rove ② sin, err, do wrong

**streak** *n.* stroke, stripe, band, line, bar, strip

**stream** ① *n.* current, course, drift, brook, creek, run ② *v.* flow, gush, spurt, pour

**strength** *n.* ① power, force, might ▷*energy* ② boldness, nerve, intensity ★**weakness**

**strenuous** *adj.* laborious, resolute, determined ▷*earnest* ★**weak**

**stress** ① *n.* tension, force, effort ▷*strain* ② *n.* accent, emphasis ③ *v.* emphasize, accentuate, highlight

**stretch** *v.* expand, reach, lengthen, elongate ▷*extend* ★**shorten**

**strict** *adj.* ① severe, rigorous, rigid, austere ▷*stern* ★**lenient** ② scrupulous, thorough, punctilious, accurate ▷*precise* ★**inaccurate**

**stride** *n. & v.* walk, step, tread, march

**strife** *n.* struggle, contest, quarrel, friction ▷*conflict* ★**peace**

**strike** ① *v.* beat, smite, collide, knock ▷*thump* ② *v.* discover, unearth ③ *n.* assault, thrust, attack ④ *n.* walkout, boycott

**striking** *adj.* eye-catching, wonderful ▷*extraordinary* ★**commonplace**

**strip** ① *v.* take off, peel, skin, shave, remove ② *n.* ribbon, stroke, streak, line

**stripe** *n.* streak, band, bar, chevron *Soldiers in the army have chevrons on their sleeves to indicate their rank,* rule ▷*strip*

**strive** *v.* endeavour, attempt, aim, compete, contend, struggle ▷*try* ★**yield**

**stroke** ① *n.* shock, blow, knock, thump ② *n.* seizure, fit, convulsion ③ *v.* pat, rub, caress, smooth, comfort

**stroll** *v. & n.* walk, promenade, saunter, tramp, ramble

**strong** *adj.* ① powerful, vigorous, hardy, muscular ▷*robust* ② solid, secure, fortified ★**weak** ③ potent, hot, spicy ▷*pungent*

**structure** *n.* ① building, edifice, erection ② construction, organization, composition

**struggle** ① *v.* endeavour, labour, battle, wrestle ★**yield** ② *n.* conflict, battle ▷*fight* ③ *n.* distress, trouble ▷*effort*

**strut** ① *n.* support, mainstay, prop ② *v.* parade, prance, swagger

**stubborn** *adj.* ① dogged, persistent, tenacious ② pig-headed, perverse, wilful ▷*obstinate* ★**docile**

**stuck-up** *adj.* vain, conceited ▷*snobbish* ★**modest**

**studious** *adj.* scholarly, learned, thoughtful ▷*diligent* ★**thoughtless**

**study** ① *v.* read, peruse, scrutinize, examine, train ▷*learn* ② *n.* learning, meditation, thought, contemplation ▷*research*

**Structures**

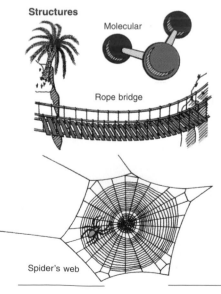

Molecular

Rope bridge

Spider's web

**stuff** ① *v.* fill, congest, pack, crowd ② *n.* textile, fabric, material, goods

**stumble** *v.* ① stagger, lurch, fall ▷*trip* ② stammer, falter ▷*stutter*

**stump** ① *v.* perplex, mystify, confuse ▷*bewilder* ② *n.* stub, tip, log, root

**stun** *v.* knock out, overpower, stupefy, dumbfound ▷*confound*

**stunt** *n.* deed, feat, achievement, deed, act, performance ▷*exploit*

**stupefy** *v.* daze, muddle, bewilder, astonish, flabbergast ▷*shock* ★**revive**

**stupendous** *adj.* astounding, amazing, overwhelming ▷*wonderful* ★**ordinary**

**stupid** *adj.* simple, stolid, dull, senseless ▷*foolish* ★**clever**

**stupidity** *n.* inanity, silliness, feebleness, foolishness ★**brilliance**

**sturdy** *adj.* rugged, stalwart, tough, robust, well-built, durable, strapping ▷*hardy* ★**weak**

**stutter** *v.* stumble, falter ▷*stammer*

**style** ① *n.* mode, vogue, fashion, way, manner, form ② *v.* name, call, christen STILE

**suave** *adj.* agreeable, elegant, polite, pleasant, sophisticated *After living in the city for many years, my sister had developed very sophisticated tastes*

**subdue** *v.* suppress, soften, tame, tone down, moderate, mellow ▷*repress*

**subject** ① *n.* (*sub*-ject) matter, topic, theme ② *n.* subordinate, dependant ③ *adj.* dependent, subordinate, liable ④ *v.* (sub-*ject*) rule over, subdue, subjugate

**submerge** *v.* plunge, immerse, sink ★**raise**

**submissive** *adj.* yielding, servile, meek ▷*obedient* ★**obstinate**

**submit** *v.* ① yield, give in, accede, surrender, hand over ② offer, tender, present

**subordinate** *adj.* junior, minor, subject, dependent, secondary ★**superior**

**subscribe** *v.* sign, enrol, register, agree, assent

**subsequent** *adj.* later, following, succeeding, after ★**former**

**subside** *v.* decline, peter out, decrease, diminish, wane, recede, ease *I used to go*

*mountaineering but my interest waned after
some years* ▷ *abate* ★**rise**

**substance** *n.* ① matter, object, stuff,
material ② essence, kernel, meaning ▷ *gist*

**substantial** *adj.* ① steady, sturdy, firm
▷ *stable* ② ample, large, real, solid
★**imaginary**

**substitute** ① *n.* alternative, makeshift,
stopgap ② *v.* swap, change, replace,
duplicate, exchange, switch

**subtle** *adj.* ① shrewd, fine, delicate
② clever, crafty, perceptive

**subtract** *v.* take away, withdraw, deduct,
remove ★**add**

**succeed** *v.* ① flourish, prosper, thrive,
triumph ★**fail** ② follow, inherit, replace
★**precede**

**success** *n.* prosperity, triumph, victory,
achievement ★**failure**

**successful** *adj.* victorious, prosperous,
fortunate, thriving ★**unlucky**

**suck** *v.* inhale, take in, draw in, imbibe

**sudden** *adj.* unexpected, abrupt, impulsive,
swift, prompt ★**gradual**

**suffer** *v.* ① bear, endure, put up with
② encounter, undergo ▷ *sustain*

**sufficient** *adj.* adequate, ample, plenty
▷ *enough* ★**deficient**

**suffocate** *v.* smother, choke ▷ *stifle*

**suggest** *v.* recommend, advise, submit, hint,
intimate, propose

**suit** ① *v.* fulfil, gratify, please, suffice,
accommodate, befit ② *n.* ensemble, outfit,
costume

**suitable** *adj.* fitting, appropriate, correct,
proper, becoming ★**unsuitable**

**suite** (*sweet*) *n.* ① set, series, succession
② apartment, rooms

**sulk** *v.* pout, grouch, brood, mope

**sulky** *adj.* glum, morose, churlish, moody
▷ *sullen* ★**genial**

**sullen** *adj.* gloomy, heavy, dismal, cheerless
▷ *sulky* ★**cheerful**

**sum** *n.* amount, total, whole, entirety SOME

**summary** *n.* synopsis, précis, abstract,
summing-up, outline, analysis

**summit** *n.* peak, pinnacle, top, apex, zenith,
acme, culmination ★**base**

**summon** *v.* call, beckon, command, invite,
muster ★**dismiss**

**sumptuous** *adj.* profuse, costly, gorgeous,
splendid ▷ *lavish* ★**frugal**

**sundry** *adj.* different, separate, several,
diverse, assorted ▷ *various*

**sunny** *adj.* bright, cheerful, light, clear
▷ *radiant* ★**gloomy**

**superb** *adj.* magnificent, stately, gorgeous
▷ *grand* ★**commonplace**

**supercilious** *adj.* contemptuous, haughty,
arrogant ▷ *snobbish* ★**modest**

**superficial** *adj.* slight, imperfect, shallow,
skin-deep ▷ *trivial* ★**profound**

**superfluous** *adj.* in excess, inessential,
extra, spare ▷ *surplus* ★**essential**

**superior** *adj.* ① better, greater, higher,
loftier ▷ *excellent* ② eminent, conspicuous,
principal ★**inferior**

**supersede** *v.* succeed, replace, displace,
suspend, usurp *The president's authority
was usurped by the military* ★**continue**

**supervise** *v.* superintend, control, manage,
run, administer, handle ▷ *direct*

**supple** *adj.* lithe, pliable, flexible, bending

**supplement** ① *n.* addition, complement,
sequel, postscript ② *v.* supply, add, fill

**supply** ① *v.* provide, furnish, yield,
contribute, purvey ★**retain** ② *n.* hoard,
reserve ▷ *stock*

**support** ① *v.* uphold, bear, sustain,
maintain, help ▷ *favour* ★**oppose** ② *v.*
hold up, prop, strut, brace ③ *v.* endure,
tolerate, suffer ④ *n.* maintenance, upkeep

**suppose** *v.* assume, presume, believe,
imagine, imply ▷ *consider*

**suppress** *v.* restrain, extinguish, destroy,
stop ▷ *quell* ★**incite**

**supreme** *adj.* dominant, highest, greatest,
maximum ★**lowly**

**sure** *adj.* ① certain, positive, definite
② secure, steady, safe ③ permanent,
abiding, enduring ★**uncertain**

**surface** *n.* ① area, expanse, stretch
② outside, exterior, covering, façade,
veneer ★**interior**

**surge** ① v. swell, rise, heave, rush ② n. ripple, billow, wave SERGE

**surly** adj. morose, cross, testy, touchy, crusty ▷*sullen* ★**affable**

**surmise** v. guess, speculate, conjecture, suspect ▷*presume* ★**know**

**surpass** v. eclipse, outdo, outstrip, excel, exceed ▷*beat*

**surplus** n. excess, remainder, balance, residue ★**shortcoming**

**surprise** ① v. startle, astonish, amaze ▷*astound* ② n. amazement, astonishment ▷*wonder*

**surrender** v. quit, give up, yield, submit ▷*relinquish*

**surround** v. enclose, encircle, encompass

**survey** ① v. (sur-*vey*) look at, examine, scrutinize ▷*study* ② v. estimate, measure ③ n. (*sur*-vey) assessment, appraisal

**survive** v. live, exist, continue, outlast, abide

**susceptible** adj. sensitive, impressionable, inclined, capable ★**insensitive**

**suspect** ① v. (sus-*pect*) disbelieve, doubt, distrust ② adj. (*sus*-pect) unbelievable, questionable, dubious, iffy

**suspend** v. ① interrupt, delay, adjourn, postpone, arrest ▷*stop* ★**continue** ② swing, dangle ▷*hang* ★**drop**

**suspense** n. anticipation, waiting, abeyance *The club couldn't decide on a new leader, so the matter was left in abeyance,* stoppage, uncertainty ▷*tension* ★**decision**

**suspicious** adj. incredulous, sceptical, doubtful, suspecting ★**trustful**

**sustain** v. ① uphold, keep, maintain, provide for ② suffer, undergo, experience ③ nourish, nurture, feed

**swagger** v. ① parade, prance, arrogance ▷*strut* ② brag, bluster ▷*boast*

**swallow** ① v. absorb, consume, eat, digest, devour, knock back, drink, ▷*gulp* ② n. mouthful, gulp ③ n. bird

**swamp** ① n. fen, bog, marsh, morass, quagmire ② v. submerge, submerse, overflow, deluge ▷*drench*

**swap** v. exchange, switch, trade, barter

**swarm** ① n. throng, horde, shoal, flock, crowd ② v. teem, abound, jam, mass, crowd, cluster

**swarthy** adj. dusky, dark, brown, tawny

**sway** ① v. swing, rock, totter, lean, incline ▷*waver* ② n. rule, authority, control ▷*influence*

**swear** v. ① promise, warrant, affirm, attest ② curse, damn, blaspheme

**sweat** v. perspire, ooze, leak, exude, swelter *During that time of the year it was very hot and we sweltered all day*

**sweep** v. brush, scrub, clean, scour

**sweet** adj. ① sugary, syrupy, luscious ★**sour** ② melodic, tuneful, musical, mellow ★**discordant** ③ gentle, tender, mild, lovable ★**unpleasant** ④ fragrant, pure, clean, fresh, wholesome, aromatic ★**putrid**

**swell** v. expand, distend, inflate, bulge ▷*enlarge* ★**contract**

**swerve** v. veer, deviate, skid, skew, lurch ▷*waver*

**swift** adj. speedy, rapid, quick ▷*fast* ★**slow**

**swill** ① v. swig, consume, imbibe, tipple ▷*gulp* ② n. refuse, garbage, waste

**swim** v. bathe, wade, paddle, float, glide

**swindle** ① n. trick, fraud, blackmail, racket ② v. hoodwink, deceive, hoax, dupe, fleece, rip off, bamboozle ▷*cheat*

**swine** n. pig, boar, sow, porker, hog

**swing** ① v. hang, suspend, dangle, lurch, reel ② n. tempo, time

**switch** ① v. change, exchange, alter, trade, substitute, swap ② n. lever, pedal, control

**swivel** v. pivot, spin, rotate, revolve, turn

**swoop** v. pounce, descend, stoop, plummet, plunge

**sword** n. rapier, blade, foil, épée, cutlass, sabre, steel SOARED

**symbol** n. character, figure, numeral, letter, sign, token, emblem CYMBAL

**sympathetic** adj. thoughtful, understanding, kind, affectionate ★**indifferent**

**synopsis** n. outline, summary, résumé, digest, review

**system** n. ① method, plan, order, scheme, arrangement, routine ② network, organization: *a hierarchical system*

# T t

**table** *n.* ① board, stand, slab, tablet, counter, stall ② list, catalogue, schedule, index, statement

**tablet** *n.* ① pill, capsule, lozenge ② board, table, pad

**tack** ① *n.* drawing-pin, thumbtack, nail, pin, brad ② *n.* aim, direction, set ③ *v.* affix, fasten, join, stitch

**tackle** ① *n.* outfit, gear, rig, harness ② *v.* grasp, halt, intercept, seize ③ *v.* deal with *I dealt with the problem of the school fund shortage,* undertake, set about

**tact** *n.* diplomacy, judgement, skill, discretion *If you want your secret to be kept, you had better not rely on his discretion* TACKED

**tactful** *adj.* diplomatic, wise, subtle, prudent ▷*discreet* ★**tactless**

**tactics** *n.* strategy, campaign, method, procedure

**tactless** *adj.* inconsiderate, gauche, clumsy, boorish ▷*inept* ★**tactful**

**tag** *n.* label, ticket, docket, slip, sticker

**taint** *v.* sully, tarnish, infect, stain, soil, contaminate ▷*defile* ★**purify**

**take** *v.* ① grasp, grab, seize, procure ② receive, accept, obtain ③ carry, convey, lead, conduct ④ interpret, understand

**take place** *v.* occur, happen, befall *Our parents were concerned about what might befall us when we left school*

**tale** *n.* story, fable, anecdote, yarn, narrative TAIL

**talent** *n.* knack, genius, gift, ability, aptitude ★**stupidity**

**talk** ① *v.* speak, say, utter, gossip ② *v.* describe, comment on, talk about ③ *n.* speech, chatter, conversation ④ *n.* lecture, speech, discourse

**tall** *adj.* lanky, lofty, big, high, towering, giant ★**short**

**tally** *v.* ① count, enumerate, compute ② agree, conform, coincide ★**disagree**

**tame** ① *adj.* domesticated, gentle, mild, docile *Although we found it in the woods, the kitten was docile* ★**savage** ② *adj.* flat, dull, boring, tedious ③ *v.* train, discipline, domesticate

**Tame**

*Although we found it in the woods, the kitten was docile*

**tamper with** *v.* meddle, interfere, damage, tinker, fiddle

**tang** *n.* smell, scent, aroma, flavour, savour, taste, smack

**tangible** *adj.* concrete, solid, substantial, real, material ★**spiritual**

**tangle** *n. & v.* twist, muddle, jumble, knot

**tantalize** *v.* tease, taunt, thwart, disappoint ▷*frustrate* ★**satisfy**

**tantrum** *n.* rage, fit, hysterics, storm

**tap** ① *v.* pat, hit, knock, rap, strike ② *n.* spout, cock, nozzle, bung, faucet

**tape** *n.* ribbon, filament, braid, strip, riband

**taper** *v.* dwindle, narrow, contract, decline, wane, narrow ★**widen** TAPIR

**tardy** *adj.* slow, sluggish, reluctant, slack ▷*late* ★**prompt**

**target** *n.* goal, aim, ambition, purpose, butt, end, victim, prey

**tariff** *n.* tax, rate, toll, duty, payment, price list, levy

**tarnish** *v.* stain, sully *Mark's reputation at school was sullied after he was accused of stealing,* spot, darken, blemish, rust ★**brighten**

**tarry** *v.* delay, stall, wait, loiter ▷*linger* ★**hurry**

**tart** ① *adj.* acid, sour, sharp, pungent ② *n.* pie, quiche, pastry, flan

**task** *n.* job, stint, chore, assignment, undertaking

**taste** ① *n.* bite, mouthful, flavour, savour, tang ② *v.* try, sip, sample, relish

**tasteful** *adj.* artistic, graceful, elegant, smart ▷*refined* ★**tasteless**

**tasteless** *adj.* ① flavourless, insipid ② gaudy, inelegant ▷*vulgar* ★**tasteful**

**tasty** *adj.* appetizing, piquant, savoury ▷*delicious* ★**disgusting**

**tattle** *v.* gossip, tittle-tattle, blab, prattle

**taunt** *v.* jibe, reproach, rebuke, ridicule, scoff at ▷*sneer* ★**compliment**

**taut** *adj.* tense, tight, stretched ▷*rigid* ★**relaxed** TAUGHT

**tawdry** *adj.* flashy, loud, gaudy, showy ▷*vulgar* ★**superior**

**tax** ① *n.* levy, duty, impost, tithe, toll ② *v.* load, oppress, overburden TACKS

**teach** *v.* instruct, educate, tutor, coach, guide, train, drill

**teacher** *n.* educator, professor, lecturer, schoolmaster, schoolmistress, coach, tutor

**team** *n.* party, group, gang, crew, company TEEM

**tear** *v.* ① rip, rend, tatter, shred ② dash, bolt, rush, sprint TARE

**tearful** *adj.* weepy, moist, wet, sobbing, sad

**tease** *v.* annoy, harass, vex, irritate, torment ▷*tantalize* ★**soothe** TEAS, TEES

**tedious** *adj.* wearisome, tiresome, irksome, exhausting ▷*boring* ★**fascinating**

**teem** *v.* abound, swarm, overflow, increase, be full ★**lack** TEAM

**tell** *v.* ① disclose, speak, state, talk, utter ② discern, discover, distinguish

**temper** ① *n.* temperament, disposition, nature, humour ② *n.* anger, annoyance, passion ③ *v.* moderate, soften, weaken, restrain, soothe, assuage

**temporary** *adj.* short, limited, impermanent, brief ★**permanent**

**tempt** *v.* entice, invite, attract, persuade ▷*lure* ★**deter**

**tenacious** *adj.* ① stubborn, firm, obstinate, unwavering ★**weak** ② adhesive, glutinous

**tenant** *n.* occupant, householder, occupier

**tend** *v.* ① take care of, manage, serve, guard, nurse, cultivate, nurture, attend ★**neglect**

② affect, lean, incline, verge ★**diverge**

**tendency** *n.* disposition, leaning, inclination, bent ★**aversion**

**tender** ① *adj.* delicate, soft ▷*fragile* ② *adj.* mild, kind, sympathetic ▷*gentle* ③ *adj.* raw, painful, sore ④ *v.* proffer *Charlotte proffered her services as a babysitter,* present, volunteer, bid

**tense** *adj.* tight, strained, taut, nervous, edgy ★**relaxed** TENTS

**tension** *n.* strain, stress, rigidity, suspense, worry ★**relaxation**

**term** ① *n.* expression, denomination, title, phrase ② *n.* time, season, spell *We stayed in Hong Kong for a spell during our trip to the Far East,* duration ③ *v.* entitle, call, dub

**terminate** *v.* cease, stop, end, conclude ▷*finish* ★**begin**

**terrible** *adj.* frightful, terrifying, fearful, dreadful ▷*horrible* ★**superb**

**terrify** *v.* petrify, shock, appal, alarm ▷*frighten* ★**reassure**

**territory** *n.* region, area, expanse, dominion, land ▷*country*

**terror** *n.* alarm, panic, horror, dismay ▷*fright* ★**confidence**

**terse** *adj.* brief, concise, short, pithy, abrupt ▷*curt* ★**long-winded**

**test** ① *n.* examination, trial, check, proof, experiment ② *v.* examine, try out, check, quiz, analyse

**testy** *adj.* irritable, bad-tempered, touchy, peevish ▷*cross* ★**genial**

**tether** *n.* rope, cord, lead, leash, chain

**text** *n.* contents, reading, passage, clause

**thanks** *n.* gratitude, credit, appreciation

**thaw** *v.* ① melt, fuse, liquefy, soften ★**freeze** ② unbend, relax

**theft** *n.* robbery, fraud, larceny, plundering

**theme** *n.* subject, text matter, topic

**theory** *n.* idea, supposition, concept, hypothesis, surmise, speculation

**therefore** *adv.* consequently, hence, accordingly, thus

**thick** *adj.* ① dense, solid, bulky, compact ② stiff, set, congealed ③ viscous, gummy, stodgy ★**thin**

**thief** *n.* crook, robber, burglar, bandit, pirate

**thin** *adj.* ① slender, slim, slight, lean, skinny ★**fat** ② wafer-like, delicate, flimsy ③ watery, dilute, unsubstantial ★**thick**

**thing** *n.* article, object, something, being, substance

**think** *v.* ① ponder, consider ▷*reflect* ② conceive, imagine ▷*fancy* ③ surmise, conclude ▷*reckon*

**thirsty** *adj.* parched, dry, craving, burning

**thorn** *n.* barb, prickle, bramble, thistle

**thorough** *adj.* outright, absolute, complete, utter ★**haphazard**

**though** *conj.* although, even though, notwithstanding, however, yet

**thought** *n.* reflection, consideration, study, concept, deduction

**thoughtful** *adj.* ① pensive, studious, contemplative ② considerate, kind, heedful, careful ★**thoughtless**

**thoughtless** *adj.* heedless, careless, rash, neglectful ▷*indiscreet* ★**thoughtful**

**thrash** *v.* ① whip, flog, hit ② stir, pitch *The sea was rough – each wave pitched the small boat closer to the rocks,* toss

**thread** *n.* filament, twist, yarn, fibre

**threadbare** *adj.* ① shabby, ragged, worn ② commonplace, hackneyed, stale ★**fresh**

**threaten** *v.* intimidate, bully, blackmail ▷*menace* ★**reassure**

**Thrash**

*The sea was rough – each wave pitched the small boat closer to the rocks.*

**thrifty** *adj.* frugal, careful, economical, saving, sparing ★**wasteful**

**thrilling** *adj.* exciting, gripping, stimulating

**thrive** *v.* prosper, flourish, succeed, grow, increase ★**decline**

**throb** ① *n.* tick, beat, palpitation ② *v.* beat, palpitate, vibrate

**throng** ① *n.* crowd, horde, mob ② *v.* pack, crowd, swarm, fill

**throttle** *v.* choke, smother, gag ▷*strangle*

**through** *prep.* by way of, by means of, as a result of

**throw** *v.* fling, cast, hurl, project, propel, thrust ★**keep** THROE

**thrust** *v. & n.* push, project, drive, force, prod, jab, lunge

**thug** *n.* hoodlum, bandit, assassin, mugger, ruffian, tough, hooligan

**thump** *v. & n.* beat, hit, knock, bang, wallop

**thunderstruck** *adj.* open-mouthed, amazed, astounded, staggered

**thus** *adv.* accordingly, so, therefore, consequently

**thwart** *v.* frustrate, balk, baffle, hinder, obstruct ★**assist**

**ticket** *n.* pass, label, card, coupon, token

**tickle** *v.* ① caress, stroke, pat, brush ② titillate, convulse, amuse ③ delight, gratify

**tide** *n.* stream, current, drift, ebb, flow TIED

**tidings** *n.* information, intelligence, report, advice ▷*news*

**tidy** *adj.* ① neat, well-kept, spruce, orderly ② ample, large, substantial, sizable

**tie** ① *v.* join, attach, secure *Be sure to secure the gate so the dogs can't get out,* unite ▷*fasten* ② *n.* cravat, necktie, bow tie ③ *n.* bond, connection ④ deadheat, stalemate

**tight** *adj.* ① fast, close, compact, tense ▷*taut* ★**loose** ② miserly, tightfisted, mean ▷*stingy* ★**generous**

**tighten** *v.* strain, tauten, constrict, cramp, crush ▷*squeeze* ★**loosen**

**till** ① *prep.* until, up to, as far as ② *v.* plough, cultivate, tend ③ *n.* cash-drawer, cash-register

**tilt** *v. & n.* slant, slope, incline, lean, list, tip

**time** *n.* ① period, duration, season, age, era, term, span ② metre, measure, tempo, rhythm THYME

**timid** *adj.* fearful, afraid, timorous, diffident, modest ▷*shy* ★**bold**

**tinge** *v.* & *n.* colour, tincture, tint, stain, shade

**tingle** *v.* thrill, throb, tickle, vibrate

**tinker** *v.* meddle, fiddle *Bill fiddled with the old clock for ages, trying to make it work,* patch up, potter, trifle

**tinkle** *v.* jingle, jangle, ring, clink

**tint** *n.* dye, hue, tinge, shade ▷*colour*

**tiny** *adj.* small, diminutive, puny, wee ▷*little* ★**huge**

**tip** ① *n.* apex, peak, point, extremity ▷*top* ② *n.* gratuity, gift, donation, reward ③ *n.* information, hint, tip-off ④ *v.* list, lean, tilt ▷*slope*

**tipsy** *adj.* inebriated, drunk, drunken

**tire** *v.* exhaust, bore, fatigue, harass, weaken

**tiresome** *adj.* wearisome, tedious, boring ▷*humdrum* ★**interesting**

**titbit** *n.* delicacy, morsel, dainty, snack, treat, scrap

**title** *n.* ① name, denomination, term, style, designation ② claim, interest *When my father died, I was left an interest in his business,* ownership

**toady** *v.* fawn, crawl, grovel, crouch, cringe

**toast** ① *n.* pledge, compliment, salutation ② *v.* brown, roast, heat

**together** *adv.* collectively, jointly, as one, simultaneously, at the same time, collectively ★**separately**

**toil** ① *v.* & *n.* struggle, labour, travail ▷*work* ★**relaxation**

**token** *n.* memento, keepsake, symbol, omen ▷*souvenir*

**tolerable** *adj.* endurable, supportable, bearable, passable ★**unbearable**

**tolerant** *adj.* forbearing, indulgent *Sally's parents are very indulgent with her and buy her whatever she wants,* liberal, easy-going ▷*lenient* ★**intolerant**

**tolerate** *v.* accept, bear with, put up with, endure, suffer ▷*allow* ★**resist**

**toll** ① *v.* ring, strike, chime, clang ② *n.* charge, duty, tax, levy

**tone** *n.* ① pitch, loudness, noise, note ② emphasis, accent, inflection ③ temper, manner, attitude ④ colour, cast, hue, shade

**too** *adv.* ① also, as well, besides ② extremely, very, unduly

**tool** *n.* ① implement, utensil, machine, agent ② pawn, puppet, cat's-paw, stooge TULLE

**top** *n.* ① summit, pinnacle, peak ② lid, cover, stopper, cap ③ upper surface ★**bottom** ④ *n.* spinning toy ⑤ *adj.* highest, topmost, best, uppermost *After climbing for four days, we reached the uppermost part of the range*

**topic** *n.* subject, motif, question ▷*theme*

**topical** *adj.* contemporary, popular, up-to-date, current

**topple** *v.* collapse, founder, overturn, totter ▷*fall*

**topsy-turvy** *adj.* upside-down, overturned, confused, chaotic

**torment** *v.* & *n.* pain, distress, plague ▷*torture* ★**ease**

**torrent** *n.* flood, stream, cascade, cataract, waterfall ★**trickle**

**torture** *v.* agonize, rack, anguish ▷*torment*

**toss** *v.* fling, hurl, pitch, cast, project, heave ▷*throw*

**total** ① *n.* aggregate, whole, sum, completion ② *v.* add, tot up, reckon ③ *adj.* complete, entire

**totally** *adv.* completely, absolutely, entirely, utterly ★**partially**

**touch** ① *v.* feel, finger, fondle, handle, stroke ② *v.* move, affect, concern ③ *v.* beat, hit, collide with ④ *v.* adjoin *Our house is situated at a spot where three counties adjoin,* meet, border ⑤ *n.* tinge, hint, suspicion

**touchy** *adj.* peevish, petulant, snappish ▷*moody* ★**genial**

**tough** ① *adj.* hard, strong, vigorous, rugged, sturdy ② *adj.* arduous, difficult ③ *n.* hooligan, bruiser, bully

**tour** *n.* trip, journey, jaunt, excursion, voyage, ride, visit

## Titles

admiral
ambassador
archbishop
baron baroness
brigadier
cardinal
chancellor colonel
commodore
constable count
countess czar
czarina
dame deacon
dean don doña
duchess duke
earl emir emperor
general governor
graf
infanta
kaiser khan king
knight
lady laird lama
lieutenant lord
madame
maharajah
maharani
major mandarin

marchioness
margrave marshal
master mayor
mikado miss
mogul monsieur
monsignor
pasha pope priest
prince
princess provost
queen
rabbi regent
senator señor
señora señorita
sergeant signor
signora signorina
shah sheik shogun
sheriff sir sultan
sultana
taoiseach
vicar viceroy
viscount viscountess

**Toys**

Wheeled toy
ancient Egypt

Top and whip
1700s

Electronic game
1900s

Doll
1800s

**tournament** *n.* contest, championship, competition ▷*match*

**tow** *v.* haul, drag, tug, haul, heave ▷*pull* TOE

**tower** ① *v.* soar, dominate, surmount ② *n.* turret, spire, belfry

**toy** ① *n.* plaything, doll, game ② *v.* play, tinker, fiddle, twiddle

**trace** ① *v.* trail, track, follow, pursue, discover ② *v.* sketch, draw, copy ③ *n.* trail, track, spoor ④ *n.* drop, speck, vestige

**track** *v.* search out, follow ▷*trace*

**tract** *n.* ① area, space, extent, plot ② booklet, leaflet, pamphlet TRACKED

**trade** ① *v.* barter, exchange, buy, sell, patronize ② *n.* occupation, work, livelihood, business

**tradition** *n.* custom, convention, practice

**traffic** ① *n.* business, barter ▷*trade* ② transport, vehicles, movement

**tragedy** *n.* catastrophe, disaster, adversity ▷*calamity* ★**comedy**

**tragic** *adj.* disastrous, catastrophic, miserable, wretched ▷*deplorable* ★**comic**

**trail** *n.* spoor, track ▷*trace*

**train** ① *v.* teach, educate, instruct, drill, school ② *n.* chain, procession, series

**traitor** *n.* rebel, mutineer, renegade, quisling, betrayer

**tramp** ① *n.* vagabond, wanderer, vagrant, dosser, hobo ▷*beggar* ② *n.* jaunt, stroll, ramble ③ *v.* roam, rove, range, walk, travel

**trample** *v.* tread on, walk on, flatten ▷*crush*

**tranquil** *adj.* peaceful, placid, serene, restful ▷*calm* ★**restless**

**transaction** *n.* business, performance, dealing, negotiation, proceeding

**transfer** *v.* move *My sister is being moved to the head office after her promotion*, displace, change ▷*exchange*

**transmit** *v.* dispatch, forward, relay ▷*send* ★**receive**

**transparent** *adj.* clear, lucid, crystal, diaphanous, see-through, evident

**transport** ① *v.* carry, convey, conduct, transfer ▷*move* ② *n.* transportation

**trap** ① *v.* ensnare, catch, net ② *n.* snare, pitfall, noose, decoy ▷*ambush*

**trash** *n.* junk, debris, rubble, garbage ▷*rubbish* ★**treasure**

**travel** ① *v.* & *n.* trek, voyage, cruise ▷*journey*

**treacherous** *adj.* ① traitorous, unfaithful, false, deceptive ▷*disloyal* ★**faithful**

**tread** *v.* ① dangerous, risky, precarious, tricky ★**reliable** ② step, walk, tramp, march, go ③ stride, gait, walk, step

**treason** *n.* treachery, betrayal, sedition

**treasure** ① *n.* hoard, fortune, riches, wealth ② *v.* appreciate, esteem ▷*value*

**treat** ① *v.* deal with, handle, manage, serve ② *v.* regale, entertain ③ *v.* doctor, attend ④ *n.* banquet, entertainment, fun

**treaty** *n.* agreement, covenant, alliance

**tremble** *v.* quake, quaver, shudder, flutter ▷*shake*

**tremendous** *adj.* ① immense, enormous ▷*huge* ② terrible, dreadful, awful

**tremor** *n.* quiver, shake, flutter, ripple ▷*vibration*

**trench** *n.* ditch, moat, trough, gully, gutter

**trend** *n.* tendency, inclination, direction

**trespass** ① *v.* infringe, overstep, intrude ② *n.* offence, sin, transgression

**trial** *n.* ① endeavour, testing, experiment ② ordeal, grief, suffering ③ essay, proof ④ hearing, lawsuit

**tribe** *n.* clan, family, race, group, set

**tribute** *n.* ① ovation, compliment, praise ② dues, toll, tithe, tax

**trick** ① *n.* fraud, artifice, wile, cheat, deception ② *n.* jape, prank, frolic ③ *n.* juggling, stage magic, conjuring ④ *v.* deceive, defraud

**trickle** *v.* leak, ooze, seep, drip, drop, dribble

**trifle** ① *n.* bauble, plaything, foolishness, nonsense ② *v.* dabble, idle, play with

**trifling** *adj.* paltry, petty, worthless, slight ▷*trivial* ★**important**

**trim** ① *v.* prune, clip, shorten, crop ② *v.* ornament, smarten, decorate ③ *adj.* tidy, neat, orderly ★**scruffy**

**trinket** *n.* bauble, bead, jewel, ornament, toy

**trip** *n.* ① journey, excursion, jaunt ▷*tour* ② *v.* stumble, fall, slip

**tripe** *n.* rubbish, trash, nonsense, twaddle *This is a silly story; I've never read such twaddle*

**trite** *adj.* hackneyed, ordinary, corny ▷*stale* ★**novel**

**triumph** *n.* victory, success, achievement ▷*conquest* ★**defeat**

**trivial** *adj.* trifling, common, unimportant, ordinary, useless ▷*trite* ★**important**

**troop** ① *n.* band, gang, group, pack, team, unit ② *v.* flock, crowd, swarm TROUPE

**trophy** *n.* prize, award, cup, souvenir

**trot** *v.* canter, jog, scamper, scurry

**trouble** ① *n.* disturbance, annoyance, calamity, misfortune ▷*misery* ② *v.* disturb, annoy, harass ▷*distress* ★**delight**

**true** *adj.* ① accurate, precise, factual, correct ★**inaccurate** ② faithful, loyal, constant ③ pure, real ▷*genuine* ★**false**

**trunk** *n.* ① body, torso, stem, stalk ② chest, case, box ③ proboscis *The tapir's proboscis is not as large as the elephant's trunk*, nose, snout

**trust** ① *n.* faith, confidence, belief ② *v.* believe in, credit, depend on ★**doubt** TRUSSED

**trustful** *adj.* trusting, innocent, naive ▷*gullible* ★**cautious**

**trustworthy** *adj.* dependable, credible, honourable ▷*reliable* ★**unreliable**

**truth** *n.* ① reality, fact, precision ▷*accuracy* ★**falsehood** ② integrity, faith, honour ▷*fidelity* ★**deceit**

**truthful** *adj.* reliable, frank, open, candid, straight ▷*honest* ★**false**

**try** ① *v.* endeavour, attempt ▷*strive* ② *v.* examine, try out ▷*test* ★**abandon** ③ *n.* trial, attempt, effort

**trying** *adj.* bothersome, annoying, irritating, troublesome ▷*irksome*

**tub** *n.* basin, bowl, pot, barrel, keg, tun

**tube** *n.* pipe, spout, duct, hose, shaft

**tuck** *v.* insert, stuff, fold, pack, pleat, hem

**tug** *v.* drag, tow, haul, heave ▷*pull* ★**push**

**tumble** *v.* drop, descend, trip, topple, stumble ▷*fall*

**tumult** *n.* noise, rumpus, racket, uproar, disturbance, disorder ★**peace**

**tune** *n.* melody, harmony, air, strain ▷*song*

**tunnel** *n.* subway, shaft, passage, gallery

**turn** ① *v.* spin, revolve, whirl ▷*rotate* ② *v.* bend, curve ▷*twist* ③ *v.* change, alter ▷*convert* ④ *v.* spoil ▷*sour* ⑤ *n.* stint, spell, chance ⑥ *n.* rotation, cycle, gyration ▷*revolution* TERN

**twaddle** *n.* balderdash, nonsense, drivel, rigmarole, piffle ▷*bunkum* ★**sense**

**twinge** *n.* pain, pang, spasm, gripe ▷*ache*

**twinkle** *v.* glitter, gleam, glisten, glimmer ▷*sparkle*

**twist** *v.* ① bend, curve, turn ② warp, contort, writhe ③ wind, intertwine *The octopus intertwined its legs around the large clam*

**twitch** *v.* jerk, jump, jiggle, blink, flutter

**type** ① *n.* kind, sort, character, description ② *n.* prototype, model, pattern ③ *n.* letter, symbol ④ *v.* typewrite, keyboard

**typical** *adj.* characteristic, symbolic, regular, stock, representative ★**abnormal**

**tyrant** *n.* despot, autocrat, dictator, martinet

# U u

**ugly** *adj.* unsightly, ungainly, frightful, ghastly, hideous, horrid, nasty ★**beautiful**

**ultimate** *adj.* furthest, farthest, most distant, extreme, eventual ▷*final*

**umpire** *n.* referee, judge, mediator

**unabashed** *adj.* brazen, unconcerned, undaunted ▷*composed* ★**sheepish**

**unable** *adj.* helpless, incapable, powerless ★**able**

**unaccustomed** *adj.* inexperienced, unfamiliar ▷*strange* ★**familiar**

**unaffected** *adj.* natural, sincere, true, artless ▷*naive* ★**impressed**

**unafraid** *adj.* courageous, dauntless, intrepid ▷*fearless* ★**afraid**

**unanimous** *adj.* harmonious, consenting, agreeing ▷*united*

**unassuming** *adj.* diffident, reserved, quiet, simple ▷*modest* ★**forward**

**unattached** *adj.* single, free, loose ▷*separate* ★**committed**

**unattended** *adj.* alone, unwatched, ignored ▷*abandoned* ★**escorted**

**unavoidable** *adj.* inevitable, irresistible, certain ▷*necessary* ★**uncertain**

**unaware** *adj.* ignorant, unheeding, unknowing, forgetful ▷*oblivious* ★**aware**

**unbalanced** *adj.* ① top-heavy, lopsided, uneven ② insane, unhinged *He seems to have become unhinged ever since he lost his job,* crazy, eccentric

**unbearable** *adj.* unacceptable, intolerable ▷*outrageous* ★**acceptable**

**unbiased** *adj.* impartial, fair, just ▷*neutral* ★**prejudiced**

**uncanny** *adj.* weird, ghostly, unearthly, creepy ▷*eerie*

**uncertain** *adj.* doubtful, vague, chancy, indefinite ▷*dubious* ★**certain**

**uncivilized** *adj.* primitive, barbaric, coarse, gross ▷*vulgar* ★**civilized**

**uncomfortable** *adj.* awkward, embarrassed, cramped, self-conscious ★**comfortable**

**uncommon** *adj.* rare, scarce, infrequent, extraordinary ▷*unusual* ★**common**

**unconscious** *adj.* ① ignorant, unheeding ▷*unaware* ② insensible, senseless, stunned ★**conscious**

**unconventional** *adj.* unorthodox, peculiar *I have my own peculiar way of looking at things,* individualistic ▷*eccentric* ★**conventional**

**uncouth** *adj.* crude, coarse, clumsy, vulgar ▷*boorish* ★**polite**

**uncover** *v.* expose, discover, show, divulge ▷*reveal* ★**conceal**

**under** ① *adv.* underneath, below, beneath ② *prep.* less than, lower than, subject to

**undergo** *v.* endure, tolerate, bear, suffer ▷*sustain*

**underground** *adj.* secret, private, hidden, subversive

**underhand** *adj.* stealthy, undercover, deceitful ▷*sneaky* ★**honest**

**underneath** *adj.* beneath, under ▷*below* ★**above**

**underrate** *v.* undervalue, understate, disparage, belittle ★**exaggerate**

**understand** *v.* comprehend, appreciate, grasp, sympathize, take in, follow ▷*realize* ★**misunderstand**

**understudy** *n.* stand-in, deputy, substitute, reserve, replacement

**undertake** *v.* attempt, commence, contract, embark on ▷*tackle*

**undesirable** *adj.* objectionable, distasteful ▷*unpleasant* ★**desirable**

**undignified** *adj.* improper, inelegant, clumsy ▷*unseemly* ★**graceful**

**undo** *v.* unfasten, disentangle, unravel, free ▷*release* ★**fasten**

**undress** *v.* disrobe, strip, remove, take off ▷*divest* ★**dress**

**unearthly** *adj.* eerie, uncanny, supernatural ▷*ghostly*

**uneasy** *adj.* uncomfortable, restive, self-conscious, edgy ★**calm**

**unemployed** *adj.* unoccupied, redundant, out of work

**uneven** *adj.* irregular, rough, bumpy,

lopsided, unequal ★**even**

**unexpected** *adj.* abrupt, impulsive, chance, surprising ▷*sudden* ★**normal**

**unfair** *adj.* prejudiced, one-sided, partial, unjust ★**fair**

**unfaithful** *adj.* faithless, untrue, dishonest ▷*false* ★**faithful**

**unfamiliar** *adj.* alien, obscure, fantastic, bizarre ▷*strange* ★**familiar**

**unfasten** *v.* release, open, unlatch, untie ▷*undo* ★**fasten**

**unfinished** *adj.* incomplete, imperfect, lacking, crude ★**finished**

**unfit** *adj.* unqualified, unsuitable, incapable, unsuited ★**suitable**

**unfold** *adj.* open, expand, develop, reveal, disclose, unwrap ★**withhold**

**unforeseen** *adj.* surprising, sudden, accidental ▷*unexpected* ★**predictable**

**unforgettable** *adj.* memorable, impressive, noteworthy, exceptional

**unfortunate** *adj.* deplorable, lamentable, adverse, hapless ▷*unlucky* ★**fortunate**

**unfriendly** *adj.* antagonistic, surly, cold ▷*hostile* ★**friendly**

**ungainly** *adj.* gawky, awkward, graceless, unwieldly ▷*clumsy* ★**graceful**

**ungrateful** *adj.* thankless, selfish, ungracious, ill-mannered ★**grateful**

**unhappiness** *n.* depression, misery, sadness

**unhappy** *adj.* miserable, dismal, luckless *Try as he might, the luckless Tom was almost last in the race,* melancholy ▷*sad* ★**happy**

**unhealthy** *adj.* ① unwholesome, harmful ② sick, ill, diseased ★**healthy**

**uniform** ① *n.* regalia, livery *It was a very grand affair, with the footmen in full livery,* costume, dress ② *adj.* stable, steady, unchanging, level ★**varied**

**unimportant** *adj.* puny, trivial, insignificant ▷*petty* ★**important**

**unintentional** *adj.* inadvertent, involuntary, unwitting ▷*accidental* ★**deliberate**

**union** *n.* ① alliance, association, league ② agreement, accord, harmony ③ fusion, blend, compound

**unique** *adj.* original, exceptional, exclusive,

single, sole ★**commonplace**

**unit** *n.* entity, single, one, individual

**unite** *v.* join, combine, connect, merge, blend, fuse ★**separate**

**united** *adj.* joined, combined, undivided ▷*unanimous* ★**separated**

**unity** *n.* union, harmony, uniformity, agreement ★**disagreement**

**universal** *adj.* general, all-embracing, entire, worldwide *Our company has products that are sold worldwide*

**unjust** *adj.* partial, prejudiced, unfair, wrong ▷*biased* ★**just**

**unkempt** *adj.* dishevelled, shabby, sloppy, slovenly, ungroomed ▷*scruffy* ★**neat**

**unkind** *adj.* inhuman, heartless, brutal, callous ▷*cruel* ★**kind**

**unknown** *adj.* hidden, mysterious, undiscovered, dark ★**familiar**

**unless** *conj.* if not, except when

**unlike** *adj.* unrelated, dissimilar, distinct ▷*different* ★**similar**

**unlikely** *adj.* rare, improbable, doubtful, incredible, unheard of ▷*dubious* ★**likely**

**unlucky** *adj.* unfortunate, luckless, ill-fated, unhappy ★**lucky**

**unnatural** *adj.* ① artificial, stilted, strained

### Uniform

*It was a very grand affair, with the footmen in full livery.*

② inhuman, cruel ▷*heartless* ★**natural**
**unnecessary** *adj.* non-essential, excess, superfluous ▷*needless* ★**necessary**
**unoccupied** *adj.* ① uninhabited, empty, deserted ▷*vacant* ② idle, spare ▷*unemployed* ★**occupied**
**unpleasant** *adj.* disagreeable, displeasing, objectionable ▷*offensive* ★**pleasant**
**unpopular** *adj.* obnoxious *I was glad to leave the party, for I had been forced to talk to some obnoxious people,* detested, shunned, rejected ▷*disliked* ★**popular**
**unqualified** *adj.* ① unable, incompetent, inadequate ▷*unfit* ② complete, thorough, absolute
**unreal** *adj.* imaginary, fictional, artificial, false, fanciful ★**real** UNREEL
**unreasonable** *adj.* ① extravagant, excessive, extreme ★**moderate** ② far-fetched, absurd, foolish ★**rational**
**unreliable** *adj.* untrustworthy, undependable, irresponsible ▷*fickle* ★**reliable**
**unrest** *n.* ① defiance, disquiet, protest, rebellion ② anxiety, distress, worry ★**calm**
**unrestricted** *adj.* unrestrained, unlimited, open, free, unhindered ★**limited**
**unripe** *adj.* green, immature, callow *I was just a callow youth in those days, but I hope I have learned something since then,* unseasoned, unready ★**ripe**
**unrivalled** *adj.* inimitable, unequalled, matchless, peerless ★**inferior**
**unruly** *adj.* disorderly, troublesome, restive ▷*rowdy* ★**orderly**
**unseemly** *adj.* incorrect, indecent, improper, unbecoming, shocking ★**seemly**
**unselfish** *adj.* generous, liberal, charitable, hospitable ▷*kind* ★**selfish**
**unstable** *adj.* unsteady, shaky, inconstant, fickle, volatile ★**stable**
**unsuitable** *adj.* improper, unacceptable, unfitting, inconsistent ★**suitable**
**untidy** *adj.* bedraggled, disorderly, muddled, messy ▷*slovenly* ★**tidy**
**untie** *v.* unfasten, unravel, free, release ▷*undo* ★**tie**

**until** *prep.* till, as far as, up to
**untimely** *adj.* inopportune, ill-timed, premature ★**opportune**
**unusual** *adj.* strange, queer, exceptional, quaint, curious ▷*odd* ★**normal**
**unwilling** *adj.* averse, disinclined, grudging, opposed ▷*reluctant* ★**willing**
**upheaval** *n.* disturbance, disruption, overthrow, turmoil, shake-up
**uphold** *v.* sustain, keep up, endorse ▷*support*
**upkeep** *n.* maintenance, care, conservation, support, expenses ★**neglect**
**upper** *adj.* higher, superior, elevated, uppermost ★**lower**
**upright** *adj.* ① sheer, steep, perpendicular ★**horizontal** ② honourable *Josephine was one of the most honourable people I ever met,* ethical, virtuous ★**dishonest**
**uproar** *n.* hubbub, noise, disorder, tumult, turmoil ▷*clamour*
**upset** ① *v.* bother, perturb, unsettle, annoy ② *v.* overthrow, overturn, topple ③ *adj.* disturbed, confused, worried
**upside-down** *adj.* ① overturned, upturned ② chaotic, muddled, jumbled
**urge** ① *v.* goad, plead, spur, beseech ★**deter** ② *n.* encouragement, compulsion ▷*impulse*
**urgent** *adj.* important, earnest, intense, vital ★**trivial**
**use** ① *v.* employ, practise, apply ② *v.* consume, exhaust, deplete, expend ③ *n.* usage, wear
**useful** *adj.* valuable, favourable, practical, beneficial ★**useless**
**useless** *adj.* trashy, paltry, futile *Trying to train a cat to fetch is a futile activity,* inefficient ▷*worthless* ★**useful**
**usual** *adj.* common, general, habitual, familiar ▷*normal* ★**exceptional**
**utensil** *n.* tool, implement, instrument, apparatus, device
**utilize** *v.* employ, apply, exploit ▷*use*
**utmost** *adj.* extreme, supreme, greatest, ultimate, last, distant
**utter** ① *adj.* thorough, absolute, complete ② *v.* declare, pronounce, speak ▷*say*
**utterly** *adv.* extremely, completely, entirely, fully, wholly

# V v

**vacant** *adj.* ① empty, unoccupied, exhausted ★**occupied** ② stupid, blank, expressionless, mindless

**vacation** *n.* holiday, rest, recess

**vagabond** *n.* vagrant, tramp, loafer, beggar, rover, hobo

**vague** *adj.* indefinite, imprecise, inexact, uncertain ▷*obscure* ★**certain**

**vain** *adj.* ① conceited, arrogant ▷*proud* ★**modest** ② fruitless, useless, worthless ▷*futile* VANE, VEIN

**valiant** *adj.* stout, valorous, worthy, gallant ▷*brave* ★**cowardly**

**valid** *adj.* genuine, authentic, official *No one is allowed into the meeting without an official pass,* proper

**valley** *n.* gorge, dale, dell, glen, vale

**valour** *n.* courage, fortitude, heroism, gallantry ▷*bravery* ★**cowardice**

**valuable** *adj.* ① costly, precious, priceless, expensive ★**worthless** ② meritorious *She was awarded the medal for meritorious service during the war,* righteous, worthy

**value** ① *n.* worth, benefit, merit, price ② *v.* appreciate, esteem, prize, treasure ③ *v.* appraise, assess, rate, estimate

**van** *n.* truck, vehicle, wagon, cart

**vandalize** *v.* damage, sabotage, harm, ruin

**vanish** *v.* ① disappear, fade, dissolve ★**appear** ② exit, depart, go

**vanity** *n.* pride, conceit, pretension, egotism ★**modesty**

**vanquish** *v.* conquer, defeat, overpower, subdue ▷*beat*

**vapour** *n.* steam, fog, mist, moisture, smoke

**variable** *adj.* changeable, fickle, unsteady, fitful, wavering ★**invariable**

**varied** *adj.* various, diverse *She was a woman of diverse interests,* miscellaneous, mixed, assorted ★**uniform**

**variety** *n.* ① assortment, array, mixture, medley *The singers entertained us with a medley of popular songs* ② sort, type,

## Vehicles

| | | |
|---|---|---|
| Ambulance | Rickshaw | Train |
| Automobile | Scooter | Trap |
| Bicycle | Sedan | Trolley bus |
| Bulldozer | Stagecoach | Truck |
| Bus | Surrey | |
| Cab | Tank | |
| Car | Taxi | |
| Cart | Tractor | |
| Chariot | Tram | |
| Coach | | |
| Fire engine | | |
| Go-cart | | |
| Hearse | | |
| Jeep | | |
| Limousine | | |
| Lorry | | |
| Motorcycle | | |

kind, class, category, species, breed, brand

**various** *adj.* mixed, different, many ▷*varied*

**vary** *v.* differ, alter, change, diversify, diverge

**vase** *n.* jug, jar, beaker ▷*pitcher*

**vast** *adj.* great, enormous, extensive, huge, wide ▷*immense* ★**narrow**

**vault** ① *n.* grave, mausoleum, cellar, crypt, dungeon ② *v.* jump, clear, bound, leap, hurdle, spring

**veer** *v.* swerve, skid, turn, tack, deviate, change, tack

**vehement** *adj.* impassioned, fiery, passionate, ardent, eager, zealous ▷*strong* ★**indifferent**

**vehicle** *n.* ① car, conveyance, automobile, carriage, cart ② agency, means, expedient

**veil** ① *n.* cloak, cover, wimple, curtain ② *v.* hide, conceal, shade, screen ★**expose** vale

**vein** *n.* ① seam, strain, streak, stripe, thread, course ② disposition, mood, style, phrasing VAIN

**velocity** *n.* rate, pace, tempo, rapidity, impetus *After I won the school prize, I had greater impetus to follow my studies* ▷*speed*

**venerable** *adj.* respectable, revered, august,

dignified, honoured, wise, grave ▷*sage*

**vengeance** *n.* reprisal, retaliation ▷*revenge*
★**pardon**

**venomous** *adj.* ① poisonous, toxic, vitriolic
② spiteful, malicious, hostile ▷*vindictive*

**vent** ① *v.* discharge, emit, express, let fly,
release ② *n.* aperture, duct, opening, outlet

**ventilate** *v.* ① aerate, cool, fan, blow ②
express, debate, discuss, examine

**venture** ① *n.* enterprise, undertaking,
endeavour ② *v.* risk, bet, hazard ▷*chance*

**verbal** *adj.* stated, said, expressed, spoken,
unwritten, word-of-mouth ★**written**

**verdict** *n.* decision, judgement, finding,
conclusion, opinion

**verge** ① *n.* border, brink, edge, boundary
② *v.* incline, tend, border, come close to

**verify** *v.* confirm, declare, authenticate,
corroborate *The witness corroborated the
story told by the defendant* ★**discredit**

**versatile** *adj.* adaptable, variable,
adjustable, handy ★**inflexible**

**verse** *n.* poem, rhyme, stave, canto, jingle,
doggerel *Call this stuff poetry? It's just
doggerel!*

**version** *n.* account, form, interpretation,
adaptation, type

**vertical** *adj.* upright, erect, sheer,
perpendicular, steep ★**horizontal**

**very** ① *adv.* extremely, exceedingly, greatly,
intensely, absolutely ② *adj.* exact, real,
true, actual, genuine

**vessel** *n.* ① bowl, pot, canister, container,
basin, jar ② craft, ship, boat

**vestige** *n.* remains, remnant, hint, glimmer,
residue, trace

**veteran** ① *n.* old-timer, master, old hand,
expert ★**novice** ② *adj.* experienced,
practised, adept ★**inexperienced**

**veto** ① *v.* ban, reject, prohibit, stop, forbid
★**approve** ② *n.* embargo *The United
Nations placed an embargo on the selling
of arms to the two countries,* prohibition,
disapproval ★**assent**

**vex** *v.* annoy, provoke, trouble, irritate,
harass ▷*displease* ★**soothe**

**vibrate** *v.* shake, quiver, oscillate, fluctuate,

throb, shudder, resonate ▷*tremble*

**vice** *n.* evil, failing, fault ▷*sin* ★**virtue**

**vicinity** *n.* area, environs, neighbourhood
▷*surroundings*

**vicious** *adj.* evil, sinful, malignant,
immoral, vile ▷*wicked* ★**virtuous**

**victim** *n.* sufferer, scapegoat, martyr, prey,
pawn, dupe

**victor** *n.* winner, conqueror, champion,
prize-winner ★**loser**

**victory** *n.* success, triumph, achievement
▷*conquest* ★**defeat**

**view** ① *n.* landscape, sight, panorama,
spectacle ② *n.* estimation, belief, theory,
opinion ③ *v.* watch, see, behold, witness

**vigilant** *adj.* attentive, wary, alert, guarded
▷*watchful* ★**lax**

**vigour** *n.* energy, vim, stamina, might, power
▷*strength* ★**weakness**

**vigorous** *adj.* forceful, energetic, powerful,
dynamic ▷*active* ★**weak**

**vile** *adj.* low, wretched, contemptible,
miserable, nasty, evil ▷*despicable*
★**noble**

**villain** *n.* blackguard, knave *You are nothing
but a knave who is out to steal my money,*
sinner, rascal ▷*rogue* ★**hero**

**vim** *n.* stamina, zip, strength ▷*vigour*

**vindicate** *v.* warrant, sustain, support,
defend, establish ▷*justify* ★**accuse**

**vindictive** *adj.* vengeful, unforgiving,
grudging, spiteful ▷*malicious* ★**merciful**

**violate** *v.* ① disobey, oppose, defy, resist,
infringe ★**obey** ② abuse, defile, outrage,
desecrate

**violent** *adj.* furious, rabid, rampant,
forcible, tempestuous ★**calm**

**virile** *adj.* manly, masculine, vigorous,
vibrant ▷*strong* ★**weak**

**virtually** *adv.* almost, nearly, practically,
substantially

**virtue** *n.* goodness, honesty, chastity, purity
▷*quality* ★**vice**

**virtuous** *adj.* chaste, innocent, honourable,
moral ▷*righteous* ★**wicked**

**visible** *adj.* perceptible, discernible,
apparent, exposed, obvious ★**invisible**

**vision** *n.* ① apparition, spectre, ghost, mirage ② concept, revelation, foresight

**visit** ① *n.* call, sojourn, stay, excursion ② *v.* call on, drop in, tarry, stay

**visitor** *n.* guest, company, tourist, caller

**visual** *adj.* seeable, observable, visible

**vital** *adj.* ① essential, indispensible, crucial ▷*necessary* ② alive, vibrant, virile, dynamic *Our team won a number of games after we had been trained by the new dynamic coach*, vivacious, energetic

**vitality** *n.* stamina, virility ▷*strength*

**vivacious** *adj.* lively, spirited, vital, animated, merry ▷*sprightly* ★**languid**

**vivid** *adj.* ① clear, bright ▷*brilliant* ② vigorous, strong, lucid ★**dull**

**vocal** *adj.* articulate, eloquent, spoken, strident, vociferous ★**quiet**

**vocation** *n.* occupation, calling, job, mission, career, pursuit

**vogue** *n.* style, fashion, mode, popularity

**voice** ① *n.* speech, articulation, utterance ② *n.* choice, preference, opinion ③ *v.* utter, express, proclaim, pronounce

**void** ① *adj.* bare, barren, empty ② *adj.* invalid, cancelled, useless ③ *n.* cavity, chasm, space, opening, nothingness

**volatile** *adj.* ① lively, changeable, fickle, giddy ② elusive, fleeting, evaporable

**volley** *n.* discharge, fusillade, barrage, shower

**volume** *n.* ① bulk, capacity, mass, quantity ▷*amount* ② loudness, amplitude ③ book, edition, tome

**voluntary** *adj.* free-willed, optional, intended, gratuitous ★**compulsory**

**vomit** *v.* spew, disgorge, puke, throw up

**vote** ① *n.* ballot, election, poll, referendum ② *v.* ballot, poll, choose, elect

**vow** ① *v.* promise, swear, assure, vouch, testify ② *n.* oath, pledge, promise

**voyage** *n.* journey, cruise, passage, trip

**vulgar** *adj.* ① common, coarse, crude, indelicate, rude ★**elegant** ② native, ordinary, common

**vulnerable** *adj.* unprotected, unguarded, exposed, defenceless, tender ★**strong**

# W w

**wad** *n.* bundle, chunk, block, plug

**waddle** *v.* wobble, totter, shuffle, toddle

**wag** ① *v.* waggle, shake ▷*vibrate* ② *n.* wit, humorist, joker

**wage** ① *n.* fee, pay, salary, remuneration ② *v.* carry out, fulfil, undertake

**wager** ① *v.* gamble, bet, speculate, chance, hazard ② *n.* pledge, stake, bet

**wagon** *n.* cart, truck, van ▷*vehicle*

**waif** *n.* orphan, stray, foundling *In the old days, children were abandoned in the streets, but some people set up homes for such foundlings*

**wail** ① *v.* deplore, weep, grieve, lament ▷*cry* ★**rejoice** ② *n.* lamentation, weeping, grief, moan, howl

**wait** *v.* ① expect, await, bide, stay, stop ▷*linger* ② attend, serve WEIGHT

**waive** *v.* relinquish, disclaim, disown, forego, defer ▷*renounce* WAVE

**wake** *v.* awaken, stimulate, excite ▷*arouse*

**wakeful** *adj.* ① restless, awake ② alert, wary, watchful

**walk** ① *v.* advance, march, step, progress, move ② *n.* stroll, hike ▷*ramble* ★**run** ③ *n.* lane, alley, way ④ *n.* sphere, field, career *I started my career in the field of journalism, but I later went into politics*

**wallow** *v.* ① flounder, stagger, tumble ② delight, enjoy, revel

**wan** *adj.* pale, ashen, feeble, sickly, pallid ▷*weak* ★**robust**

**wand** *n.* mace, baton, stick, sceptre, rod

**wander** *v.* stray, meander, roam, stroll, deviate, saunter

**wane** *v.* droop, decline, decrease, lessen, ebb *As the little boat neared the rocks, Fred's courage ebbed away*, sink ★**wax** WAIN

**wangle** *v.* fiddle, contrive, fix, arrange

**want** ① *v.* desire, covet, crave, need, require ② *n.* need, necessity, demand ③ *n.* dearth, deficiency ▷*scarcity* ★**plenty**

**wanton** *adj.* ① unscrupulous, irresponsible

② playful, frolicsome, wild ③ dissolute, immoral

**war** *n.* hostilities, fighting, bloodshed, enmity, strife, combal ★**peace** WORE

**ward** *n.* ① pupil, minor, charge ② district, quarter WARRED

**ward off** *v.* prevent, forestall, avoid, stop ▷*avert*

**wardrobe** *n.* ① locker, cupboard, closet ② outfit, clothes, apparel

**warm** ① *adj.* tepid, hot, lukewarm ② *adj.* sympathetic ▷*warmhearted* ③ *adj.* eager, hot, zealous ④ *v.* heat, bake, cook, prepare

**warn** *v.* caution, admonish, advise, alert, apprise WORN

**warning** *n.* caution, admonition, forewarning, alarm, tip

**warp** *v.* contort, bend, twist, kink, deform, distort ★**straighten**

**warrant** ① *v.* guarantee, certify, justify, permit, allow ② *n.* assurance, permit, licence, authority *She produced documents that showed her authority on the board of directors*

**wary** *adj.* cautious, alert, careful, heedful ▷*prudent* ★**rash**

**wash** ① *v.* bathe, scrub, rinse, cleanse, wet ② *n.* washing, cleaning

**waste** ① *n.* rubbish, debris, trash, garbage ② *v.* squander, spend, lavish, fritter ③ *v.* wither, decay, shrivel, perish WAIST

**wasteful** *adj.* lavish, prodigal, spendthrift ▷*extravagant* ★**economical**

**watch** ① *v.* note, observe, guard ★**ignore** ② *v.* inspect, look at, oversee ③ *n.* timepiece ④ *n.* guard, sentry, watchman

**watchful** *adj.* attentive, observant, vigilant ▷*wary* ★**inattentive**

**water** *v.* wet, bathe, wash, douse, drench, sprinkle, spray

**wave** ① *v.* brandish, flourish, waft, swing ② *n.* breaker, billow, undulation WAIVE

**waver** *v.* falter, hesitate, vacillate *There's no time to vacillate; make up your mind* ★**decide**

**wax** *v.* increase, rise, grow, expand, enlarge ★**wane**

**way** *n.* ① route, road, path, passage, track ② technique *The company introduced a new technique for making glass,* procedure, method, style WEIGH

**wayward** *adj.* contrary, perverse, obstinate ▷*stubborn* ★**docile**

**weak** *adj.* ① feeble, frail, puny, helpless, delicate ② foolish, soft, senseless, stupid ③ thin, watery, insipid ④ fragile, flimsy, tumbledown ★**strong** WEEK

**weaken** *v.* enfeeble, relax, sag, flag ▷*languish* ★**strengthen**

**weakness** *n.* defect, fault, frailty, flaw ★**strength**

**wealth** *n.* riches, luxury, prosperity, money, opulence ★**poverty**

**wealthy** *adj.* rich, affluent, prosperous, opulent ★**poor**

**wear** *v.* ① dress in, don ② rub, scrape, waste, consume ③ last, endure, remain WARE

**weary** ① *adj.* exhausted, tired, fatigued ★**fresh** ② *v.* exhaust, tire, bore ★**refresh**

**weather** *n.* climate, clime, conditions

**weave** *v.* braid, plait, unite, blend

**web** *n.* net, tissue, webbing, textile, netting

**wed** *v.* marry, join, link, splice, tie the knot

**wedge** ① *n.* block, chock, lump, chunk ② *v.* crowd, force, jam, push, thrust, squeeze

**wee** *adj.* little, small, minute ▷*tiny* ★**large**

**weep** *v.* blubber, snivel, sob, whimper *The lost puppy was found at last, whimpering in a corner* ▷*cry* ★**rejoice**

**weigh** *v.* balance, estimate, ponder, examine, consider WAY

**weight** *n.* ① load, pressure, burden, heaviness ② importance, onus, significance, gravity WAIT

**weighty** *adj.* heavy, hefty, ponderous, onerous ★**trivial**

**weird** *adj.* eerie, supernatural, unearthly, mysterious ▷*uncanny*

**welcome** ① *adj.* pleasing, desirable ▷*agreeable* ② *v.* greet, accost, hail, salute ③ *n.* greeting, salutation, acceptance

**welfare** *n.* well-being, comfort, happiness, benefit, advantage ★**harm**

**well** ① *adj.* robust, healthy, hearty, sound

## Weather Conditions

**Hot weather**
close drought heat-wave
hot humid muggy sultry
sweltering torrid tropical

**Cold weather**
arctic bitter blizzard
brisk chilly cold cold snap
cool freezing frost
glacial hail icy nippy subzero

**Overcast weather**
cloudy dark foggy
hazy misty
murky overcast
smoggy

**Windy weather**
blowy blustery
breeze draught
flurry gale
gusty hurricane tornado
turbulent windy

**Wet weather**
deluge
downpour
drizzle
mizzle
precipitation
rainy
showers
sleet slush
snowing
soaking

★**ill** ② *adv.* properly, suitable, adequately, accurately ★**badly** ③ *n.* fountain, spring

**well-off** *adj.* comfortable, prosperous ▷*wealthy* ★**poor**

**wet** *adj.* ① moist, damp, watery, drenched ② *adj.* drizzling, showery, raining ③ *v.* soak, moisten, dampen

**wheedle** *v.* coax, cajole, inveigle *We were inveigled into buying some of the local lace,* persuade ★**coerce**

**whet** *v.* ① sharpen, hone, strop ★**blunt** ② excite, stimulate, rouse ★**dampen**

**whim** *n.* fancy, humour, desire, urge, notion, impulse

**whine** *v.* ① howl, wail, whimper, moan ② complain, grouse, grumble, whinge

**whip** *v.* ① flog, lash, thrash, chastise, spank ② whisk, mix, blend

**whirl** *v.* pirouette, twirl, spin, rotate, revolve, whir, gyrate ▷*twist*

**whisk** *v.* beat, brush, hasten, hurry, sweep ▷*whip*

**whisper** ① *n.* murmur, hint, suggestion, breath ② *v.* breathe, murmur, divulge, buzz, intimate ★**shout**

**whistle** *n. & v.* cheep, chirp, warble, call

**whole** *adj.* ① all, entire, total, intact ② sound, complete, unbroken ★**part** HOLE

**wholesome** *adj.* healthful, nutritious, beneficial, sound, good ★**noxious**

**wicked** *adj.* infamous, corrupt, depraved, unrighteous, sinister, sinful ▷*evil* ★**virtuous**

**wickedness** *n.* corruption, depravity, iniquity, sinfulness, villainy ▷*evil*

**wide** *adj.* broad, ample, extended, spacious,

roomy, extensive, vast ★**narrow**

**widespread** *adj.* prevalent, far-flung, extensive, sweeping, universal *The use of a universal language would be of great help in the United Nations* ★**limited**

**wield** *v.* ① brandish, flourish, manipulate ② control, command, exert, maintain

**wild** *adj.* ① savage, ferocious, fierce, untamed ★**tame** ② violent, unrestrained, boisterous ★**civilized** ③ careless, insane, reckless ★**sane**

**wilderness** *n.* desert, jungle, wasteland, wilds, outback

**will** ① *n.* resolution, decision, zeal, accord ② *n.* order, wish, command, request, demand ③ *n.* legacy, testament ④ *v.* choose, desire, elect

**wilful** *adj.* temperamental, headstrong, deliberate ▷*obstinate* ★**docile**

**willing** *adj.* disposed, zealous, ready, earnest ▷*agreeable* ★**unwilling**

**wilt** *v.* wither, waste, sag, dwindle ▷*ebb*

**wily** *adj.* cunning, sly, tricky, deceitful ▷*crafty* ★**sincere**

**win** *v.* succeed, gain, get, acquire, procure ▷*triumph* ★**lose**

**wince** *v.* shrink, quail, flinch *My little sister didn't flinch once when she had her vaccination,* start ▷*cringe*

**wind** (rhymes with *pinned*) *n.* breeze, blast, gust, gale

**wind** (rhymes with *mind*) *v.* coil, turn, twist, bend WINED

**wink** *n.* & *v.* blink, flutter, flicker, glint

**winner** *n.* champion, master ▷*victor*

**wipe** *v.* clean, brush, mop, remove, swab

**wire** *n.* ① cable, telegraph, telegram ② cable, cord, flex

**wisdom** *n.* judgement, discretion, tact, thought, reason ★**folly**

**wise** *adj.* sensible, profound, astute, subtle, discreet ▷*sage* ★**foolish**

**wish** ① *v.* desire, crave, want, hanker for, long for ② *n.* command, will, desire, liking

**wistful** *adj.* ① pensive, musing, wishful ② forlorn, melancholy, soulful

**wit** *n.* ① fun, humour, levity, pleasantry, banter, ② brains, sense, judgement, intelligence ★**stupidity**

**witch** *n.* enchantress, sorceress, crone, hag

**withdraw** *v.* ① retire, retreat, depart, leave ▷*flee* ② extract, take out

**withdrawn** *adj.* unsociable, retiring, reclusive, aloof, solitary ★**sociable**

**wither** *v.* waste, fade, pine, languish, shrivel. wilt ▷*shrivel*

**withhold** *v.* retain, reserve, restrain, hold back ▷*keep* ★**grant**

**within** *adj.* inside, interior, inner

**withstand** *v.* resist, oppose, confront, stand up to ▷*defy* ★**support**

**witness** ① *n.* spectator, onlooker, bystander *One of the bystanders at the accident came forward to give evidence,* signatory ② *v.* behold, observe, see, attest

**witty** *adj.* funny, jocular, waggish, amusing ▷*comical* ★**dull**

**wizard** *n.* sorcerer, magician, conjurer

**woe** *n.* sorrow, sadness, grief, misery, trouble ★**joy**

**woman** *n.* lady, girl, female, wife

**wonder** ① *n.* marvel, miracle, rarity, curiosity ② *n.* bewilderment, surprise, amazement ▷*awe* ③ *v.* speculate, question, marvel, muse, conjecture

**wonderful** *adj.* marvellous, fabulous, spectacular, superb ▷*splendid* ★**commonplace**

**woo** *v.* make love, court, pursue, chase

**wood** *n.* ① timber, planks, lumber ② forest, woods, copse, woodland, grove, thicket WOULD

**word** *n.* ① expression, term, utterance ② pledge, promise ③ tidings, news, information, bulletin, statement

**work** ① *n.* toil, drudgery, labour, grind ② *n.* task, job, stint, chore ③ *v.* operate, function, manipulate, run, drive

**world** *n.* globe, earth, sphere, planet

**worry** ① *v.* bother, annoy, disturb ▷*trouble* ★**soothe** ② *n.* vexation, anxiety, concern, fear ★**delight**

**worsen** *v.* aggravate, decline, deteriorate, degenerate ★**improve**

## Borrowed Words

**Boomerang**

**Modern French**
police
rendezvous
liaison
menu

**Dutch**
boss
brandy
decoy
landscape

**Scandinavia**
fjord
geyser

lemming
ombudsman
ski

**Italian**
balcony
cameo
fiasco
influenza

**German**
blitz
delicatessen
dollar
kindergarten

**Chinese**
kowtow
sampan
typhoon
wok

**Japanese**
bonsai
judo
karate
origami

**Turkish**
coffee
kiosk

**Spanish**
armada
fiesta
macho
patio
siesta
sombrero

**Afrikaans**
aardvark
apartheid

boer
trek
veldt

**Inuit**
anorak
igloo
kayak
parka

**Gaelic**
blarney
bog
brat
brogue
smithereens

**Aztec**
avocado
cocoa
tomato

**Arabic**
admiral
alcohol
algebra
alkali
sherbet
sofa
zero

**Aboriginal languages**
boomerang
dingo
budgerigar
kangaroo

**Persian**
bazaar
caravan
divan
paradise

tulip
turban

**Hindi**
bungalow
chintz
cot
pyjamas
thug
veranda

**Native American**
chipmunk
moccasin
moose
papoose
wigwam

**worship** ① *v.* revere, adore, esteem, honour, praise ★despise ② *n.* adoration, devotion, reverence

**worth** *n.* value, benefit, merit, calibre *This year's students were of a high calibre,* dignity

**worthless** *adj.* valueless, paltry, trifling, useless ▷*cheap* ★valuable

**worthwhile** *adj.* valuable, helpful, useful, beneficial ★useless

**worthy** *adj.* upright, admirable, excellent, honest, fine ★vile

**wound** ① *v.* hurt, injure, gash, pain, distress ▷*harm* ★heal ② *n.* injury, bruise, harm

**wrangle** *v.* & *n.* squabble, fight, row, scrap ▷*quarrel* ★accord

**wrap** *v.* fold, envelop, enclose, cover, clothe, conceal ★unfold RAP

**wrath** *n.* fury, ire, rage, passion ▷*anger* ★pleasure

**wreck** ① *v.* demolish, smash, ruin, destroy, spoil, ravage ★repair ② *n.* derelict, hulk, shipwreck, ruin

**wrench** *v.* twist, wring, strain, sprain, pull

**wrestle** *v.* struggle, battle, combat, grapple, tussle ▷*fight*

**wretch** *n.* vagabond, blackguard, villain, rogue, ruffian, rascal ▷*scoundrel*

**wretched** *adj.* ① dejected, abject, miserable ▷*despicable* ② saddening, pathetic ▷*pitiful* ★joyful

**wriggle** *v.* twist, writhe, squirm, worm *My hamster wormed his way under the couch and it took some time before we could get him back out,* dodge

**wring** *v.* choke, squeeze, throttle, strangle, twist RING

**wrinkle** *n.* & *v.* crease, pucker, ruffle, rumple, crinkle, furrow

**write** *v.* inscribe, pen, sign, scrawl, scribble RIGHT, RITE, WRIGHT

**writer** *n.* ① scribe, penman, clerk ② author, essayist, narrator, playwright, poet, dramatist, columnist, hack

**writhe** *v.* wind, twine, weave, twist, squirm ▷*wriggle*

**written** *adj.* recorded, set down, documentary, transcribed

**wrong** ① *adj.* unjust, unfair, immoral, wicked ② *adj.* false, mistaken, erroneous ③ *v.* injure, hurt, abuse ④ *n.* offence, atrocity, iniquity, sin, injustice ★right

**wry** *adj.* crooked, askew, awry, aslant, twisted, distorted ★straight RYE

# Y y

**yank** *v.* draw, pull, snatch ▷*jerk*

**yap** *v.* ① bark, yelp ② prattle, blather, gossip, jaw

**yard** ① *n.* courtyard, court, quadrangle, garden ② three feet

**yarn** *n.* ① story, account, tale, narrative ② thread, wool, linen, twist

**yawn** *v.* gape, open

**yearly** *adj.* ① annual, perennial, per annum *We shall pay a salary of £50,000 per annum* ② *adv.* every year, annually

**yearn** *v.* ache, crave, desire, pine, hunger for ★**dislike**

**yell** *v.* shriek, squawk, whoop, screech, shout ▷*bellow* ★**whisper**

**yield** ① *v.* produce, provide, furnish, supply ② *v.* surrender, give in, submit ★**withstand** ③ *v.* abdicate, resign, renounce ④ *n.* crop, harvest, product, output

**yielding** ① *adj.* obedient, submissive, unresisting ★**stubborn** ② plastic, malleable, flexible ★**solid**

**yoke** ① *v.* join, couple, link, harness ② *n.* chain, bondage *The children of Israel moved out of bondage in the land of Egypt,* enslavement YOLK

**yokel** *n.* bumpkin, rustic, boor, peasant

**young** *adj.* youthful, tender, juvenile, junior, little ★**old**

**youngster** *n.* child, youth, boy, girl, kid, teenager, lad, adolescent

**youth** *n.* ① adolescence, prime, salad days ★**age** ② lad, boy ▷*youngster*

**youthful** *adj.* boyish, girlish, young, spry, juvenile, lively ★**aged**

**Yule** *n.* Christmas

# Z z

**zany** *adj.* crazy, daft, droll, goofy, eccentric, wacky, loony ▷*funny* ★**serious**

**zeal** *n.* devotion, eagerness, enthusiasm, keenness, ardour ★**apathy**

**zealous** *adj.* devoted, fervent *Dave was a fervent supporter of the school's football team,* fanatical, earnest ▷*eager* ★**apathetic**

**zenith** *n.* climax, height, apex, peak

**zero** *n.* nothing, nought, nil, nullity, zip, aught

**zest** *n.* ① relish, gusto, appetite, keenness ② flavour, piquancy, taste ③ rind, peel

**zone** *n.* area, district, region, tract, sector

**zoom** *v.* flash, fly, shoot, streak, hurtle, whizz

# Words and Synonyms in the English Language

No one can say for sure how many words there are in the English language. A large up-to-date dictionary might include as many as 460,000 entries. Of course, no single person knows or uses all of these words. Native speakers of English might use from 5,000 to 50,000 words and recognize many more. In our daily lives we can often get by with anywhere from a few hundred to a few thousand words. But if we limit ourselves to such a low number, we will soon find that we cannot always say or write precisely what we mean.

Fortunately, many words in English are synonyms – words that mean the same thing or nearly the same thing. And so there are many different words to choose from in order to express yourself clearly and in an interesting manner. Your Thesaurus can help you to find just the word you are looking for to make your writing more interesting to read and to explain yourself more exactly. Sometimes your Thesaurus will simply remind you of a word that you already know but couldn't think of. At other times it might suggest a new word that will help express your meaning more precisely or with more energy and variety. Because the Thesaurus doesn't tell you the meaning of words, it is always a good idea to check a dictionary to make sure that any word that is new to you means what you want it to mean in your sentence. (The opposite is also true – a dictionary will tell you what words mean, but it might not suggest other choices the way your Thesaurus does.)

## Where do all these words come from?
The English language is very rich in synonyms. Over the past 1600 years it has changed and grown as new words develop and as others are borrowed from different languages. Many of our most common words are native to English and have been used since the first Anglo-Saxons settled in the island of Britain in the fifth century (*man, wife, child, lord, lady, daisy, think, come, home, shirt, word, busy, to, in, ask*). Other common words were borrowed from the Scandinavian settlers who came to Britain during the next few centuries (*sky, scowl, shin, skirt, window*).

In 1066 the French-speaking Normans conquered England. For the next 300 years French was the language of the rulers of England, the aristocracy. During this period speakers of English began to use many French words in their speech and today thousands of these French borrowings have become ordinary English words themselves (*language, conquer, beauty, debt, govern, joy, host, count, plenty, memory*).

Yet when students went to school during these early centuries, they didn't go to study English as we do today, or even French, but to study Latin and then Greek. It is not surprising, therefore, that English now includes many words that came from Latin and Greek. From Latin we get such words as *history, bishop, educate, compose, intelligent, element, solar,* and *pedestrian*. From Greek come *elephant, synonym, system, anthology* and *geography*. Many of these Greek words came to English through Latin. Modern scientific words are often composed of Greek and Latin elements: *thesaurus, telephone, television, bicycle, radio, dinosaur, pneumonia.*

The age of exploration, travel and conquest that began in the 1400s greatly increased the number of English words as travellers, soldiers and settlers came into contact with people speaking different languages all over the world. There are thousands of words that we use today without ever thinking of their widespread origins. Below, for example, are some of our words for different types of storm and the languages they come from:

| | |
|---|---|
| English: *storm* | Scandinavian: *squall* |
| Spanish: *tornado* | Arabic: *monsoon* |
| Latin: *tempest* | Taino (Caribbean): *hurricane* |
| Greek: *cyclone* | Chinese: *typhoon* |

# All Sorts of Synonyms

Synonyms don't just come from borrowing words from other languages. People in different places often use different words to mean the same thing. A recent example is found in the words for the bumps that are put on some roads and car parks to keep cars from going too fast. In Britain these are known as *sleeping policemen* but in the U.S. they are called *speed bumps*. Or consider the little insects whose tails light up on summer evenings. Since the 1600s these have been known as *fireflies*, but in the U.S. they are also called *lightning bugs*. In various parts of the U.S., *dragonflies* are known as *mosquito hawks*, *darning needles*, and *snake doctors*. In Britain, a road intersection that goes around a circle is called a *roundabout*, but in most of the U.S. it is called a *traffic circle* – yet in New England it is called a *rotary*. Depending on where you live in the U.S. you might sell your old toys at a *tag sale*, a *garage sale*, a *yard sale*, or a *lawn sale*. Here in Britain you would sell them at a *car boot sale*, because the British sell such things from the *boots* of their cars. What's the *boot* of a car? In the U.S. they call it the *trunk*.

But most synonyms in your Thesaurus are not based on regional or national differences. Synonyms are words that have similar meanings. Their meanings may overlap, but they do not usually express exactly the same thing. Synonyms cluster around a single sense but have different shades of meaning. One of the things your Thesaurus does best is help you to find the right word with just the right shade of meaning so that you can say what you want in the best way. Some words may be formal and some informal. Some may be used in one situation but not in another.

For example, the words *friend*, *companion*, *ally*, and *pal* are all words for someone you like or are friendly with, but each one suggests something slightly different. A *friend* is someone you like, but a *pal* is someone you are particularly close to. The word *ally*, on the other hand, suggests someone who agrees with your position in some matter.

*Ally* often refers to one country that is on friendly terms with another country and it also suggests the opposite of *enemy*. Thus, a country can be your *friend* and *ally*, but not your *pal* or *companion*. Your *pal*, however, should not only be your *friend* and *companion*, he or she should also be a good *ally*. Each time you choose a synonym you need to think a little about which of the choices in your Thesaurus is the best one for you at the moment. You may know right away when you see it, or you may need to look up some of the choices in a dictionary.

## Finding the Differences among Synonyms

On the following pages some entries from your Thesaurus are expanded to show how to choose the word that means the closest to what you wish to say. Definitions are given to show how the synonyms are related and how they are different. Example sentences are included to show one way, at least, in which the word is commonly used. In these expanded entries the main entry is in CAPITALS and its synonyms are listed below it in **bold**. Each synonym is then followed by its meaning and an example sentence. Compare these expanded entries with the entries in the main part of your Thesaurus.

| Word | Meaning | Example |
|------|---------|---------|
| FRIEND *n.* | someone you know and like; someone who is not your enemy | *All his **friends** came to the party.* *If you can't trust your **friends**, who can you trust?* |
| **companion** | a person or animal who spends a lot of time with you | *Allen has been my constant **companion** for three weeks.* |
| **associate** | someone you work with or often mix with socially | *Her **associates** included the mayor and everyone on the council.* |
| **ally** | a country or person who agrees to help and support another | *Denmark and Portugal are two of the closest **allies** of Great Britain.* |

| | | |
|---|---|---|
| **crony** | an informal word for someone who has been a close friend for a long time | *One of my old **cronies** showed up at the school reunion.* |
| **pal** | an informal word for a close friend | *My **pals** and I go fishing every Saturday.* |
| **chum** | an informal word for a close friend | *We've been **chums** for three years.* |

| | | |
|---|---|---|
| HISTORY *n.* | a record, and often an interpretation, of past events and developments | *She wrote a **history** of jazz.* <br> *The doctor wanted to know my medical **history**.* |
| **narration** | a detailed telling of what happened | *The **narration** of his escape took over an hour.* |
| **account** | a description, report, or explanation | *Paul gave us an **account** of his trip to Peru.* |
| **saga** | a long tale of heroic events | *The book is a **saga** of three generations of a seafaring family.* |
| **story** | a description of real or imaginary events | *He especially likes **stories** about animals.* |
| **chronicle** | a record of events in the order they happened | *The Prime Minister kept a **chronicle** of her years in office.* |

| | | |
|---|---|---|
| LIFT *v.* | to move up to a higher position | *This box is too heavy for me to **lift**.* |
| **raise** | to move or lift to a high position | *If you know the answer, **raise** your hand.* |
| **erect** | to raise something to an upright position | *We **erected** our tent near the river.* |
| **hoist** | to lift up something, especially with ropes and pulleys | *They had to **hoist** the girders to the top of the new skyscraper.* |

| | | |
|---|---|---|
| **elevate** | to raise or lift up to a higher place or rank | *She was **elevated** to the post of Managing Director.* |
| **hold up** | to prop up or keep from falling | *He was so tired he could hardly **hold up** his head.* |

| | | |
|---|---|---|
| MAXIMUM *adj.* | the greatest allowed or possible | *This bus carries a **maximum** load of 42 passengers.* |
| **supreme** | of the highest rank, power or importance; most excellent | *Many people have been willing to make the **supreme** sacrifice and die for the freedom of others.* |
| **highest** | having the greatest height or importance | *The president holds the **highest** elected office in the country.* |
| **most** | greatest in quantity, amount, or degree | *The big dipper is the **most** exciting ride in the park.* |
| **greatest** | largest in number, quantity, degree, intensity, etc | *The **greatest** gift you can give me is your respect.* |
| **top** | of the highest quality, amount, or degree | *The salesman promised me a **top** price for my old car.* |
| **largest** | greatest in size or quantity; biggest | *The **largest** known volcano is on Mars.* |

| | | |
|---|---|---|
| PLACID *adj.* | having a calm appearance | *The lake was **placid** as we canoed through the mist.* |
| **peaceful** | calm and quiet; at peace | *He spent a **peaceful** afternoon reading in the shade.* |
| **quiet** | without noise or bustle | *The city becomes **quiet** in the middle of the night.* |

| | | |
|---|---|---|
| **serene** | not disturbed or troubled | *The serene expression on her face helped us to calm down.* |
| **mild** | not extreme in any way | *We had a mild winter last year.* |
| **restful** | quiet, soothing, and peaceful | *We had a restful holiday at the seaside.* |
| RECIPE *n.* | a list of ingredients and instructions for preparing something, especially a particular food | *I have a wonderful recipe for chocolate cheesecake.* |
| **formula** | a general rule or principle; a set method for doing something | *His formula for success is to get up early, dress neatly and be polite.* |
| **method** | a logical, orderly arrangement of steps for doing something | *She has a very effective teaching method.* |
| **prescription** | written directions for preparing or using a medicine | *The doctor gave me a prescription for penicillin.* |
| SPEED *n.* | rate of movement or action; quickness | *The car careered down the hill at great speed.* |
| **velocity** | the speed at which an object is travelling | *The train travels at a constant velocity of 120 kilometres per hour.* |
| **rapidity** | a fast rate of motion or occurrence | *The rapidity of her answers showed her great confidence.* |
| **pace** | rate of movement, progress, occurrence, etc | *We climbed the trail at a steady pace.* |
| **dispatch** | (*old usage*) promptness; efficient quickness | *Let's finish this job with dispatch.* |

| | | |
|---|---|---|
| **tempo** | rate of activity; pace | *The **tempo** of city life is too fast for me.* |

| | | |
|---|---|---|
| VALID *adj.* | legally acceptable for use | *You need a **valid** licence to drive a car.* |
| **genuine** | authentic; not artificial or fake | *This letter bears the **genuine** signature of Emily Brontë.* |
| **authentic** | not false or imitation | *She has an **authentic** Scottish accent.* |
| **official** | established or made legal by someone in authority | *No one is allowed in here without an **official** pass.* |
| **proper** | fit, suitable, or appropriate | *He did not have the **proper** visa for entering China.* |

# Name Synonyms

Even names have synonyms! Many names have different forms in
other languages. Some nicknames don't even look or sound like the
original names they come from, like *Ned* and *Nell* for *Edward* and
*Helen*. Sometimes these nicknames become first names themselves,
like *Peggy* and *Robin*, originally nicknames for *Margaret* and *Robert*.
For these reasons, many names that we hear around us every day are
what we might call 'name synonyms'. Below is a list of a few
common names given in their English forms followed by some of their
synonyms. Female names are shown in *italic* type (*Alexandra*); male
names are shown in roman type (Alec). A few names that are used for
both males and females have been underlined.

| | |
|---|---|
| **Alexander** | <u>Alex</u>, Alec, *Alexandra*, *Alexa*, Alexandre, Alejandro, *Alexandrina* |
| **Anthony** | Tony, Antonio, *Antonia*, *Toni*, Antony |
| **Arthur** | Arturo, Art |
| *Christina* | <u>Chris</u>, *Chrissy*, Christian, *Christine*, *Kristen*, *Kirsten*, *Kirstie*, *Tina*, *Christie* |
| **Christopher** | <u>Chris</u>, Kit |
| **David** | Dave, Davy, Dafydd, Dai, Dewi |
| **Derek** | Derrick, Dietrich, Terry |
| *Dorothy* | *Dora, Dolly, Dorothea, Dot, Dottie* |
| **Edward** | Ned, Ted, Eduardo, Edvard, Duarte |
| *Elizabeth* | *Eliza, Isabel, Elsa, Lisa, Elsie, Elspeth, Lilian, Bessy, Betty, Libby, Liz, Lizzy* |
| **Francis** | *Frances*, Frank, Francesco, *Francesca*, François, *Françoise*, *Francine*, Franz |
| **Frederick** | Fred, Freddie, *Frederica*, Friedrich |
| **George** | *Georgia*, Georges, Jorge, Jurgen, Jerzy, *Georgina*, *Georgiana*, *Georgette* |
| **Gerald** | Geraldo, Jerry |
| *Helen* | *Helena, Elena, Ellen, Nell* |

| | |
|---|---|
| **James** | Jaime, Jacob, Jacques, Jake, *Jacqueline*, Seamus, Iago, Hamish, Jim, Jimmy, <u>Jamie</u> |
| *Jane* | *Joan, Joanne, Jeanne, Jean, Siobhán, Juana* (*see* **John**) |
| **Jeffrey** | Geoffrey, Jeff, Geoff |
| **John** | Ian, Sean, Shawn, Jean, Juan, Giovanni, Johann, Johannes, Hans, Ivan, Evan, Jack, *Jackie* (*see* **Jane**) |
| **Jonathan** | Jon, Jonny |
| *Katherine* | *Catherine, Kate, Cathy, Katie, Kathleen, Caitlin, Katrine, Catrin, Katya, Katrinka, Kitty, Kit* |
| *Margaret* | *Marguerite, Margarita, Margery, Margot, Meg, Greta, Gretchen, Rita, Pearl, Margie, Maggie, Peggy, Peg* |
| **Mark** | Marco, Marcos, Marcus |
| *Mary* | *Maria, Marie, Miriam, Marion, Marian, Máire, Moira, Mia, Mitzi, May* |
| *Mathilda* | *Maud, Tilly, Mattie* |
| **Nicholas** | Nicolo, Nikolai, Nick, Klaus |
| *Nicola* | *Nicole, Nicolette, Nicky* (*see* **Nicholas**) |
| **Patrick** | *Patricia,* <u>Pat</u>*, Trisha, Trish, Patsy,* Padraig, Paddy |
| **Paul** | *Paula,* Pablo, Paolo, Paulo, *Pauline, Paulette* |
| **Richard** | Ricardo, Rick, Dick |
| **Robert** | *Roberta,* Roberto, Rupert, <u>Robin</u>, Rob, Bob |
| **Stephen** | Steven, Steve, *Stephanie, Steffany,* Stefan, Stefano, Estéban, Étienne, <u>Stevie</u> |
| *Susan* | *Sue, Susanna, Suzanne, Shoshana, Suzie, Suzette* |
| **Thomas** | Tommaso, Tom, *Thomasina, Tamsin* |
| **William** | Will, Bill, Guglielmo, Guillaume, Wilhelm, *Wilhelmina, Wilma, Willa* |

# Homonyms

Homonyms are words that sound the same but that mean different things. Many homonyms are spelt the same, such as the adjective *faint* (indistinct) and the verb *faint* (to collapse). In your Thesaurus, homonyms that are spelled the same are usually listed as different numbered senses of the entry word, as you will see if you look up **faint**. There are also homonyms that sound the same but are spelled differently. This kind of homonym is listed in small capital letters at the end of the whole entry. Thus, you will see that the entry for **faint** ends with the word FEINT. This means that although *feint* sounds like *faint*, it means something different. Your Thesaurus includes these homonyms in order to help you find the one you are looking for. For example, *choose* and *chews* are homonyms. **Choose** is entered in your Thesaurus, but if you need another word for *chews*, you should look at the entry for **chew**.

Below is a list of many common homonyms.

| | |
|---|---|
| air / heir | blue / blew |
| aloud / allowed | boar / bore |
| alter / altar | board / bored |
| bait / bate | bold / bowled |
| band / banned | bow / bough |
| baron / barren | bowl / boll |
| base / bass | boy / buoy |
| bay / bey | braid / brayed |
| beach / beech | brake / break |
| bear / bare | brood / brewed |
| bearing / baring | bruise / brews |
| beat / beet | build / billed |
| beer / bier | buy / by / bye |
| billed / build | cash / cache |
| birth / berth | cast / caste |
| bite / byte | cause / caws |
| block / bloc | cell / sell |

cellar / seller

censor / censer

cent / sent / scent

chaste / chased

choose / chews

chute / shoot

cite / sight / site

chord / cord / cored

coarse / course

coax / cokes

colonel / kernel

compliment / complement

core / corps

council / counsel

coward / cowered

creak / creek

cue / queue

current / currant

cymbal / symbol

daze / days

dear / deer

dense / dents

dew / due

die / dye

dire / dyer

discreet / discrete

earn / urn

faint / feint

fair / fare

fate / fête

fawn / faun

faze / phase

feat / feet

file / phial

flair / flare

flee / flea

flow / floe

flower / flour

fold / foaled

for / four / fore

foul / fowl

freeze / frees / frieze

gamble / gambol

gate / gait

gauge / gage

graze / grays

great / grate

guest / guessed

guilt / gilt

guise / guys

hail / hale

hall / haul

handsome / hansom

hear / here

heard / herd

heed / he'd

heir / air

heroine / heroin

hew / hue

high / hi

higher / hire

him / hymn

hoard / horde

hoarse / horse

hold / holed

holy / wholly

hose / hoes

humorous / humerus

idle / idol

instance / instants

intense / intents
jam / jamb
key / quay
knave / nave
knead / need
knight / night
knot / not
know / no
lane / lain
lapse / laps
lax / lacks
leaf / lief
leak / leek
least / leased
lessen / lesson
liar / lyre
lie / lye
load / lode / lowed
loan / lone
loot / lute
low / lo
made / maid
magnet / magnate
mail / male
manner / manor
mantel / mantle
marshal / martial
maze / maize
mean / mien
meat / meet / mete
medal / meddle
metal / mettle
might / mite
mince / mints
miner / minor

mode / mowed
morning / mourning
new / knew
none / nun
oh / owe
one / won
pact / packed
pail / pale
pain / pane
pair / pear / pare
past / passed
patience / patients
pause / paws
peace / piece
peal / peel
pedal / peddle
peer / pier
phrase / frays
plain / plane
pour / pore
praise / prays / preys
pray / prey
pride / pried
principal / principle
prize / pries
rack / wrack
rain / reign / rein
raise / raze
rap / wrap
rapt / rapped / wrapped
read / reed
real / reel
residence / residents
rest / wrest
review / revue

rhyme / rime
right / write / rite / wright
ring / wring
road / rode / rowed
roll / role
rough / ruff
row / roe
rude / rood / rued
rye / wry
sail / sale
see / sea
seem / seam
seen / scene
seize / seas / sees
sense / cents / scents
sew / so / sow
sheer / shear
side / sighed
size / sighs
slay / sleigh
slow / sloe
some / sum
sore / soar
sole / soul
staid / stayed
stake / steak
stare / stair
stationary / stationery
steal / steel
straight / strait
style / stile
surge / serge
sweet / suite
sword / soared
symbol / cymbal

tact / tacked
tale / tail
taut / taught
tax / tacks
team / teem
tear / tare
tease / teas / tees
tense / tents
throw / throe
time / thyme
to / too / two
tool / tulle
tow / toe
tract / tracked
trust / trussed
turn / tern
unreal / unreel
use / ewes
vain / vein / vane
veil / vale
wade / weighed
wait / weight
waive / wave
wane / wain
war / wore
ward / warred
warn / worn
waste / waist
way / weigh / whey
weak / week
wear / where / ware
weather / whether
weave / we've
wee / we
weed / we'd

wet / whet
wheel / we'll / weal
whine / wine
which / witch
whoa / woe
whole / hole
wild / whiled
wind / wined / whined
wood / would
worn / warn
wretch / retch
wrote / rote
yoke / yolk
you / ewe
Yule / you'll